ArtScroll Mesorah Series®

Rabbi Nosson Scherman / Rabbi Meir Zlotowitz

General Editors

yom kippur

YOM KIPPUR — ITS SIGNIFICANCE, LAWS, AND PRAYERS / A PRESENTATION ANTHOLOGIZED FROM TALMUDIC AND TRADITIONAL SOURCES.

Published by

Mesorah Publications, ltd

Overview by
Rabbi Nosson Scherman

Laws by
Rabbi Hersh Goldwurm

Insights and Prayers by
Rabbi Avie Gold

FIRST EDITION
First Impression . . . August, 1989
Second Impression . . . August 1990
Third Impression . . . June 1993
Fourth Impression . . . July 1995
Fifth Impression . . . June 1997
Sixth Impression . . . June 1999
Seventh Impression . . . May 2001
Eighth Impression . . . August 2005
Ninth Impression . . . August 2009

Published and Distributed by
MESORAH PUBLICATIONS, Ltd.
4401 Second Avenue
Brooklyn, New York 11232

Distributed in Europe by
LEHMANNS
Unit E, Viking Business Park
Rolling Mill Road
Jarrow, Tyne & Wear NE32 3DP
England

Distributed in Australia & New Zealand by
GOLDS WORLD OF JUDAICA
3-13 William Street
Balaclava, Melbourne 3183
Victoria Australia

Distributed in Israel by
SIFRIATI / A. GITLER — BOOKS
6 Hayarkon Street
Bnei Brak 51127

Distributed in South Africa by
KOLLEL BOOKSHOP
Ivy Common 105 William Road
Norwood 2192, Johannesburg, South Africa

ARTSCROLL MESORAH SERIES®
"YOM KIPPUR" / Its Significance, Laws, and Prayers
© Copyright 1989, by MESORAH PUBLICATIONS, Ltd.
4401 Second Avenue / Brooklyn, N.Y. 11232 / (718) 921-9000 / www.artscroll.com

ISBN 10: 0-89906-216-4
ISBN 13: 978-0-89906-216-7

Typography by Compuscribe at ArtScroll Studios, Ltd.

Printed in the United States of America by Noble Book Press
Bound by Sefercraft, Quality Bookbinders, Ltd. Brooklyn, N.Y.

Leon Setton

יהודה בן אסתר הכהן ע"ה

March 17, 1984 / י"ד אדר ב' תשמ"ד

*Born on Yom Kippur, he lived up to the
message of that day all his life.*

*At peace with his fellow Jews and a zealot in
the cause of harmony, he was a worthy heir of
Aaron, the first Kohen.*

*"Blessed is my Lord for every single day" –
בָּרוּךְ ה' יוֹם יוֹם – was his constant refrain.
Every day is a new gift, and we are challenged
to use it well, as the Giver wished.
Leon Setton lived up to the challenge.*

*His memory inspires us to be worthy
of his legacy.*

*Mrs. Claire Setton
and family*

ᥰ᥍ Preface

The Days of Awe conclude with, Yom Kippur, the festival when there are no festivities, when we rejoice with trepidation, when we approach Hashem and realize how far we have removed ourselves from His Presence. Torah Scrolls are carried about the synagogue and embraced by the congregation; Kol Nidrei is recited in its haunting centuries-old chant; the congregation stands erect in tallis and kittel like the ministering angels. All these are powerful stimulants to repentance. All testify to the delicate balance between the Jew's eternal confidence in God's mercy and his fear that the inadequacy of his deeds makes him fall far short of the minimum threshold of performance.

In this volume, Mesorah Publications proudly presents a selection of Yom Kippur highlights to the reader. The goal of the book's authors is to provide color, background, meaning, and authenticity to observances and aspects of this profound and meaningful day. It is often said and just as often forgotten that people let the most important activities of their lives become habitual. This dismal part of human nature is particularly disturbing at times like Yom Kippur, when Jews are called upon to examine themselves, shed their failings, reconcile their differences, and elevate their awareness, aspiration, and performance.

It is our profound hope that his book will help its readers explore and absorb the message of Yom Kippur — and even more, that it will help them personify the goals of the day.

The Book contains four sections:

☐ The **Overview**, like others in the ArtScroll Series, presents a hashkafah/philosophical perspective on major concepts of the day.

☐ The **Insights** offers a fascinating collection of rabbinic thought, homilies, interpretation, and inspirational stories.

☐ The **Laws and Customs** offers a digest of the laws that apply to the individual, at home and in the synagogue.

☐ The **Prayers** concentrate on the Blessing of the Children, Kol Nidrei, Avinu Malkeinu, and Yizkor, and are complete with the original translation and anthologized commentary that are unique to the award-winning ArtScroll Series.

The Laws and Customs were written by RABBI HERSH GOLDWURM, whose breadth of scholarship has been displayed in many tractates of the ArtScroll Mishnah, the Book of Daniel, and the ArtScroll History Series. It is a rare privilege to be associated with him and to bring his writings to the public.

The *Insights* and *Prayers* sections are by our colleague, RABBI AVIE GOLD. *In his modest, unassuming way, he has become a major — indeed, an indispensable — part of the ArtScroll Series.*

Like scores of its predecessors in the ArtScroll Series, this volume is a tribute to the graphics artistry of REB SHEAH BRANDER. *His skill is a jewel in the crown of Torah.*

We are grateful to the entire ArtScroll staff, who cope with pressures, deadlines, and inconvenience with an aplomb that is surely born of their dedication to the ideals we are privileged to serve: RABBI YEHEZKEL DANZIGER, RABBI SHIMON GOLDING, YOSEF TIMINSKY, YOSEF GESSER, MICHAEL HOREN, MRS. FAYGIE WEINBAUM, LEA FREIER, SHEILA TENNENBAUM, MRS. ESTHER FEIERSTEIN, MRS. MENUCHA SILVER, MRS. ZISSI LANDAU, BASSIE GOLDSTEIN, MRS. SURIE MALINE *and* FAIGIE ZLOTOWITZ.

Rabbi Nosson Scherman / Rabbi Meir Zlotowitz
GENERAL EDITORS

Av 5749 / August 1989

Table of Contents

✍ Observance / Selected Laws and Customs

✍ Observance / Prayers and Ritual

❧ An Overview / Yom Kippur — The Day and Its Essence

Day of Repentance
Levels of Repentance
The Gift of His Nearness
Purim and Yom Kippur
Power of the Day

– Rabbi Nosson Scherman

An Overview/
Yom Kippur — The Day and Its Essence*

דִּרְשׁוּ ה׳ בְּהִמָּצְאוֹ קְרָאֻהוּ בִּהְיוֹתוֹ קָרוֹב ... בְּיָחִיד
אֵימַת? אָמַר רַבָּה בַּר אֲבוּהַ אֵלּוּ עֲשָׂרָה יָמִים שֶׁבֵּין
רֹאשׁ הַשָּׁנָה לְיוֹם הַכִּפּוּרִים.

Seek HASHEM when He is accessible, call Him when He is near (Isaiah 55:6) ... When does this apply [even to an individual]? Rabbah bar Avuhah said: These are the ten days between Rosh Hashanah and Yom Kippur (Rosh Hashanah 18a).

I. Day of Repentance

A Necessary Gift

Without the possibility of repentance, the world could not exist, because man stumbles more than he strides.

Without the possibility of repentance, the world could not exist, because — as our common experience makes all too clear — man stumbles more than he strides. If there were no possibility of wiping the slate clean, man could have no hope of rising above his frequent sins. They would always remain to condemn him, never allowing him to escape the inevitability of judgment and punishment. For this reason, the concept of *teshuvah* [repentance] had to be created before the universe, for God would not create a world that was doomed from its inception (*Nedarim* 39b). But though the possibility of repentance always exists — *must* exist — it is uniquely acceptable during the ten days ending with Yom Kippur. During this period, God waits — anxiously and expectantly, as it were — for the Jewish *people* and the Jewish *person* to return to His embrace. He is more responsive at this time, He assists those groping for His closeness, and He regards our failure to respond to this opportunity as a transgression of uncommon magnitude.

*The Overview is based primarily on Resisei Laylah, ch. 50

Relative Merit

Sometimes a particular good deed is so important that it outweighs many sins, and vice versa.

Rambam (*Hil. Teshuvah* 3:1-3) writes that on Rosh Hashanah everyone's deeds are weighed in the heavenly scales of judgment. Those with a preponderance of good deeds are inscribed for life; those with a preponderance of sins are inscribed for death. The key factor in this is not the numbers of virtues or sins, but their relative worth. Sometimes a particular good deed is so important that it outweighs many sins, and vice versa. This explains many stories from Rabbinic literature where it is told that seemingly undistinguished people — or even some who were generally considered to be evil — were assigned to high places in God's order because of relatively few especially outstanding deeds.

Seldom do we know why people are deserving of good fortune and often we are troubled by the success of those whom we consider to be unworthy. But occasionally we understand. For example, we might be convinced that someone is totally undeserving — until we learn that, at great personal sacrifice, he had saved countless lives.

The same principle extends to the nation as a whole. The *Chafetz Chaim* would exhort his fellow Jews to extend themselves to study Torah and fulfill the commandments, even though the quality of study and observance in his time had fallen precipitously from the standards of previous centuries. To the contrary, the *Chofetz Chaim* would say that loyalty to the Torah in his time mattered more than in earlier eras. In his time, poverty, persecution, the community dislocations caused by World War I, and the inroads of various secular ideologies had made it more difficult than ever

In such times, even imperfect mitzvos are of relatively great value before God, because they come at such great effort.

to be a complete Jew. In such times, even imperfect *mitzvos* are of relatively great value before God, because they come at such great effort. Similarly, we correctly admire people of limited ability who strive mightily and achieve the utmost of their potential, even though, in absolute terms, they are less accomplished than brilliant scholars who excel the crowd with a minimum of effort. In weighing people's deeds, God, too, measures many factors, most of which are known only to Him in His ultimate wisdom.

A Time to Repent But there is a third category of people facing the judgment of Rosh Hashanah: Those who are evenly balanced between virtues and sins. Of such people *Rambam* (ibid) writes:

וְהַבֵּינוֹנִי, תּוֹלִין אוֹתוֹ עַד יוֹם הַכִּפּוּרִים, אִם עָשָׂה תְּשׁוּבָה נֶחְתַּם לְחַיִּים, וְאִם לָאו נֶחְתַּם לְמִיתָה.

As for one who is evenly balanced [between good and bad deeds], his fate is suspended until Yom Kippur. If he repents, he is sealed for life, and if not he is sealed for death.

Failure to repent is sufficient reason to condemn a sinner who was otherwise balanced between good and evil. *Rambam* maintains that failure to repent is sufficient reason to condemn a sinner who was otherwise balanced between good and evil, even though he has not increased his sins. But why? If someone fails to repent, he is *still* evenly balanced, and in such cases the Abundantly Merciful One tips the scales in favor of virtue (*Rosh Hashanah* 17a). If so, one's failure to repent should change nothing — the scales remain evenly balanced as they were, and God's mercy should decide the issue in favor of life.

Lechem Mishnah explains that the failure to repent is in itself an additional transgression, because there is a constant commandment upon every Jew to repent at all times. Thus, if someone does not repent, by his very refusal to do so, he has wantonly tipped the scales against himself.

The commandment to repent is no ordinary commandment. It is a heavenly gift that enables man to erase the past. R' Yitzchok Blazer (*Cochvei Or*) takes the point further. The commandment to repent is no ordinary commandment. It is a heavenly gift that enables man to erase the past, especially during the Ten Days of Repentance, when God is near and awaits the opportunity to forgive His errant children. A refusal to repent at such a propitious time is not merely negligent, it is insulting. It is as if God Himself comes hat in hand hoping that the sinner will look up and say, "I am truly sorry, I will change. Please forgive me." Instead, he turns his back upon God and disdains the Heavenly advance. Can there be a greater insult, or a graver sin? In such a case, it is clear why God does not tip the scales toward mercy; the sinner has forfeited his right to it.

II. Levels of Repentance

The Difficulty

It is clear from the Talmud that repentance during these ten days has a special dimension, and that it can accomplish during this period what it cannot at other times of the year. But the commandment to repent is constant; it is equally binding at all times. As we say in the prayers of Yom Kippur:

But the commandment to repent is constant; it is equally binding at all times.

וְעַד יוֹם מוֹתוֹ תְּחַכֶּה לּוֹ, אִם יָשׁוּב מִיַּד תְּקַבְּלוֹ.

Until the day of his death You await him, if he repents You will accept him immediately (Yom Kippur liturgy).

If so, what is unique about the obligation of repentance during these days, and about God's readiness to accept it?

The Talmud speaks of the sealing of God's decree in terms of נֶכְתָּם, a *deep stain* that is firmly set in a fabric. The reference is to a stain that is not limited to the surface but has worked its way in so that it permeates the material through and through. Unlike a surface stain, which can usually be removed with brushing or a bit of soap and water, a deep stain is impervious to ordinary laundering. The analogy of such a sin is applied to a Heavenly decree that has been sealed and cannot be annulled, because the decree resulted from a sin for which repentance is virtually impossible. What sort of sin is this?

Like everything in life, sin comes in many degrees and stages. Everyone makes mistakes. People err and feel sorry for what they have done. They repent and resolve never to do it again. Like a surface stain that is easily laundered, such sins lend themselves fairly easily to *teshuvah*. Or people may sin in a less superficial way. The "grime" digs in and gains a toehold beneath the surface, but it is still not absorbed through and through.

Like a surface stain that is easily laundered, such sins lend themselves fairly easily to teshuvah.

In the realm of repentance such sins are more stubborn, more habitual, more impervious to *teshuvah*, but they, too, can be removed by Torah and prayer, which are the primary tools of sincere repentance. The more ingrained the sin, the more difficult to repent, but it is always possible — unless the stain becomes so thoroughly embedded that it goes through and through, that it permeates the person to such an extent that it becomes part of him and he does not even recognize the need to repent. One does not "repent" the color of his eyes.

The more ingrained the sin, the more difficult to repent, but it is always possible — unless the stain becomes thoroughly embedded.

In spiritual terms, what does this mean? Of what sort of sin do we speak? And is even such a sin beyond all hope?

In the ordinary course of human events, people repent by, as the saying goes, "turning over a new leaf." They turn the page on the past and begin a new, better course of life. True, in terms of the ideal requirements of *teshuvah*, this method leaves much to be desired, because it does not fulfill all of the conditions of a perfect repentance, as given by Scripture and the Sages, and set forth at length by Rabbeinu Yona in *Shaarei Teshuvah*. Merely going on to a new beginning without remorse and heartbreak fails to purge the misdeeds of the past. Nevertheless, it is a legitimate means of self-betterment, of tearing oneself away from the life that had become stained and corrupted. Later, once the erstwhile sinner is firmly embarked on his new course, the remorse will come inevitably. But, as the saying goes, "the best is often the enemy of the good"; if we always resist mere improvement because it falls short of perfection, we will not only fail to be perfect, we will not even be good. The ideal repentance is usually too hard for most people to achieve. For them it is necessary to turn from the past and look ahead; to put off repairing the flawed past and move on to building a better future.

"The best is often the enemy of the good"; if we always resist mere improvement because it falls short of perfection, we will not only fail to be perfect, we will not even be good.

A Practical Course

Chiddushei HaRim once spoke to his disciples before Yom Kippur and exhorted them on the practical way to repent. A listener recorded his words in the original

Yiddish. This is what he said:

"Hillel the Elder said, אִם אֵין אֲנִי לִי מִי לִי, *If I am not for myself, who will be for me?* (*Avos* 1:14) . This means, if I will not perform the mission that is designated for me, who will do it for me? Everyone must carry out his personal mission in life. וְאִם לֹא עַכְשָׁיו אֵימָתַי, *And if not now, when?* (ibid.). When will *this* point in time — this עַכְשָׁיו, *now* — ever exist again? This minute in which we speak has never existed since the beginning of Creation, and it will never again exist in the future. Previously, there was a different "now" with its own particular mission, and later there will be a new "now" with a new mission. As the *Zohar* puts it, 'The garments that one donned in the morning one does not don in the evening . . .'

This minute in which we speak has never existed since the beginning of Creation, and it will never again exist in the future.

"One must exert himself in Torah study with all his energies, and thereby he will become attached to the Torah. There are 600,000 letters in the Torah and there are 600,000 souls in the nation of Israel. [This refers to the Kabbalistic concept that the 600,000 souls mentioned in the Torah in the census of those who left Egypt are the primary souls of the Jewish nation. From then on, all Jewish souls are derived from them.] Each of these souls is a part of the completeness of the Torah [each soul is represented by a letter], so that if someone fulfills his personal role in carrying out the Torah's commands, he becomes part of the fabric of the entire nation [i.e., he blends in with the other 599,999 souls, and all of them together form a unit, just as a Torah Scroll must have all of the required letters]. If someone becomes part of the nation, he benefits from the rest of the nation, and the more one unites himself with the nation, the more he gains from the nation. As one strives more and more to become part of the nation, he is enabled to gain something of the "now" during which every other Jew did something good [because every member of a group is enhanced by the accomplishments of all the others].

If someone becomes part of the nation, he benefits from the rest of the nation, and the more one unites himself with the nation, the more he gains from the nation.

"This is necessary because, as Hillel continues, וּכְשֶׁאֲנִי לְעַצְמִי, מָה אֲנִי?, *and if I am for myself, what am I?*, meaning that if I am separated from the nation, when will I ever be able to properly carry out the responsibilities of my personal "now"? Every instant has its own responsibility, and what has to be done now cannot be postponed until later, because every subsequent instant has its own responsibility, its own spiritual glow that each of us must bring into the world [through our performance].

"Surely, if one has committed, God forbid, an ugly sin and he concentrates on סוּר מֵרָע, *turn from evil* (*Psalms* 34:16) [meaning that he engages his mind in thinking about the sin and purging himself of its effects] — he is thinking about the ugliness that he committed, and *a person exists where his mind is!* A person's soul reposes entirely where his mind is occupied — so he is reposing in ugliness. He surely will not repent, because he will be preoccupied with mental images of the sin and it will block the emotional wellsprings of his heart. It may drag him down to depression, God forbid.

A person's soul re-poses entirely where his mind is occupied — so he is reposing in ugli-ness.

"Even if someone has not committed a very crude sin, so that his mind will not be preoccupied with such ugliness and his emotional drive for improvement will not be blocked — it is still not worthwhile to dwell on the sin in an attempt to escape from evil. It is like someone trying to sweep away mud. He pushes the mud this way, he pushes the mud that way — he remains with mud! He *did* sin, he *didn't* sin — what benefit has Heaven from this preoccupation [if it prevents him from moving ahead to an improved life]? While he was thinking about it, he could have been stringing pearls of Torah study and good deeds, so that Heaven will be benefited!

While he was thinking about it, he could have been stringing pearls of Torah study and good deeds, so that Heaven will be benefited!

"[Therefore, let us interpret the verse differently:] סוּר מֵרָע וַעֲשֵׂה טוֹב, *turn away from evil* — don't think about it — *and do good*. If you have committed bundles of sins, perform bundles of good deeds instead.

"Today, before Yom Kippur, we should feel the עֲזִיבַת הַחֵטְא, *withdrawal from sin*, through a clear mind and from the depth of the heart, but not with superficial emotion, and with a sincere resolve for the future. And we must be joyous, as Scripture says: עִבְדוּ אֶת ה' בְּשִׂמְחָה, *serve Hashem with joy* ... and the purpose of the Confession should be וְתִמְלֹךְ אַתָּה לְבַדֶּךָ, *You Hashem shall reign, alone* (*Likkutei Yehudah*).

Impediments to Teshuvah

But sometimes, people cannot succeed this way. They suffer from an apathy, a coldness that does not permit them to turn the leaf.

Ordinarily, the sort of *teshuvah* recommended by *Chiddushei HaRim* suffices to turn people around. They *can* look ahead to the future and turn their attention to the upcoming "nows," uniting themselves with the Jewish people and placing their concentration on Torah study and the performance of the commandments. But sometimes, people cannot succeed this way. They suffer from an apathy, a coldness that does not permit them to turn the leaf, that does not even permit them to open their eyes to what they lack. They are complacent. Perhaps they may even recognize intellectually that they have stumbled along the way and fallen into an abyss of spiritual contamination — but they come to enjoy the sludge and feel no misgivings about wallowing in it. Rosh Hashanah and Yom Kippur come and go, and leave them unmoved. Why is this?

Like everything in Creation, there are levels of sin. The early stages are superficial stains and can be cleansed easily. Deeper stains can be cleansed only with more strenuous effort, but they *can* be removed. But some stains become so deeply ingrained they resist all ordinary efforts. These are the kinds of sin that *Rif* (end of *Yoma*) and *Rambam* (*Hil. Teshuvah* ch. 4) codify as the Twenty-four Things that Prevent Repentance. They do not make *teshuvah* impossible — nothing can do that — but they are the sorts of sin that stand in the way of the potential penitent (ibid. 4:6).

They create the mental and emotional states that make a person so content with himself or that so anger God that the paths to improvement are impeded.

In a sense they are personality disorders; they create the mental and emotional states that make a person so content with himself or that so anger God that the paths to improvement are impeded. This is the condition that the Sages describe as a stain so deeply ingrained that it penetrates the entire fabric until ordinary cleansing cannot be effective. Just as soap and water cannot remove such stains, so Torah and commandments cannot dislodge the festering resistance nurtured by such sins.

More, such categories of sin create a chasm, a distance, between the sinner and God. The *Mabit* (*Bais Elokim*) defines repentance pithily as

קְרִיבָה לַה' מֵרִיחוּק הַחֵטְא.

Drawing close to God from the distance of sin.

But what if the distance is so great that one cannot draw near? These twenty-four sins create such a distance, a spiritual canyon between God and sinners.

Very briefly, as explained by *Rambam*, the sins fall under five separate categories, as follows:

A. *Four sins so great that God blocks the sinner's way toward repentance:*
  1. Causing the multitude to sin or preventing them from performing a commandment;
  2. Enticing an individual to sin;
  3. Standing idly by while one's child — or anyone else he can influence — slides down the path to sin;
  4. One who says, "I will sin and repent later," or "I will sin and Yom Kippur will atone for me."

B. *Five sins or attitudes that, by their very nature, stand in the way of repentance, because they make it very difficult for the sinner to accept the need to repent or to heed the admonition to do so:*

  1. One who separates himself from the community;
  2. One who disputes the wise men of his time;
  3. One who disparages the commandments;
  4. One who insults his teachers;
  5. One who hates admonitions.

C. *Five sins that prevent someone from repenting, because these sins involve other people, and the sinner will not know of whom he must beg forgiveness or to whom he must return property:*
  1. One who curses a crowd, so that he does not

know to whom to apologize;

2. One who shares in stolen goods, without knowing the victim;

3. One who does not announce and return found property;

4. One who persecutes the poor and homeless, who are forced to travel from place to place and tend to be anonymous;

5. One who accepts bribes, so that he can never know the full extent of his miscarriages of justice.

D. *Five sins from which it is difficult to repent because the violator considers them to be so trivial that they are not even sins:*

It is difficult to repent because the violator considers them to be so trivial that they are not even sins.

1. One who eats from a meal that does not suffice for his hosts;

2. One who uses the security deposit of poor people;

3. One who looks at immoral or obscene displays, and deludes himself into feeling that he has not committed an immoral act;

4. One who glorifies himself through a disparaging comparison with another person, even though his comrade was not present to suffer embarrassment;

5. One who suspects another unjustly.

E. *Five sins that entice the transgressor to commit them constantly, and that become irresistible to him:*

1. Gossip-mongering;
2. Slander;
3. Anger;
4. Harboring evil thoughts;
5. Associating with the wicked.

These five categories stand in the way of all repentance, and it is this that makes them so pernicious.

Each in its own way, these five categories stand in the way of all repentance, and it is this that makes them so pernicious. Such a sinner may pay lip service to the requirement to attend the synagogue and pray, but his prayer will be without sincerity. His mind will wander and his heart be cold, because he is far from God, and he will be prevented from drawing near by an intellectual, emotional barrier born of his insensitive, selfish deeds.

Every person knows himself, at least somewhat. He knows which sin or sins gnaw at him and defy his attempts at repentance. And if he analyzes himself and his deeds, he can always trace the problem to one of the twenty-four sins that impede repentance. He will not be able to repent unless he can hack away at the impediment. But how? He is so far from God — how can he draw near?

He will not be able to repent unless he can hack away at the impediment. But how?

The Jew's Shadow

The special quality of the Ten Days of Repentance is that God is accessible, He is near.

The period is inaugurated with the *shofar* blasts of Rosh Hashanah. The *shofar* represents an inarticulate cry from the heart, a cry from someone who has no words, because his sins may have become so indelibly ingrained, the barrier so firmly enclosing his heart, that he cannot even mouth the words of repentance. But there always remains a spark of aspiration in the Jewish heart, no matter how lifeless the spark has become — and when it is stimulated, it can flicker and flame again. The *shofar* that symbolizes this spiritual cry for help bears witness to the vitality that remains in Jewish hearts, even when there seemed to be no hope.

An allusion to this is the test found in the Mishnah (*Keilim* 17:13). There is an amphibious animal known as כֶּלֶב הַמַּיִם, literally *sea dog* (generally translated as sea otter or seal). Regarding the laws of purity and contamination, it is necessary to know whether it is a water or a land animal, since their respective laws are different. The Mishnah teaches that the sea dog is a land animal, because when it is threatened it flees from the water to the land. The principle of the Mishnah extends to people as well: It is that creatures instinctively return to their origins in time of danger. The amphibian dashes to land; the Jew calls out to God, however incoherently.

Creatures instinctively return to their origins in time of danger. The amphibian dashes to land; the Jew calls out to God, however incoherently.

The *shofar* sound is the beginning of repentance, and like every action it brings a reaction. Scripture says, 'ה צִלְּךָ, HASHEM *is your Protector* (*Psalms* 121:5), but the word צֵל can also be translated as *shadow*, and it is this translation that is used by *Shelah* and many others to explain the verse: HASHEM *is your Shadow*; just as a shadow mimics the actions of the one casting it, so God, as it were, copies the deeds of the Jews. This is the import of the Talmudic dictum that God puts on *tefillin*, and that His *tefillin* contain Scriptural verses that attest to the uniqueness of Israel (*Berachos* 6a). Again, it is the "shadow effect": If Israel is scrupulous in donning *tefillin* that contain Scriptural verses attesting to the Oneness of God, then God responds by attesting to the uniqueness of Israel.

Just as a shadow mimics the actions of the one casting it, so God, as it were, copies the deeds of the Jews.

Whatever *mitzvah* a Jew performs is reflected in God's response to him, because our deeds are important to God and He acts accordingly. If Jews are kind to one another, God is generous to Jews. When Israel prays, God takes note and answers. Thus, our prayers speak of Him as "remembering" us, although — as other prayers emphasize — the concept of "forgetfulness" cannot be associated with Him. The intent is that if *we* remember His omnipotence and mercy by pleading for His compassion, we cause *Him* to be attentive to us, as if He had suddenly "remembered" us.

The Process

The spark within the heart was dormant but not dead, and the shofar represents its inarticulate cry for life.

This process begins on Rosh Hashanah with the *shofar* blast. The spark within the heart was dormant but not dead, and the *shofar* represents its inarticulate cry for life. The spark is so weak that it is incapable of putting its longing into words, much as many of us enter the Days of Awe with intellectual awareness that our conduct has been deplorable and a vague desire to repent, but we cannot muster the desire to truly change. We feel, but we cannot translate our feelings into sincere speech, much less effective action. But a longing is present, inarticulate but present, like the thin sound of the *shofar* that is inarticulate, but comes from deep inside. The Heavenly "Shadow" reciprocates by drawing closer and enabling us to break through the barriers of indifference that had built up over the months and years.

The Torah ordains only one day of Rosh Hashanah.

During the period of the Second Temple, the Sages ordained that there be a second day, as well, to avoid confusion that might result from a delay in the testimony of witnesses who had seen the new moon. [See the ArtScroll *Mishnah Rosh Hashanah* ch. 4 for a discussion of this subject.] However, it is axiomatic in Rabbinic literature that there is more than one level of cause. The immediate cause was the practical one of delayed testimony and a resultant confusion in the Temple service, but there was an underlying cause involving the spiritual needs of the nation. So, too, commentators find hidden layers of meaning and purpose in the Rabbinic institution of the second festival day of Rosh Hashanah.

Commentators find hidden layers of meaning and purpose in the Rabbinic institution of the second festival day of Rosh Hashanah.

At first, a single day of Rosh Hashanah was sufficient to set in motion the process of repentance. As the Creator had instituted from the genesis of the universe, there would be ten steps — like the ten *sefirah*-emanations of Kabbalistic literature — until the process reached its climax with the sanctity and forgiveness of Yom Kippur. The first day of Rosh Hashanah was אִתְעֲרוּתָא דִלְעֵילָא, *an inspiration from above*, God's call for us to begin reaching out to Him, as it were. As the centuries marched on, the inspiration of the first day was no longer sufficient to move the nation toward repentance, so the Sages saw the need to institute the permanent second day of Rosh Hashanah. The second day, because it was a Rabbinic institution, is an אִתְעֲרוּתָא דִלְתַתָּא, *an inspiration from below*, representing the Jewish spiritual genius for finding ways to move upward on the ladder of closeness to God. Like all Rabbinically ordained commandments, this was an instance of Israel creating ways to inspire itself with an awareness of God's Presence and a dedication to His service. The first day appeals to Israel's mind and the second day to its heart. Then begin the stages of repentance leading up to the climax — Yom Kippur.

The first day appeals to Israel's mind and the second day to its heart.

Circumcision — Body and Heart

It is noteworthy that Abraham's circumcision took place on Yom Kippur [according to *Pirkei d'Rabbi Eliezer*, unlike other Midrashic sources which maintain that it took place on Passover]. *Harav Gedaliah Schorr* comments that this illustrates the similarity of purpose between the commandments of circumcision and Yom Kippur. Each removes a barrier that suppresses the revelation of holiness.

The physical act of circumcision consists of removing the עָרְלָה [*orlah*], *foreskin*. This small bit of surplusage is called *orlah*, a name that gives us an indication of what it represents, because wherever the term *orlah* is used in Scripture, it refers to a barrier standing in the way of a beneficial result. The first three years of a tree's produce are called *orlah*, because the Torah bars people from enjoying it in any way (*Leviticus* 19:23). A person's resistance to repentance is called עָרְלַת הַלֵּב, *the orlah of the heart.* If left to its sincerest, purest impulses, the heart should long for closeness to God and His will; it should yearn for the soul to be reunited with the holiness it enjoyed before coming in contact with the animal drives and corroding greed that characterize much of life on earth.

If left to its sincerest, purest impulses, the heart should long for closeness to God and His will.

Why, then, doesn't the heart propel man to repent? Because people tend to become habituated in sin, or luxury, or unethical practices or the gradually stultifying conviction that life cannot escape the grip of "business as usual." Once that happens, there is an emotional and intellectual barrier that stifles the heart's inner cry for repentance. That barrier is the *orlah* of the heart.

The bodily *orlah*, too, symbolizes a barrier to holiness. Adam was as close to God as a physical being can possibly be. So great was he at the time of his creation that the angels thought he was a Divine being before whom they should sing praises. No aspect of Creation was incomprehensible to him, and his body was as brilliant as the sun. Adam's closeness to God found physical expression in the fact that he was born circumcised; that is, that there was no *orlah* intervening

Adam's closeness to God found physical expression in the fact that he was born circumcised.

between him and God. Even the organ that represents man's most animal-like urge was totally harnessed to God's service. Nothing stood between Adam and God. Adam was created circumcised for he was a superior being, but by succumbing to sin, he fell prey to the natural forces that should have been his servants. Having set his sights downward toward earth, he could no longer look to the heavens as he was created to do. His personal failure created a barrier against the spirit, a barrier that was mirrored in his body, for the Sages teach that when he sinned, the symbol of his closeness to God, his circumcision, was covered by a growth of flesh (*Sanhedrin* 38b).

His personal failure created a barrier against the spirit, a barrier that was mirrored in his body.

Then Abraham revealed new vistas of recognition that Hashem was everywhere and controlled everything. He earned the privilege of being designated the father of a nation that would carry on his mission of standing up to skeptics and enemies, until the day when all nations would acknowledge Israel's Godly message. Abraham saw God everywhere. Obstructions to holiness withered away. The human race still was encumbered with the spiritual and physical *orlah* of Adam, but Abraham demonstrated that man could surmount it. God recognized this change in his spiritual essence by giving him the commandment of circumcision. [See Overview to the ArtScroll *Bris Milah*.]

But Abraham demonstrated that man could surmount it.

III. The Gift of His Nearness

A Special Day

On Yom Kippur, too, God gives us the gift of His nearness, making it possible for us to remove the barriers that our shortcomings have erected. The proportions of this nearness are truly awesome, as evidenced by the two primary historical events that symbolize the purpose of the day.

A commandment of the Torah should never be understood as merely a commemoration of a historical occurrence.

Let us be clear that, as we find often in the commentaries, a commandment of the Torah should never be understood as merely a commemoration of a historical occurrence. Just the opposite — the Torah existed before Creation, and the events that are associated with the respective commandments were ordained to coincide with those dates. For example, in God's master plan that pre-dated Creation, the fifteenth of Nissan was a time of freedom and that is why the events commemorated by Pesach occurred at that time, not that we celebrate anniversaries of events that took place in Nissan only coincidentally. Thus, by examing the events Divinely associated with Yom Kippur, we can understand God's purpose in ordaining the day.

In explaining the commandment of Yom Kippur, *Chinuch* (*mitzvah* 185) writes:

> From the beginning of the Creation of the universe, He designated and sanctified it for this purpose, and after God blessed it He designated this day for atonement. The day was sanctified and it received the power of purity from Him until it [i.e., the day itself] could assist in atonement. This is why the Sages say everywhere that Yom Kippur atones, as if to say that the day itself [even without repentance] provides atonement for less serious sins.

Yom Kippur atones, as if to say that the day itself [even without repentance] provides atonement for less serious sins.

The Midrash implies a similar thought. On the verse *It was evening and it was morning, one day* (Genesis 1:5), the Midrash comments that the term *"one day"* — rather than the seemingly more logical *first* day — implies that there was a day that was intended from the beginning of Creation to be unique. And which was this "one day"? — it was Yom Kippur. The Midrash comments further that the term יוֹם אֶחָד can be translated *the day* **of** *the Only One*, for when God was all alone — *the Only One* — He desired to rest His Presence in the worlds below (*Bereishis Rabbah* 83:10).

Harav Schorr elaborates on the uniqueness of Yom Kippur, as indicated by *Chinuch* and the Midrash. On the first day of Creation, no individual being had yet been created. On the second day, the angels, including the Satan and his forces of evil, were created, and the Satan was given the power to act as if he were an independent force, separate from God. But on the first day, there could be no doubt that God alone was the Master of all, that there were no forces of evil, and that only He was the Source of all life. It was His will that there continue to be a day when everyone with eyes to see would recognize that all power resides in God alone. That day is Yom Kippur, when, as the Sages teach, Satan's power is suspended, so that Israel can repent and renew its attachment to God. On Yom Kippur, God gives us a glimpse of the first day of Creation, when there was no evil and nothing to cast doubt on God's solitary majesty.

On the first day, there could be no doubt that God alone was the Master of all, that there were no forces of evil.

On Yom Kippur, God gives us a glimpse of the first day of Creation, when there was no evil and nothing to cast doubt on God's solitary majesty.

Two events took place on Yom Kippur. Moses came down from Mount Sinai carrying the second Tablets of the Law and the Kohen Gadol was permitted to enter the Holy of Holies, the only time any human being was permitted to enter that holiest of all places.

Moses' descent from Sinai was one of the supreme moments in Jewish history, because it signified that God had forgiven Israel for the grievous sin of the Golden Calf. It should not be forgotten that eighty days before that first day of atonement, the very existence of the nation was in doubt. Moses had found them prancing around the Golden Calf and he had smashed the first Tablets. God had expressed His intention to exterminate the nation and begin a new Jewish people with Moses' offspring. Only Moses' prayers and then the people's repentance had saved them from destruction, and his descent from heaven with the second Tablets guaranteed that God had indeed forgiven and renewed His intimacy with Israel, as it were. A renewed closeness had been achieved and, with Moses as its agent, the Jewish people had united itself with God.

Moses' descent from heaven with the second Tablets guaranteed that God had indeed forgiven and renewed His intimacy with Israel.

And on every Yom Kippur thereafter, the Kohen Gadol would enter the Holy of Holies — only one day a year and only one representative of the nation — entering the place where the Tablets were kept and which represents the Oneness of the majesty of God.

As the Scriptural account and the Talmudic discussion of it make clear, the Kohen Gadol's service was able to bring atonement upon the entire nation, but today, without a Temple and without the service of the Kohen Gadol, how can the nation achieve atonement? Is there still a way for a multitude to be forgiven thanks to the service of an individual?

According to the Talmud, there is.

The Power of an Individual

יָחִיד שֶׁשָּׁב מוֹחֲלִין לוֹ וּלְכָל הָעוֹלָם כֻּלּוֹ.

If an individual repents, God forgives him and the entire world (Yoma 86b).

To understand the atonement effected by the Kohen Gadol or by an individual penitent, we must understand the concept of עַצְמוֹ שֶׁל יוֹם מְכַפֵּר, *the very day [of Yom Kippur] brings atonement*. According to the Sages, this is so only in combination with *teshuvah*, but repen-

But repentance accomplishes more on Yom Kippur, in conjunction with the day, than it can at any other time.

tance accomplishes more on Yom Kippur, in conjunction with the day, than it can at any other time. According to Rabbi [Judah the Prince, the great and saintly leader and redacter of the Mishnah], the holiness of the day itself is sufficient to provide atonement even without repentance (*Shavuos* 13a, *Yoma* 85a). How can a day bring atonement — or even assist in bringing atonement — if a person does not merit it on his own? Surely atonement is not an automatic process!

All Jewish hearts have within them the spark of holiness, and all Jews are united as offspring of Abraham, Isaac, and Jacob. Circumstances, temptation, environment, exile, persecution — all the ills of the human condition — have frayed this unity and, indeed, caused it virtually to disappear. The present exile was caused by the sins of unjustified hatred and national dissension. It is axiomatic that the exile cannot end unless Israel manages to banish from its midst the sins that caused it. Sadly, no one familiar with the Jewish experience can deny that hatred and dissension are still

At root, however, Israel is one and the nation in its essence is good.

very much with us. At root, however, Israel *is* one and the nation in its essence is *good*. External symptoms to the contrary, the warts and blemishes on the national body are external wounds inflicted by the strains of exile, but Israel's essence remains good. And the spark within us that is our legacy from the Patriarchs is never extinguished.

The service of Yom Kippur brings out these essential truths. The Sages teach that the Kohen Gadol's incense service in the Holy of Holies provided atonement for the sin of *lashon hara*, or gossip, slander, and rumor-mongering. As noted above, these are among the sins that impede repentance and clearly few sins do more to breed hatred and destroy national unity. They teach that one of the merits that enabled him to enter that sacred place was the covenant of circumcision, the commandment that signifies our bond with God and the Patriarchs [see below]. And the service of the he-goat to Azazel signified that our sins are placed upon Esau, because Israel's sins are the fault of external factors, the evil that is represented by Esau [see below].

All of this is brought out by the uniqueness of Yom Kippur, when the Satan is stripped of his power, and when every Jew can raise himself to the level of the angels. All of this is brought out by the uniqueness of Yom Kippur — עֲצוּמוֹ שֶׁל יוֹם — the day that was created for atonement, when the Satan is stripped of his power, and when every Jew can raise himself to the level of the angels [see Overview, ArtScroll Yom Kippur Machzor].

Since all Jewish souls are united with one another and with God, the achievement of an individual has the power to exalt the rest of the nation along with himself. Moses ascended the mountain as an agent of the nation. As did the Kohen Gadol when he entered the Holy of Holies. And as does any individual Jew when he genuinely repents. When that happens, the *nation* changes, and, to a degree at least, even an individual can accomplish what the Kohen Gadol accomplished. The principle is the same. *Is there ever a Yom Kippur when there is no Jew who repents with all his heart and soul? Never.* Is there ever a Yom Kippur when there is no Jew who repents with all his heart and soul? Never — thus Israel can always hope that, collectively, it can be elevated by the achievement of one of its members.

In a related vein, *Michtav Me'Eliyahu* (vol. 3, p. 283) explains the dictum: Moses said, "On Yom Kippur I will see the glory of the Holy One, Blessed is He, and then I will atone for the Children of Israel (*Pirkei d'Rabbi Eliezer* ch. 15). When someone is able to understand to whatever degree the apparently inexplicable workings of God's providence, he becomes elevated. More than that, when he gains a perception of Heavenly justice and mercy, then all the people with whom he had come in contact and all the situations he had experienced — the sort of phenomena that may well have caused others to doubt the ways of God — these same people and events will have contributed to his new awareness of God's greatness, because it was because of them that he gained his new understanding.

All the people with whom he had come in contact and all the situations he had experienced will have contributed to his new awareness of God's greatness.

This in itself becomes a vehicle for their atonement, because all of them have contributed to the growth of the individual who perceived the glory of God. Such things happen when a person realizes that seemingly worthless people have an important role in the world. Or someone who requires unexpected surgery bemoans the inconvenience, pain, and loss of time — and under the knife an unsuspected malignancy is discovered in its early stages, and successfully removed in time. A new discovery — God is merciful! And if this is so, then it is equally true in the myriad situations when we do not understand. The wise person extrapolates and realizes that everything God does is for the good, even when we cannot understand. And if a constellation of people contribute to this new awareness, then all of them are partners effecting the revelation of His glory; if so, all derive atonement as a result.

The Torah describes Israel as יַעֲקֹב חֶבֶל נַחֲלָתוֹ, *Jacob the portion of his heritage* (*Deuteronomy* 32:9). The word חֶבֶל can be translated as *rope*, suggesting that all Jews are attached to one another as if by a single rope. If one pulls one end of the rope, he moves everything that is attached to it along its entire length. And — because all Jews are extensions of the Patriarchs — the rope's uppermost tip is attached to Jacob, whose image is engraved on the Heavenly Throne of Glory. The "rope" extends from Israel's loftiest personage on high to its least distinguished son or daughter below. All are

All Jews are attached to one another as if by a single rope. If one pulls one end of the rope, he moves everything that is attached to it along its entire length.

connected to one another, and on Yom Kippur every Jew has it in his power to pull others up with him.

IV. Purim and Yom Kippur

‫... אֵיזֶה שֵׁם טוֹב שֶׁקָּנְתָה? שֶׁכָּל הַמּוֹעֲדִים עֲתִידִים‬
‫לִבָּטֵל וִימֵי הַפּוּרִים לֹא בְּטֵלִים ... לְעוֹלָם. ר' אֱלִיעֶזֶר‬
‫אוֹמֵר אַף יוֹם הַכִּפּוּרִים לֹא יִבָּטֵל ...‬

What was the good name that [Esther] earned for herself? That all the festivals may be nullified, but the days of Purim will never be nullified ... R' Eliezer says, Yom Kippur, too, will not be nullified (Yalkut Shimoni, Esther 944).

Two Enduring Days

There is a special quality about Purim and Yom Kippur, a quality that will endure even after the Final Redemption, when the nature of the universe will change. In time to come, *Maharal* explains, the observance of the commandments may take a form other than the one we know today; the Torah is eternal, but in a new world with a heightened level of spirituality, an existence far above our experience and even our imagination, certain elements of the commandments as we know them may be altered. But not Purim and Yom Kippur. They will remain as they are. Furthermore, in the familiar dictum of the *Zohar*, the Hebrew name for Yom Kippur, ‫יוֹם כִּפּוּרִים‬, alludes to the similarity between these two seemingly *dissimilar* days: ‫יוֹם כְּפוּרִים‬, *it is a day that is* **like** *Purim*. It seems incongruous that a day of joyous abandon and a day of awesome introspection should be more similar to one another than any of the other festivals to one another. What is it about Purim and Yom Kippur that creates this relationship?

In a new world with a heightened level of spirituality, certain elements of the commandments as we know them may be altered.

The world of the future will be a world of life.

The world of the future will be a world of life. There will be a resuscitation of the dead, and the world will return to the exalted level of Adam and Eve, to the level that the Jewish people attained when they heard the voice of God and received the Ten Commandments at Mount Sinai. During those times, there was no death and no Evil Inclination as we know it today. Truth was so obvious that falsehood had no allure, and people realized that the temptation to sin is nothing more than falsehood disguised by an attractive rationale. But

Adam and Israel allowed themselves to be driven to sin, so death came into being, and it became the task of Israel and mankind to rid themselves of the delusions. Adam and Israel allowed themselves to be driven to sin, so death came into being, and it became the task of Israel and mankind to rid themselves of the delusions that had caused them to deny the truth and had dashed them down from angelic heights to vulnerable, painful mortality.

The primary characteristic of the World to Come, therefore, is life. God is the ultimate life, and when man lives up to his ultimate purpose, he will be reunited with the Source of Life. In such an existence, everything associated with man will be of a higher order. But Purim and Yom Kippur will not change — *because they are themselves manifestations of life.* Let us see why.

In the time of Mordechai and Esther, it was decreed that every Jewish man, woman, and child be murdered on a single day in the month of Adar. Haman the Amalekite was on the verge of achieving the goal of his ancestor Esau and his malevolent offspring. And his willing accomplice, King Ahasuerus, put all the forces of the world's leading power at Haman's disposal. The situation of the Jewish people was hopeless. They had but recently been exiled and dispersed. They had not an ally in the world. Derision and contempt were their lot everywhere. They were as good as dead; the months until Haman's deadline were more a torture than a reprieve.

Yom Kippur, too, would seem to be a time of *By what right can the sinner hope to escape God's judgment?* inevitable death — according to the rules of logic. By what right can the sinner hope to escape God's judgment? And what human being has not sinned? Would any of us allow a child to keep playing with a tool that he uses to smash our windows? Should God permit us to continue "playing" with a soul with which we flout Him, instead of serving Him?

As noted above, repentance pre-existed the world because God knew that man could not exist unless he had the potential of redeeming himself. Thus it is not a concept that we could regard as rational. Indeed, according to the Sages, before creating *teshuvah*, repentance, God inquired of Wisdom and Prophecy what should be done with sinners. They answered quite logically. Wisdom argued that sinners should be pursued by their evil — without any hope of forgiveness. And Prophecy argued that the sinful soul deserves to die (*Yerushalmi Makkos* 2:6). So the sinner should have no grounds for hope on Yom Kippur; God decreed otherwise.

Both festivals, Yom Kippur and Purim, transcend human "certainty"; they are united with the ultimate, Heavenly Source of life.

But Israel survived Haman's threat with renewed vigor, and it survives every Yom Kippur with God's acceptance of its repentance. In place of death there is life. This means that both festivals, Yom Kippur and Purim, transcend human "certainty"; they are united with the ultimate, Heavenly Source of life which is unaffected by the laws of logic or nature. In the World to Come, all existence will rise to that level, but Purim and Yom Kippur are already manifestations of life, so they will never change.

Triumph Over Esau

The two festivals are similar because each represents a triumph over the forces of Esau.

In another way as well the two festivals are similar in the very root of their being — because each represents a triumph over the forces of Esau. When the time came for Jacob to receive the blessings from his father Isaac, Rebecca instructed him to go to the flock וְקַח לִי מִשָּׁם שְׁנֵי גְדָיֵי עִזִּים טֹבִים, *and fetch me from there two choice, young kids from the goats* (Genesis 27:9). Noting that the service of Yom Kippur, too, includes two goats, the Midrash comments that when Rebecca spoke of the goats as being טֹבִים, *choice* or *good*, the goats would be *choice* or *good* not only for him, but for his descendants, as well, because Israel would be granted atonement on Yom Kippur though an offering of two goats. The goats of Yom Kippur are called שְׂעִיר עִזִּים, and since

Esau is known as שָׂעִיר (*Genesis* 27:11), the Sages derive

When the Kohen Gadol places the sins of Israel on the head of one of the goats, it is as if the sins are being placed upon the head of Esau. that when the Kohen Gadol places the sins of Israel on the head of one of the goats (*Leviticus* 16:22), it is as if the sins are being placed upon the head of Esau. [This difficult concept will be discussed in the Overview, ArtScroll *Vayikra* vol. II.] Thus, Yom Kippur marks the vindication of Jacob at the expense of Esau, meaning, as we shall see below, that the responsibility for Jacob's sins should properly be borne by Esau (*Bereishis Rabbah* 65:14, *Vayikra Rabbah* 21:11, 27:9).

Purim, too, is a time when a fate intended for Israel was transferred to Esau. Purim, too, is a time when a fate intended for Israel was transferred to Esau. Haman had done his work well in decreeing Israel's doom and erecting a gallows for Mordechai's execution, but in the end it was Israel that was given the right to do away with its enemies and Haman who inaugurated the gallows. As the Midrash relates, Haman complained to the king that the Jews had too many festivals, but the outcome was that he was responsible for adding another one to the Jewish calendar — and a festival whose significance and joy would endure forever! (*Maharal, Tiferes Yisrael, ch. 53*).

V. Power of the Day

רַבִּי אוֹמֵר כָּל עֲבֵרוֹת שֶׁבַּתּוֹרָה בֵּין עָשָׂה תְשׁוּבָה בֵּין
לֹא עָשָׂה תְשׁוּבָה יוֹם הַכִּפּוּרִים מְכַפֵּר, חוּץ מִפּוֹרֵק
עוֹל, וּמְגַלֶּה פָנִים בַּתּוֹרָה שֶׁלֹּא כְּהַלָכָה, וּמֵפֵר בְּרִיתוֹ
שֶׁל אַבְרָהָם אָבִינוּ, שֶׁאִם עָשָׂה תְשׁוּבָה יוֹם הַכִּפּוּרִים
מְכַפֵּר וְאִם לֹא עָשָׂה תְשׁוּבָה אֵין יוֹם הַכִּפּוּרִים מְכַפֵּר.
*Rabbi [Judah the Prince] says, Yom Kippur
atones for all the sins of the Torah, whether
one repented or whether one did not repent
— except for one who has cast off [God's]
yoke, or [intentionally] misinterpreted the
Torah, or annulled the covenant of our father
Abraham [i.e., circumcision]. Then, if he
repented, Yom Kippur atones, but if he did
not repent, Yom Kippur does not atone
(Shavuos 13a, Yoma 85b).*

Triple Bond

The Torah creates a bond between God and every Jew.

The Torah creates a bond between God and every Jew, but the health of such a bond requires three conditions: (a) The Jew must be willing to be bound; (b) there must be an agent to create the bond; and (c) the Jew must acknowledge God to Whom he is bound. A Jew who refuses to be circumcised has destroyed the covenant that gives standing and validity to the bond, thereby refusing to be bound. The Torah is the agent that unites a Jew with God, the recipient with the Giver; if he denies the validity of the Torah he severs his connection with God. And if ח"ו he throws off the yoke of God's sovereignty, he denies that there is Anyone to Whom to be bound.

Often we may be found sadly wanting in our allegiance and performance — but we do not sever the bond.

People are far from perfect, even those who generally are loyal to the Torah and perform the commandments. Often we may be found sadly wanting in our allegiance and performance — but we do not sever the bond. We are like a fruit that becomes damaged or whose stem is nicked. As long as it is still connected to the tree and the tree is healthy, the fruit will live. But if something happens that prevents it from drawing nourishment from the tree, it will shrivel and die.

Similarly the Jew. He is one with God. His shortcomings do not alter that, and on the day that God becomes universally acknowledged as One, and Satan's accusations are stilled, atonement is granted to the Jew. As long as he maintains his bond with his Creator, he is nourished by the living waters of Godliness and his sins are forgiven. His essence is intact and unsullied; damaged, perhaps, but not severed from its Source.

Let the Jew, however, deny any of the three indispensable ingredients of his attachment to God — basic faith, the Torah, or the covenant — and he is no longer part of the unit. He is a severed fruit, and no matter how healthy he may look, he is doomed. When that happens, according to Rabbi, Yom Kippur in itself cannot automatically give atonement.

But even then, there is hope. Repentance.

Because the root of repentance [תְּשׁוּבָה] is שָׁב, *return*.

Repentance is the Jew's return to his Source. He re-grafts himself to the tree of life and atonement becomes his reward.

Repentance is the Jew's return to his Source, his reunification with his Creator. He re-grafts himself to the tree of life, as it were, and atonement becomes his reward (*Maharal, Tiferes Yisrael* ch. 9).

Yom Kippur is a day of hope and life for Israel and a day of mercy and longing for God. He longs for our repentance so that He can bestow His mercy upon us, and because he does, we never lose hope that the day's verdict will be an inscription in the Book of Life. May God and Israel both achieve their goals on this and every Yom Kippur.

Menachem Av, 5749   *Rabbi Nosson Scherman*
August, 1989

❧ Background and Insights

The Scriptural Verses
The Ten Days of Repentance
Erev Yom Kippur
The Mitzvah of Eating on Erev Yom Kippur
The Day and Date of Yom Kippur
On This Very Day
Teshuvah / Repentance
Selections from Ramban's Hilchos Teshuvah
Pardon and Forgiveness
Viduy / Confession
The Five Afflictions
Some Aspects of the Prayer Services
Minchah
Ne'ilah
The Night After Yom Kippur

❧ Yom Kippur Stories

Haazinu – A Concise History of the World
The Sincerity of the Flute
The Cantonist
Yom Kippur During World War II

– Rabbi Avie Gold

◄§ Background and Insights:

The Scriptural Verses

◄§The special laws regarding Yom Kippur appear in the Torah in three separate passages.

☐ The first of these (*Leviticus 16:1-34*) appears in *parashas Acharei* and details the unique Temple Service of the day. This service is performed exclusively by the *Kohen Gadol* (High Priest). Moreover, this passage, quite appropriately, is the Torah reading for *Shacharis* of Yom Kippur.

וַיְדַבֵּר ה' אֶל מֹשֶׁה אַחֲרֵי מוֹת שְׁנֵי בְּנֵי אַהֲרֹן בְּקָרְבָתָם לִפְנֵי ה' וַיָּמֻתוּ. וַיֹּאמֶר ה'
אֶל מֹשֶׁה דַּבֵּר אֶל אַהֲרֹן אָחִיךָ וְאַל יָבֹא בְכָל עֵת אֶל הַקֹּדֶשׁ מִבֵּית לַפָּרֹכֶת אֶל פְּנֵי
הַכַּפֹּרֶת אֲשֶׁר עַל הָאָרֹן וְלֹא יָמוּת כִּי בֶּעָנָן אֵרָאֶה עַל הַכַּפֹּרֶת. בְּזֹאת יָבֹא אַהֲרֹן
אֶל הַקֹּדֶשׁ . . . וְהָיְתָה לָכֶם לְחֻקַּת עוֹלָם בַּחֹדֶשׁ הַשְּׁבִיעִי בֶּעָשׂוֹר לַחֹדֶשׁ תְּעַנּוּ אֶת
נַפְשֹׁתֵיכֶם וְכָל מְלָאכָה לֹא תַעֲשׂוּ הָאֶזְרָח וְהַגֵּר הַגָּר בְּתוֹכְכֶם. כִּי בַיּוֹם הַזֶּה יְכַפֵּר
עֲלֵיכֶם לְטַהֵר אֶתְכֶם מִכֹּל חַטֹּאתֵיכֶם לִפְנֵי ה' תִּטְהָרוּ. שַׁבַּת שַׁבָּתוֹן הִיא לָכֶם
וְעִנִּיתֶם אֶת נַפְשֹׁתֵיכֶם חֻקַּת עוֹלָם. וְכִפֶּר הַכֹּהֵן אֲשֶׁר יִמְשַׁח אֹתוֹ וַאֲשֶׁר יְמַלֵּא אֶת
יָדוֹ לְכַהֵן תַּחַת אָבִיו וְלָבַשׁ אֶת בִּגְדֵי הַבָּד בִּגְדֵי הַקֹּדֶשׁ. וְכִפֶּר אֶת מִקְדַּשׁ הַקֹּדֶשׁ
וְאֶת אֹהֶל מוֹעֵד וְאֶת הַמִּזְבֵּחַ יְכַפֵּר וְעַל הַכֹּהֲנִים וְעַל כָּל עַם הַקָּהָל יְכַפֵּר. וְהָיְתָה
זֹּאת לָכֶם לְחֻקַּת עוֹלָם לְכַפֵּר עַל בְּנֵי יִשְׂרָאֵל מִכָּל חַטֹּאתָם אַחַת בַּשָּׁנָה וַיַּעַשׂ
כַּאֲשֶׁר צִוָּה ה' אֶת מֹשֶׁה.

HASHEM spoke to Moses after the death of Aaron's two sons, when they approached before HASHEM, and they died. And HASHEM said to Moses: Speak to Aaron, your brother — he may not come at all times into the Sanctuary within the curtain, in front of the cover that is upon the Ark, so that he should not die; for in a cloud will I appear upon the cover. Only with this may Aaron come into the Sanctuary . . . This shall remain for you an eternal decree: in the seventh month, on the tenth of the month, you shall afflict yourselves and not do any work, neither the citizen nor the alien who lives among you. For through this day he will atone for you to cleanse you; from all your sins before HASHEM you shall be cleansed. It is a Sabbath of complete rest for you when you are to afflict yourselves; it is an eternal decree. The Kohen, who has been anointed or who has been given the authority to serve in place of his father, shall bring atonement; he shall don linen vestments, the sacred vestments. He shall bring atonement upon the Holy of Holies; and upon the Tent of Meeting and the Altar shall he bring atonement; and upon the Kohanim and upon all the people of the congregation shall he bring atonement. This shall be to you an eternal decree to bring atonement upon the Children of Israel for all their sins once a year; and [Aaron] did as HASHEM commanded Moses.

☐ The second Torah passage (*Leviticus* 23:26-32) that speaks of Yom Kippur appears in the section of *parashas Emor,* that discusses the festivals. It contains the commandment of affliction, i.e., fasting, and prohibition against working. These verses make no mention of the Temple service.

Although this passage would seem the logical choice for the afternoon Torah reading of Yom Kippur, it is not. Presumably this is due to the brevity of the passage, seven verses, while the Torah reading requires a minimum of nine verses.

וַיְדַבֵּר ה׳ אֶל מֹשֶׁה לֵּאמֹר. אַךְ בֶּעָשׂוֹר לַחֹדֶשׁ הַשְּׁבִיעִי הַזֶּה יוֹם הַכִּפֻּרִים הוּא מִקְרָא קֹדֶשׁ יִהְיֶה לָכֶם וְעִנִּיתֶם אֶת נַפְשֹׁתֵיכֶם וְהִקְרַבְתֶּם אִשֶּׁה לַה׳. וְכָל מְלָאכָה לֹא תַעֲשׂוּ בְּעֶצֶם הַיּוֹם הַזֶּה כִּי יוֹם כִּפֻּרִים הוּא לְכַפֵּר עֲלֵיכֶם לִפְנֵי ה׳ אֱלֹהֵיכֶם. כִּי כָל הַנֶּפֶשׁ אֲשֶׁר לֹא תְעֻנֶּה בְּעֶצֶם הַיּוֹם הַזֶּה וְנִכְרְתָה מֵעַמֶּיהָ. וְכָל הַנֶּפֶשׁ אֲשֶׁר תַּעֲשֶׂה כָּל מְלָאכָה בְּעֶצֶם הַיּוֹם הַזֶּה וְהַאֲבַדְתִּי אֶת הַנֶּפֶשׁ הַהִוא מִקֶּרֶב עַמָּהּ. כָּל מְלָאכָה לֹא תַעֲשׂוּ חֻקַּת עוֹלָם לְדֹרֹתֵיכֶם בְּכֹל מֹשְׁבֹתֵיכֶם. שַׁבַּת שַׁבָּתוֹן הוּא לָכֶם וְעִנִּיתֶם אֶת נַפְשֹׁתֵיכֶם בְּתִשְׁעָה לַחֹדֶשׁ בָּעֶרֶב מֵעֶרֶב עַד עֶרֶב תִּשְׁבְּתוּ שַׁבַּתְּכֶם.

HASHEM spoke to Moses saying: But on the tenth day of this month it is a Day of Atonement; there shall be a holy convocation for you, and you shall afflict yourselves; you shall offer a fire-offering to HASHEM. You shall not do any work on this very day, for it is a Day of Atonement to atone for you before HASHEM, your God. For any soul who will not be afflicted on this very day will be cut off from its people. And any soul who will do work on this very day, I will destroy that soul from among its people. You shall not do any work; it is an eternal decree throughout your generations in all your dwelling places. It is a day of complete rest for you and you shall afflict yourselves, on the ninth of the month in the evening — from evening to evening — shall you rest on your rest day.

☐ The third Torah passage (*Numbers* 29:7-11) is in *parashas Pinchas,* in the section that details the *mussaf* offerings of each festival. As is the case of the other festivals, these verses are read as *Maftir* on Yom Kippur morning.

וּבֶעָשׂוֹר לַחֹדֶשׁ הַשְּׁבִיעִי הַזֶּה מִקְרָא קֹדֶשׁ יִהְיֶה לָכֶם וְעִנִּיתֶם אֶת נַפְשֹׁתֵיכֶם כָּל מְלָאכָה לֹא תַעֲשׂוּ. וְהִקְרַבְתֶּם עֹלָה לַה׳ רֵיחַ נִיחֹחַ פַּר בֶּן בָּקָר אֶחָד אַיִל אֶחָד כְּבָשִׂים בְּנֵי שָׁנָה שִׁבְעָה תְּמִימִם יִהְיוּ לָכֶם. וּמִנְחָתָם סֹלֶת בְּלוּלָה בַשֶּׁמֶן שְׁלֹשָׁה עֶשְׂרֹנִים לַפָּר שְׁנֵי עֶשְׂרֹנִים לָאַיִל הָאֶחָד. עִשָּׂרוֹן עִשָּׂרוֹן לַכֶּבֶשׂ הָאֶחָד לְשִׁבְעַת הַכְּבָשִׂים. שְׂעִיר עִזִּים אֶחָד חַטָּאת מִלְּבַד חַטַּאת הַכִּפֻּרִים וְעֹלַת הַתָּמִיד וּמִנְחָתָהּ וְנִסְכֵּיהֶם.

On the tenth day of this seventh month, there shall be a holy convocation for you and your shall afflict yourselves; you shall do no work. You shall offer an elevation-offering to HASHEM for a satisfying aroma — one young bull, one ram, seven lambs in their first year; they shall be unblemished for you. And their meal-offering shall be fine flour mixed with oil — three tenth-ephah for the bull, two tenth-ephah for the one ram. A single tenth-ephah for each lamb of the seven lambs. One he-goat for a sin-offering; aside from the sin-offering of the atonement and the continual elevation-offering, with its meal-offering; and their libations.

The Ten Days of Repentance

Suspended in Judgment

◆§Three Books are opened on Rosh Hashanah: One for the completely wicked; one for the completely righteous; and one for those between. The completely righteous are immediately inscribed for life; the completely wicked are immediately inscribed for death; those between remain suspended between Rosh Hashanah and Yom Kippur. If they prove worthy, they are inscribed for life, if not they are inscribed for death (*Rosh Hashanah* 16b).

At first glance we may interpret the fate of those between as a sort of suspension of judgment. Since they are neither all good nor all bad, they are given a ten-day chance to clear their records. If they repent, their slate is cleaned and they are given a verdict of life. If not, they are given a verdict of death.

However, a more literal reading of the Talmud dictates a different approach. The words תְּלוּיִם וְעוֹמְדִים, usually rendered "remain suspended," literally mean "hang and stand."

Their verdict is pronounced on Rosh Hashanah and since they are not completely righteous, they are sentenced to death. But since they are not completely wicked, their sentence is postponed until Yom Kippur. It is as if they were made to stand on the gallows, the noose on their necks, suspended in the air — but with a chair under their feet. They "hang and stand."

Should they prove worthy by repenting between Rosh Hashanah and Yom Kippur, the noose is removed from their neck. Should they not prove worthy, the chair is removed (*Mei'imrei Shlomo*).

A Test of Love and Awe

◆§Although the Torah decrees only one fast day, Yom Kippur itself, many righteous people accept additional fasts upon themselves in the days and weeks preceding Yom Kippur. Some even fast every day beginning with the Sunday before Rosh Hashanah (but excluding Rosh Hashanah, Shabbos, and Erev Yom Kippur).

According to *Kisvei HaArizal*: During the Ten Days of Repentance each Jew can discover the extent to which he loves and fears God, for according to the intensity of his love and awe will he be aroused to return to Hashem. A person who epitomizes awe of God will begin fasting even before Rosh Hashanah. Those on a lower plane will begin between Rosh

Hashanah and Yom Kippur. While those on a still lower level will fast only on Yom Kippur itself. But should there be a one who considers Yom Kippur as but an ordinary day, his soul has no share among the souls of Israel. It is for this reason that one who eats on Yom Kippur is deserving of *kares,* spiritual excision. And this is the meaning of the verse: *For any soul who will not be afflicted on this very day will be cut off from his people* (*Leviticus* 23:29). If no affliction can be found in a soul on this sanctified and sanctifying day, that is proof that such a soul no longer belongs among the Jews.

Erev Yom Kippur

Preparing for Atonement

◆§The preparations for atonement and for *teshuvah* on Yom Kippur have been proceeding since the days before. And in addition to the *selichos* (penitential prayers), the special changes in the prayers, and the extra *zehirus* (carefulness in *mitzvos*) which are customary during the latter days of Elul and throughout the Ten Days of Repentance, there are a number of preparatory acts reserved especially for Erev Yom Kippur. Some are customs, others are laws. These preparatory acts are: *kaparos* (the atonement ritual), *piyus* (reconciliation), *tevilah* (immersion in a *mikveh*), *viduy* (confession of sins), and *tzedakah* (charity).

The Kaparos Ritual

◆§The ancient ritual of *Kaparos*/Atonement is cited by the early *Geonim* (see *Rosh, Yoma* 8:23; *Tur Orach Chaim* 605).

The ritual is designed to imbue people with the feeling that their lives are at stake as Yom Kippur approaches, and that they must repent and seek atonement. The ceremony symbolizes that our sins cry out for atonement, and that our good deeds and repentance can save us from the punishment we deserve. The form of the ritual calls for a chicken to be moved in a circular motion around the penitent's head. The chicken is later slaughtered [symbolizing the concept that a sinner deserves to give up his soul for not having used it to do God's will] and either the chicken or its cash value is given to the poor, for charity is an indispensable part of repentance — and the combination of the two can achieve atonement.

In giving the *kaparos* chicken to the poor, one must be extremely careful not to embarrass the recipient or to cause him to feel that the donor is ridding himself of his sins and placing them on this poor man's head (*Matteh Ephraim*).

The entrails are left for birds and animals, because this shows the same kind of compassion that we pray God will show us.

□ Technically, any animal should be acceptable for the *kaparos* ritual. However, in order that the ritual not be misconstrued as a sacrificial offering — an act prohibited in the absence of the *Beis HaMikdash* — the animal used for *kaparos* may not be one that is suitable for such sacrifices, e.g., a dove. Chickens were chosen because the Hebrew word גֶּבֶר means both *man* and *rooster*. Thus, use of this particular bird alludes to the person performing the ritual.

In the original and preferable form, a white rooster was taken for a male and a white hen for a female, because the color white symbolizes atonement (see *Isaiah* 1:18). Nevertheless, it is forbidden to make strenuous efforts to find white birds, lest it appear that one is following the idolaters' practice of using only white birds in their ceremonies (see *Avodah Zarah* 13b-14a). [Further details of this ritual appear in the section "Laws and Customs" §45-53.]

Reconciliation

◆§If *kaparos* is a custom stemming from the time of the *Geonim, piyus, reconciliation* (lit., "appeasement"), has its basis in Mishnah (*Yoma* 8:9):

> For sins between man and God, Yom Kippur provides atonement; but for sins between man and his fellow man, Yom Kippur does not provide atonement, until he appeases that man. This did R' Elazar ben Azariah expound: *"From all your sins before HASHEM shall you be cleansed"* (*Leviticus* 16:30) — for sins between man and God, Yom Kippur provides atonement, but for sins between man and his fellow man, Yom Kippur does not provide atonement, until he appeases that man.

The Talmud relates that Rav, having once angered R' Chaninah, went every year for thirteen years to appease him on Erev Yom Kippur. *Rosh* (end of *Yoma*) and *Tur* (*Derech Chaim* 606) infer from this: "Therefore, on Erev Yom Kippur every man should set his heart on appeasing everyone against whom he has transgressed." [Details regarding the *mitzvah* of reconciliation appear in "Laws and Customs" §60-70.]

Immersion

◆§The custom of *tevilah,* immersion in a *mikveh* (ritual bath), on Erev Yom Kippur also has its source in the time of the *Geonim*. There are two reasons for this immersion in the *mikveh*: purification from ritual impurity and preparation for *teshuvah*. Although *R' Saadiah Gaon* ruled that one should recite the blessing " ... Who sanctified us by His commandments and commanded us concerning *tevilah"* for this immersion, the other *Geonim* and the *poskim* disagree, ruling that this *tevilah* should be performed without reciting the blessing. [For further details, see "Laws and Customs" §77-81].

Confession

~§The obligation of *viduy,* confession, on Erev Yom Kippur is a basic law. We read in *Tosefta Yoma:*

> The *mitzvah* of *viduy* on Erev Yom Kippur [is] at nightfall; but the Sages said, a person should confess before he eats and drinks, lest his mind become confused in the midst of eating and drinking; he should confess after eating and drinking, for maybe a mishap (transgression) occurred at the meal. And even though he confessed after he ate and drank, he should confess at *Maariv.*

The requirement of confession before eating is the basis of the current custom of reciting *viduy* at the conclusion of the silent *Shemoneh Esrei* of *Minchah,* then after *Minchah* returning home to eat the final meal before the feast.

This *Tosefta* is the subject of a dispute (cited by *Ran*) among the *Rishonim.* Most of them interpret the words עִם חֲשֵׁכָה, *at nightfall,* to mean after Yom Kippur has begun, so that the essential time for this *viduy* is at *Maariv* of Yom Kippur. When the Sages decreed, from fear of possible confusion, that one should confess before the meal, they did not decree that there should be yet another *viduy* after the meal besides the confession. The words " . . . he should confess after eating" refer to *Maariv* itself.

There is, however, another opinion which holds that the essential law requires one to confess before the beginning of the time of atonement, so as to enter the day in a state of *teshuvah.* "At nightfall," according to this opinion, means immediately before Yom Kippur begins, so that there will be no time to sin between the *viduy* and the beginning of the day, i.e., nightfall. From fear of possible confusion the Sages decreed that one should confess before the meal as well, but in so decreeing they did not abolish the *viduy* which is said at the essential time; that is, at the end of the day. Thus, according to this opinion one must confess twice before night — once before the meal and once after it — and then confess a third time after nightfall, at *Maariv.* [Details concerning *Minchah* of Erev Yom Kippur and the confession appear in "Laws and Customs" §82-89.]

Tzedakah

~§It is customary to distribute charity on the afternoon before Yom Kippur. *Mateh Ephraim* (607) writes:

> In most communities it is the custom to distribute *tzedakah* to the poor as one walks to the synagogue for the *Minchah* Prayer. Also, those responsible for the other *tzedakah* funds in the community sit in the forechamber of the synagogue and there the members of the congregation give *tzedakah,* each man according to his ability.

In many synagogues today, a number of plates or *pushkas,* each for donations to a different charity, are laid out on the *bimah* at *Minchah* time. This permits everyone to fulfill the *mitzvah* of *tzedakah* numerous times.

The Mitzvah of Eating on Erev Yom Kippur

Accounted as Fasting

⊷§The fast of Yom Kippur begins already, in a special way, on Erev Yom Kippur. As the Talmud (*Yoma* 81a) expounds:

וְעִנִּיתֶם אֶת נַפְשֹׁתֵיכֶם בְּתִשְׁעָה לַחֹדֶשׁ, *And you shall afflict your souls on the ninth of the month* (*Leviticus* 23:32).

Do we fast on the *ninth*? Is it not on the *tenth* that we fast? Rather, the Torah tells us that whoever eats and drinks on the ninth, is accounted by Scripture as if he fasted on both the ninth and the tenth.

The relationship of the *mitzvah* of eating and drinking on the ninth to the *mitzvah* of affliction on the tenth does not consist merely in the fact that "it is accounted by Scripture as if he fasted." Rather, the *mitzvah* itself serves as a preparation for the coming day's fast. *Rosh* (*Yoma* 8:22) explains: The Talmud means that we should prepare ourselves in the ninth of the month, strengthening ourselves through eating and drinking so that we will be able to afflict ourselves the next day. This shows the love of the Holy One, Blessed is He, for Israel; it is like a man who has a darling son (יֶלֶד שַׁעֲשׁוּעִים), and decrees that the boy must afflict himself on a certain day; but he insists that the lad be given food and drink the day before, so that he will be able to withstand the fast.

The "Affliction of Eating"

⊷§There seems to be an obvious difficulty in the statement of our Sages — that since the Torah commanded us, *And you shall afflict your souls on the ninth of the month,* the Torah intends to make it a *mitzvah* to eat on Erev Yom Kippur. If that was the intention, why did God not command us explicitly to eat and drink on the ninth? In explanation the *Dubno Maggid* says that human nature being what it is, if the commandment were to be stated in this way, people might eat and drink so much that we might (God forbid!) not have a *minyan* for *Kol Nidrei*. Since, however, the commandment is stated as an "affliction," so many laws and customs hallow the eating on this day that the *mitzvah* of eating becomes indeed as much an act of serene Divine service as the *mitzvah* of fasting.

The Obligation of Women

●§This special quality of the *mitzvah* of eating on Erev Yom Kippur — that it constitutes "preparation" for the coming fast — gives rise to a halachic question. There is a general rule that women are exempt from מִצְוַת עֲשֵׂה שֶׁהַזְּמַן גְּרָמָא, *a positive mitzvah for which a definite time is specified.* But since eating on Erev Yom Kippur is a time-related positive *mitzvah,* we may ask whether women are obligated by this *mitzvah* or not. On the other hand, since the nature of this *mitzvah* is "preparation" for the fast, then just as they are obligated by the fast itself, [which involves a negative (or prohibitive) *mitzvah* and as such is applicable to women,] so also women should be obligated by the preparation.

In his responsa, R' Akiva Eger remains undecided on this question, concluding, "It requires further thought when time is available." He arrived at this state of doubt through an actual case that came before him (*Teshuvos R' Akiva Eger* 16):

A certain woman who was ill, and who according to her doctors would be harmed by eating, wished nevertheless to fulfill the *mitzvah* of eating on Erev Yom Kippur. Her father sought R' Akiva Eger's opinion. One is touched by the simple and moving words with which the sage replied:

> In regard to your daughter who is ill, and for whom all food is harmful, and who for several weeks has taken her entire nutrition through medicines, חָלִילָה וְחָלִילָה, far, far be it from her that she should eat! And as to the statement of my distinguished correspondent that his daughter is both learned and exacting in following the word of God, and it will be difficult to persuade her in this matter, I advise that you request one or two attendants of the local *beis din* to inform her that a letter has arrived from me enjoining her by a strict decree that she should not eat anything more than to which she is accustomed to eating every day.

The Obligation of the Sick

●§A grandson of R' Akiva Eger, the author of *Ksav Sofer,* discusses a different problem. If one is dangerously ill, so that he is forbidden to fast on Yom Kippur, is he obligated by the *mitzvah* of eating on Erev Yom Kippur? Here the situation is exactly the reverse of the question concerning women. If the reason for eating is preparation for the fast, then the sick person is exempt since he is exempt from the fast; but if the eating is in itself a *mitzvah,* then the sick person is obligated. Accordingly, *Ksav Sofer* points out, in the specific case of a woman who is ill, so that she cannot fast on Yom Kippur, she must necessarily be exempt from the *mitzvah* of eating on Erev Yom Kippur, for no matter which way we define the mitzvah of eating — either as subsidiary to the fast [from which she is exempt] or independent of it [making it a time-related positive *mitzvah*] — she will be exempt (*Teshuvos Ksav Sofer, Orach Chaim* 112).

The Meal

◆§In discussing this *mitzvah,* the *Acharonim* raise questions about a number of its details. *Minchas Chinuch* (*mitzvah* 313) states, for example, that the obligation to eat on Erev Yom Kippur need not necessarily be fulfilled by eating bread [as required on *Shabbos* or *Yom Tov*], but that other types of food are also sufficient.

□ *Netziv* considers why it is that no blessing is recited over this *mitzvah* of eating. He concludes that it is because the eating is not a *mitzvah* in its own right, but rather serves as a preparation for the fast of the following day — and one does not recite a blessing for a preparatory act (*Ha'amek She'elah* 167).

□ Despite the fact that the *mitzvah* is to eat, the *poskim* write that one should take care to eat light foods, such as poultry and fish. And in fact we find that from earliest times it has been customary to eat poultry and fish on this day (*Orach Chaim* 608:4; *Levush* 604).

שְׁלוּחֵי מִצְוָה אֵינָן נִזּוֹקִין /
Performers of a Mitzvah Will not Be Harmed

◆§In connection with the special desirability of fish for this meal, *Tur* cites a story related by the Midrash:

It once happened that the [non-Jewish] governor of a certain city sent his servant out to buy fish. The servant could find only one fish, and offered a gold coin for it. A Jewish tailor who was on the spot offered a higher price, and the bidding continued back and forth until the price had risen to five gold coins, at which point the governor's servant relinquished the fish to the tailor. Returning to his master, the servant recounted the whole incident.

The governor sent for the tailor and asked him, "What is your trade?"

"A tailor," was the reply.

"And why did you pay five gold coins for a fish worth one gold coin — and not only that, but you wrested it from the hand of my servant?"

The tailor answered, "And how could I do other than buy it, even if it had cost ten gold coins, in order to eat it on a day such as this, when God has commanded us to eat and drink, and when we are confident that He will forgive our sins?"

Replied the governor, "In that case, you have done well" — and released the tailor, who went his way in peace.

Extending the Fast Day

◆§The Torah has commanded us to extend the fast of Yom Kippur by adding a *tosefes,* a segment of time taken from the preceding afternoon, during which we refrain from food and drink. This *tosefes* of Yom Kippur, then, after the preparatory stage of eating, constitutes the second stage of the *mitzvah* of the fast. The Talmud (*Beitzah* 30a) states that this *tosefes,* as regards fasting, is a Scripture commandment. Elsewhere (*Rosh Hashanah* 9a; *Yoma* 81b) the Talmud derives this obligation from various verses. No fixed amount of time has been assigned to this *tosefes;* but some time before dusk one is required לְהוֹסִיף מֵחוֹל עַל הַקֹּדֶשׁ, *to add from the non-sacred to the sacred* (*Orach Chaim* 608:1).

There is a disagreement among the *Rishonim* as to whether the *tosefes* of *Shabbos* and *Yom Tov* is Scriptural or Rabbinic; and the same disagreement exists concerning the *tosefes* of *Yom Kippur* with respect to forbidden labor. But, as stated above, with respect to the fast, there is no dispute; all agree that the *tosefes* on Yom Kippur is of Scriptural authority.

בִּרְכַּת הַבָּנִים / Blessing of the Children

◆§It is customary for parents to bless their children, young and old, before leaving for the synagogue, after the final Erev Yom Kippur meal. The flow of Divine beneficence and blessing which comes with the onset of this sacred day makes this a particularly auspicious time for such blessings. Both hands should be placed upon the head of the child to signify that the blessing is conveyed with complete generosity of spirit. Each parent may add personal blessings to the customary text (see page 126) as he sees fit (*Bais Yaakov*).

The Day and Date of Yom Kippur

The Tenth Day of Tishrei

The Midrash (*Seder Olam Rabbah* 6) gives this chronology (accompanied by the relevant proof verses) of the period between the Receiving of the Torah at Mount Sinai and the following tenth day of Tishrei:

> On the seventh day [of Sivan] after receiving the *Luchos* (Tablets containing the Ten Commandments), Moses ascended the mountain which the cloud had been covering for six days in order to cleanse Moses. He remained on the mountain forty days and forty nights. On the fortieth day, which was the seventeenth of Tammuz, he descended, discovered the nation sinning with the Golden Calf, and broke the *Luchos*. He ascended the mountain for the second time on the eighteenth of Tammuz to seek compassion for Israel. He remained there for another period of forty days and forty nights, until, at the end of that period, God was appeased. Then He told Moses to [descend,] hew a second set of Tablets and then ascend Mount Sinai for the third time. Moses did so. He descended on the twenty-eighth of Av and hewed the two Tablets. On the twenty-ninth of Av he ascended and the Torah was

taught to him anew; as it says: *So I stood on the mountain as during the first period, forty days and forty nights; and HASHEM listened to me that time also; and HASHEM did not desire to destroy you* (Deuteronomy 10:10). From this verse we derive that just as the first forty-day period was favorable, so was the third forty-day period, but the second forty-day period was a time of Divine anger. Moses descended for the third and final time on the tenth of Tishrei, which was to be Yom Kippur, and informed the people that he had found favor before the Omnipresent. Therefore, this day was established as a decree and a remembrance for all generations, as it says: *This shall be to you an eternal decree* (Leviticus 16:34).

☐ Another Midrash (*Tanna D'vei Eliyahu Zuta* 4) describes Moses' descent from the mountain that Yom Kippur:

During the final forty-day period that Moses ascended Mount Sinai to bring the Torah to his people, Israel declared each day as a day of fasting [they would eat only at night]. But on the eve of the fortieth day they did not break their fast, instead, they continued fasting all through the night — in order that the Evil Inclination not gain the upper hand.[1] The next morning on the tenth of Tishrei, they arose early and stood before Mount Sinai waiting to greet Moses. They cried when they saw Moses, and Moses cried when he saw them. And that crying ascended on high. At that moment, the compassion of the Holy One, Blessed is He, was aroused and the Holy Spirit informed them of good tidings and consolations, "My children, I swear by My great Name that this crying shall be for you a crying of joy; and this day shall be for you a day of forgiveness, atonements and pardon — for you, for your children, for your children's children, to the end of all generations."

☐ Moreover, when God forgives Israel's sin, He is not sad hearted; rather, He celebrates with great joy, and He says to the mountain and hills, to the springs and the valleys, "Come and celebrate with Me with great joy, for I am about to forgive the sins of Israel" (*Tanna D'vei Eliyahu Rabbah* 1).

The Day of the Week

◁§ **לֹא אָדּ״וּ רֹאשׁ**, *Lo adu Rosh,* is the concise halachic statement for the principle underlying the formulation of the calendar; namely, Rosh Hashanah may never fall on Sunday, Wednesday or Friday. [The word **אָדּ״וּ** is a combination of the letters א=1; ד=4; and ו=6, which stand for the first, fourth, and sixth days of the week.] This principle is stated by

---

1. On two previous occasions, both associated with the giving of the Torah, the nation was bested by the Evil Inclination. First, on the day they were to receive the Torah, the people should have remained awake in anticipation of the great event. Yet the people not only slept that night, but they overslept. Second, forty days later, when they despaired of Moses' return, they sinned with the Golden Calf.

Rambam (*Hil. Kiddush HaChodesh* 7:1) who explains it with a series of astronomical considerations (ibid. 7:7). *Ravad* finds a much simpler explanation based on certain Talmudic discussions (*Rosh Hashanah* 20a; *Yerushalmi Succah* 4:1). Stated tersely, *Ravad* teaches that if Rosh Hashanah were to fall on Sunday, then Hoshana Rabbah (on the twenty-first of Tishrei) would be on a Sabbath, and we would not be able to fulfill the ceremony of *Hoshanos*. If Rosh Hashanah were on Wednesday, then Yom Kippur (the tenth of Tishrei) would fall on Friday, and if Rosh Hashanah were on Friday, Yom Kippur would be on Sunday. Both cases would entail the observance of two consecutive days — the Sabbath and Yom Kippur — on which it would be forbidden to cook fresh food and to bury the dead. The year is therefore fixed in such a manner that such occurrences are avoided.

☐ Another reason why Yom Kippur cannot fall on Sunday, Tuesday or Friday is developed by *Bris Kehunas Olam*.

The Mishnah (*Keilim* 17:14) teaches:

> Some things created on the first day [i.e., Sunday of Creation] can contract *tumah* [ritual impurity]; on the second day, there is no *tumah*; on the third, there is *tumah*; on the fourth and fifth there is no *tumah* . . . and whatever was created on the sixth day can contract *tumah*.

The Mishnah means: On the Sunday of Creation, God created earth and water and both earthenware vessels and water can contract *tumah*. Monday's creation was the firmament in which there can be no *tumah*. On Tuesday, the trees were created, and wooden vessels can contract *tumah*. On Wednesday, God created the heavenly lights to which *tumah* does not apply. On Thursday, He created the birds and the fish; vessels made of their skin, bones or feathers cannot contract *tumah*. On Friday, all species of beasts and animal, as well as man, were created, and vessels made from their skin or bones can contract *tumah*.

Now since Yom Kippur is a day of purity, it can fall out only on a day of purity — Monday, Wednesday, Thursday or Saturday — but not on Sunday, Tuesday or Friday.

בְּעֶצֶם הַיּוֹם הַזֶּה / On This Very Day

The Greatness of Yom Kippur

◆§R' Yisrael Salanter used to exclaim, "If we were given such a wondrous day like Yom Kippur — a day on which man is forgiven for all his sins — only once in seventy years, we would have a great asset. How great then is our wealth when we have Yom Kippur once each year!"

☐ Yom Kippur contains within itself the entire year. Every hour of Yom Kippur represents many days, and every minute comprises many hours. [Thus, one who repents sincerely on Yom Kippur may be considered as having repented for the entire year] (*Or HaMeir*).

☐ The chassidic master R' Shmelke of Nikolsburg once said, "If given the choice I would prefer never to die [despite the eternal reward in the World to Come]. For in the World to Come there is no Yom Kippur. And how can a Jew live without Yom Kippur? Of what value is a life without *teshuvah?*"

☐ Yom Kippur is a foretaste of the World to Come. Just as there is neither eating nor drinking in the spirituality of the World to Come, so is there neither eating nor drinking on Yom Kippur. But Yom Kippur has one thing more to offer than does the World to Come, namely, *teshuvah* (*R' Shlomo of Karlin*).

כִּי בַיּוֹם הַזֶּה — For Through This Day

⧯§A verse that in its Scriptural context sums up the purpose of the *Kohen's Gadol's* [High Priest's] service in the *Beis HaMikdash* on Yom Kippur has been reinterpreted and applied to God's forgiving our sins on this day. As such, the verse has become one of the major focal points of the Yom Kippur *machzor*.

The Torah states:

כִּי בַיּוֹם הַזֶּה יְכַפֵּר עֲלֵיכֶם לְטַהֵר אֶתְכֶם, מִכֹּל חַטֹּאתֵיכֶם לִפְנֵי ה׳ תִּטְהָרוּ.
For through [performing the Temple service on] *this day, he* [the Kohen Gadol] *will atone for you, to cleanse you; from all your sins before* Hashem, *you shall be cleansed* (*Leviticus* 16:30).

This same verse in the *machzor* is retranslated: *For through this day, He* [God] *will atone for you . . .* In an era when we cannot perform the Temple service, the verse, as used in the liturgy, cannot refer to the *Kohen Gadol,* but must be understood as an allusion to the fact that עַצּוּמוֹ שֶׁל יוֹם, *the very day of Yom Kippur,* brings atonement. That is, God forgives Israel in merit of the day. (See *Toras Kohanim* and *Malbim* to *Leviticus* 16:30.)

☐ A question has been raised regarding this verse. Why the redundant תִּטְהָרוּ, *you will be cleansed,* after the verse has just stated לְטַהֵר אֶתְכֶם, *to cleanse you?*

Noam Megadim finds the answer to this question in a Talmudic passage that interprets the words לִפְנֵי ה׳, *before* Hashem, as a reference to the *Beis HaMikdash.* We may explain our verse with this same meaning. If we do *teshuvah* in the full measure required of us, we will merit the rebuilding of the Temple. The verse teaches us this lesson: If "He will atone for you, to cleanse you," in the present Temple-less era, then you will live to see the rebuilt *Beis HaMikdash* where "before HASHEM you shall be cleansed."

☐ A similar explanation, but with an esoteric twist, is based on the kabbalistic teaching that God reveals His conduct through a variety of Divine manifestations, each of which is known as one of God's "Names." Moreover, every sin committed on earth causes a blemish, so to speak, in one of the Divine Names. [Thus we find in one of the personal prayers sometimes recited during the weekday *Shemoneh Esrei,* וּתְמַלֵּא כָּל הַשֵּׁמוֹת שֶׁפָּגַמְתִּי, *And make whole all of the Names that I have blemished*.] But when one repents wholeheartedly, his sins are wiped out and the blemishes are removed from the Divine Names. In this vein we may interpret: יְכַפֵּר עֲלֵיכֶם לְטַהֵר אֶתְכֶם, [when] *He will atone for you to cleanse you,* and then, even those blemishes which you have caused לִפְנֵי ה׳, *before HASHEM* [i.e., in His Divine Name], תִּטְהָרוּ, *you will have cleansed* (*HaYashar VehaTov*).

☐ *Ben Poras Yosef* proposes another interpretation:

There are two roads to atonement. The preferred way is for man to arouse himself to repentance through fasting, prayer and good deeds. HASHEM and His heavenly court will then assist him along the path he has chosen. [As the Talmud (*Shabbos* 104a) states succinctly: בָּא לְטַהֵר מְסַיְּעִים אוֹתוֹ, *if one comes to be cleansed, they help him.*] This road to atonement is called אִתְעֲרוּתָא דִלְתַתָּא, *an awakening from below.*

In the second way, man does not bring himself to repentance until he has been nudged from above. The spur may come in the form of Divine retribution for some sin, as a heavenly message in a dream, or in any of various different ways. This road to atonement is called אִתְעֲרוּתָא דִלְעֵלָּא, *an awakening from above.*

Our verse alludes to both types of *teshuvah.* The first part of the verse states: *For through this day He will atone for you, to cleanse you* — "He will atone," implies an awakening from above. For no mention is made of *teshuvah;* no hint is given of a previous self-awakening to repentance. However, the preferred way is described in the latter clause of the verse: "[If you repent] *from all of your sins before HASHEM* [arouses you to *teshuvah*, then] *you shall be cleansed.*"

Between Man and God; Between Man and Man

⋙§The Mishnah (*Yoma* 8:9) explains the closing clause of this verse:

אֶת זוֹ דָּרַשׁ רַבִּי אֶלְעָזָר בֶּן עֲזַרְיָה: „מִכֹּל חַטֹּאתֵיכֶם לִפְנֵי ה׳ תִּטְהָרוּ״ — עֲבֵרוֹת שֶׁבֵּין אָדָם לַמָּקוֹם, יוֹם הַכִּפּוּרִים מְכַפֵּר; עֲבֵרוֹת שֶׁבֵּין אָדָם לַחֲבֵרוֹ, אֵין יוֹם הַכִּפּוּרִים מְכַפֵּר, עַד שֶׁיְּרַצֶּה אֶת חֲבֵרוֹ.

This did R' Elazar ben Azariah expound: From all of your sins before HASHEM, shall you be cleansed — for sins between man and God, Yom

Kippur provides atonement, but for sins between man and his fellow man, Yom Kippur does not provide atonement, until he appeases that man.

A Sabbath of Sabbaths

◄§A man once asked the chassidic master, R' Tzvi Hirsch of Rimanov, "How does Yom Kippur, of which it is written שַׁבָּת שַׁבָּתוֹן, *a Sabbath of Sabbaths*, (*Leviticus* 16:31) differ from every *Shabbos* about which it is also written *a Sabbath of Sabbaths* (*Exodus* 35:2)?"

R' Tzvi Hirsch replied, "Regarding *Shabbos* it is written, *a Sabbath of Sabbaths unto* HASHEM, but about Yom Kippur it is written, *a Sabbath of Sabbaths unto you*. For on Yom Kippur we draw the sanctity of the heavens down to earth."

The Hairy and the Bald Brothers

◄§Jacob contrasted himself with his brother Esau: "Esau is a hairy man, while I am a smooth-skinned man" (*Genesis* 27:11). The Sages (*Yalkut Shimoni* 114) explain this verse as an allusion to Yom Kippur. In the usual order of things, one cannot rectify all of his mistakes in one fell swoop. Each misdeed must be corrected, each wrong step retraced, each sin atoned for. Yet Yom Kippur was presented to Israel as a day of atonement, a day on which all their transgressions and shortcomings are forgiven at one time. But this day was given only to Israel — as it is written: "For through this day, He will atone for **you,** to cleanse **you**" (*Leviticus* 16:30).

This can be understood through the parable of two brothers — one bald, one hairy — who were working on the winnowing floor. Straw, stubble and dust covered both brothers. Yet, there was a difference. With one quick wipe the bald brother's head was clean, while the hairy brother had to work hard at removing each piece of straw from his head.

"Esau is a hairy man." He cannot readily cleanse himself of the stubble of sin. Jacob is "a smooth-skinned man," and through but a single Yom Kippur can be cleansed and purified.

Teshuvah / Repentance

Teshuvah on Yom Kippur Vs. Teshuvah All Year

◄§According to Rabbeinu Yonah we are commanded to repent our sins at every opportunity, all through the year. This *mitzvah* is derived from the verse, וְשַׁבְתָּ עַד ה' אֱלֹהֶיךָ, *And you shall return to* HASHEM, *your God* (*Deuteronomy* 30:2). The special *mitzvah* of *teshuvah* on Yom Kippur, however, appears in the verse, כִּי בַיּוֹם הַזֶּה . . . מִכֹּל חַטֹּאתֵיכֶם לִפְנֵי ה' תִּטְהָרוּ, *For through this day . . . from all your sins before* HASHEM, *you shall be cleansed* (*Leviticus* 16:30).

Note that the year-round *mitzvah* of repentance is declared by the word וְשַׁבְתָּ, *and you shall return.* This is the basis for our calling repentance תְּשׁוּבָה, *teshuvah,* and the penitent בַּעַל תְּשׁוּבָה, *one who has repented* (or, *one who has mastered teshuvah*). But the verse that teaches us regarding repentance on Yom Kippur uses the word תִּטְהָרוּ, *you shall be cleansed.* Not merely "returning to Hashem," as during the rest of the year; rather, "cleansing before Hashem."

"Many and varied are the levels of *teshuvah,*" and each person may approach God according to his level of *teshuvah.* Nevertheless, every *teshuvah,* regardless of how slight or how intense, effects forgiveness to some degree. However, the soul is not completely cleansed of the sin until one cleanses his heart with the full measure of *teshuvah.* This may be compared to laundering a soiled white garment. Even a minute amount of washing will remove some of the grime, but only with great effort — the proper combination of cleansers, water, rubbing, etc. — will the garment become sparkling clean and return to its original whiteness (*Rabbeinu Yonah* 1:9).

So it is also with the *teshuvah* of Yom Kippur. Throughout the year, every minimum attempt at repentance removes some grime of sin and serves to fulfill, to a degree, the *mitzvah* of וְשַׁבְתָּ, *you shall return.* Nevertheless, on Yom Kippur, we are commanded to remove every last bit of dirt, to cleanse our souls with wholehearted repentance. This *mitzvah* requires more than a mere perfunctory declaration of penitence (*Pachad Yitzchak*).

Yom Kippur Without Teshuvah

⧫§The Talmud (*Shevuos* 13a) records a dispute regarding the efficacy of Yom Kippur as a means of achieving atonement for one who does not repent his sins:

> Rabbi Yehudah HaNassi says: For all sins mentioned in the Torah, whether or not one repents, Yom Kippur brings atonement, except for three: one who casts off the yoke by denying the fundamental beliefs of Judaism; one who treats the Torah with audacity by expounding false interpretations of the Torah; and one who denies the covenant of circumcision. For these three, if one repents, Yom Kippur atones; but if one does not repent, Yom Kippur does not atone.

Another opinion is ascribed to R' Yehudah:

> I would think that Yom Kippur atones for both those who repent and those who do not repent, but this can be disproved. For we may compare Yom Kippur to the sacrificial sin- and guilt-offerings, all of which atone. Now just as sin- and guilt-offerings atone only for those who repent, similarly Yom Kippur atones only for those who repent.
>
> But, we may rejoin, how can we compare them? Sin- and guilt-offerings do not atone for intentional sins only for inadvertent ones, while

Yom Kippur atones for both intentional and inadvertent sins. The answer is that the Torah states, אַךְ, *but,* and the general rule is that the word אַךְ implies an exclusion, i.e., some sins are excluded from atonement on Yom Kippur, namely, the sins of those who do not repent.

גְּדוֹלָה תְּשׁוּבָה / Great Is Repentance

⋖§The Talmud (*Yoma* 86a) speaks of the greatness of *teshuvah*:

☐ R' Chama the son of R' Chanina said: Great is repentance, for it brings healing to the world, as it is said: *I will heal their rebelliousness, I will love them freely* (Hoshea 14:5).

☐ R' Chama the son of R' Chanina asked: In the first part of a verse (Jeremiah 3:22) it is written, *Return you rebellious children,* i.e., you who were formerly rebellious; while in the second part of that same verse it is written, *I will heal your rebelliousness* [implying that they are still rebellious]. He answered: There is no contradiction. The first part speaks of repentance out of love; the second, of repentance out of fear.

☐ R' Yehudah asked: It is written, *Return, you rebellious children, I will heal your rebelliousness.* But it is also written, *For I [HASHEM] have become Master over you, and I have taken you, one from a city and two from a family* (Jeremiah 3:14). He answered: There is no contradiction. The first verse speaks of repentance out of love or fear; the second, of repentance out of suffering.

☐ R' Levi said: Great is repentance, for it reaches up to the Throne of Glory, as it is said: *Return, O Israel, unto HASHEM, your God* (Hoshea 14:2).

☐ R' Yochanan said: Great is repentance, for it overrides a prohibition of the Torah, as it is said: *If a man should send his wife away, and she go from him and become another man's wife, may he ever return to her again? Will not that land be greatly polluted? But you have been promiscuous with many companions; yet return to Me — the word of HASHEM* (Jeremiah 3:1).

☐ R' Yonasan said: Great is repentance, for it brings about redemption, as it is said: *A redeemer shall come to Zion, and to those of Jacob who repent from willful sin* (Isaiah 59:20). How is it that "a redeemer shall come to Zion"? Because of "those of Jacob who repent from willful sin."

☐ Resh Lakish said: Great is repentance, for because of it premeditated sins are accounted as errors, as it is said: *Return, O Israel, unto HASHEM, your God; for you have stumbled in your iniquity* (Hoshea 14:2). "Iniquity" is premeditated, and yet he calls it "stumbling." But is this so? Has not Resh Lakish said that repentance is great, for because of it premeditated sins are accounted as merits, as it is said: *But when a wicked man returns from his wickedness and practices justice and charity, he shall live because of them* (*Ezekiel* 33:19)? There is no contradiction. The latter verse speaks of repentance out of love; the first of repentance out of fear.

☐ R' Shmuel bar Nachmani said in the name of R' Yonasan: Great is repentance, because it prolongs the years of a man, as it is said: *But when a wicked man returns from his wickedness . . . he shall live from them* (*Ezekiel* 33:19).

☐ R' Yitzchak said: In *Eretz Yisrael* they said in the name of Rabbah bar Mari: Come and see how the conduct of one of flesh and blood differs from that of the Holy One, Blessed is He. In the conduct of flesh and blood, if one angers his fellow, it is questionable whether he can be pacified by him or not. And even if he can be pacified, it is questionable whether or not he will be pacified by mere words, as it is said: *Take with you words, and return to* HASHEM (*Hoshea* 14:3). Furthermore, He even accounts it to him as a good deed, as it is said: *and take that which is good* (ibid.). Still more, Scripture accounts it to him as if he had sacrificed bulls, as it is said: *Let our lips compensate for the sacrificial bulls* (ibid.). Perhaps you will say this refers to obligatory bulls? Therefore it is said: *I will heal their rebelliousness, I will love them freely* (ibid. v. 5).

☐ It was taught: R' Meir used to say: Great is repentance, for on account of an individual who repented, the sins of all the world are forgiven, as it is said: *I will heal their rebelliousness, I will love them freely, for My anger is turned away from him* (ibid.). It does not say "from them," but "from him."

Selections from Rambam's Hilchos Teshuvah

☐ **1:1** — Should a person transgress any *mitzvah* of the Torah — whether positive or negative, whether intentionally or inadvertently — when he repents and returns from his sin, he must confess before God, Blessed is He, as it is written: *If a man or a woman shall commit* (*any of the sins of man*) *. . . let them confess their sins that they have committed . . .* (*Numbers* 5:6-7). This refers to verbal confession; and that confession is a positive *mitzvah*.

How does one confess? He should say, "I beg of You, Hashem, I have erred; I have been iniquitous; I have willfully sinned against You. And such and such have I done. But now I am contrite and ashamed of my actions. I shall never again repeat them." This is the essence of confession. However, increasing the length and breadth of one's confession is a praiseworthy trait . . .

☐ **1:3** — Today, when the *Beis HaMikdash* is not standing and we do not have the atonement of the sacrificial altar, there is nothing but *teshuvah*.

For *teshuvah* atones for all sins. Even if one has been wicked for his entire lifetime but does *teshuvah* at the end, we do not mention any of his wickedness to him, as it says, *The wicked one will not stumble over his wickedness on the day he repents from his wickedness* (*Ezekiel* 33:12). Additionally, the essence of the Day of Yom Kippur atones for penitents, as it says: *For through this day He will atone for you* (*Leviticus* 16:30).

☐ **2:1** — What is complete *teshuvah*? When one who has transgressed is faced with the opportunity to repeat his sin and he has the power to do so, yet he refrains — neither because of fear nor because of weakness — but because he wishes to repent. For example, a man who has had an illicit relationship with a woman and at a later date finds himself secluded with her, his desire for her and his physical strength remaining the same, and in the same state in which he had previously sinned, yet he refrains and does not transgress — he is the complete penitent. It is of him that Solomon said: *Remember your Creator in the days of your youth[ful passion*] (*Ecclesiastes* 12:1).

Nevertheless, if one does not repent until his old age, at a time when he is no longer able to do that which he had done earlier, although his *teshuvah* is not of the highest degree, it avails him and he is a penitent.

Even if one has sinned his entire lifetime, but repents on the day of his death and dies in a state of repentance, all his sins are forgiven, as it says: *As long as the sun, the light, the moon and stars have not darkened, and the clouds have returned after the rain* (ibid. v. 2), which refers to the day of death. Thus, if one "remembers his Creator" and repents before he dies, he shall be forgiven.

☐ **2:2** — And how does one repent? A sinner should abandon his sinfulness, drive it from his thoughts and conclude in his heart that he will never do it again, as it says: *Let the wicked man abandon his way . . .* (*Isaiah* 55:7). Additionally, he should regret the past as it says: *For after I repented, I regretted* (*Jeremiah* 31:18). [Let him do all this to such a degree that] the Knower of Secrets will bear witness that he will never repeat the sin in question, as it says: *Take with your words and return to HASHEM. Say unto Him . . . '[Bear witness for us that] we shall no longer refer to our handiwork as our god'* (*Hoshea* 14:3-4). And he must also confess with his lips and declare those things that he has concluded in his heart.

☐ **2:3** — If one confesses verbally, but does not resolve in his heart to abandon his sinful ways, he is like one who immerses himself in a *mikveh* while holding an impure creature. And so it is said: *One who confesses and abandons [his sins] shall obtain mercy* (*Proverbs* 28:13). And he must specify the sin, as it says: *I beg of You, this nation has sinned a great sin, they have made for themselves a golden idol* (*Exodus* 32:31).

☐ **2:4** — Among the methods of *teshuvah* are: The penitent should continually call to Hashem, with crying and with supplications; he should distribute charity according to his means; he should distance himself from that with which he sinned; he should change his name, as if to say, "I am someone else, not that man who did those deeds"; he should change all his actions for the better, to the straightforward path; and he should go into exile, for exile brings atonement for sin by humbling a person and making him modest and of humble spirit.

☐ **2:5** — It is very praiseworthy for the penitent to confess publicly, to announce his wanton acts and to expose the sins he has committed against other people. He should tell others, "In truth, I have sinned against so and so, and I have done such and such acts to him. But today I repent and regret."

If one haughtily refuses to make his sins known and instead hides his wanton acts, his *teshuvah* is not complete, as it says: *He who covers his wanton acts will not succeed* (Proverbs 28:13).

The aforesaid applies only to sins between one man and another. But sins between man and God need not be publicized. Indeed, it is brazenness to reveal them. Rather, such a sinner should repent before God, Blessed is He, and enumerate his sins before Him. However, he should confess publicly without specifying which sins he committed. And it is good for him not to reveal his sins [of this type], as it says: *Praiseworthy is one whose wantonness is forgiven, whose sin is covered over* (Psalms 32:1).

☐ **2:6** — Although *teshuvah* and prayer avail at all times, during the ten days from Rosh Hashanah to Yom Kippur it avails even more, and is accepted immediately, as it says: *Seek HASHEM when He is to be found* (Isaiah 55:6).

The aforesaid applies only to an individual. But regarding the congregation as a whole, whenever they do *teshuvah* and pray wholeheartedly, they are answered, as it says: *As HASHEM, our God, whenever we call to Him* (Deuteronomy 4:7).

☐ **2:7** — Yom Kippur is a time of *teshuvah* for everyone — for the individual, and for the masses. It is a deadline for forgiveness and atonement for Israel. Therefore all are obligated to do *teshuvah* and to confess on Yom Kippur.

The *mitzvah* of confession on Yom Kippur should be performed in the afternoon of the day before Yom Kippur, prior to eating the meal before the fast. This is done lest one choke during the meal before he has confessed. But although he has confessed before eating, he must repeat his confession on the night of Yom Kippur during *Maariv*, and he must confess again during *Shacharis*, during *Mussaf*, during *Minchah*, and during *Neilah*.

In which part of the prayer service does one recite the confession? The individual at the conclusion of his *Amidah* prayer; the *chazzan* in the fourth blessing of his *Amidah* prayer.

☐ **2:8** — The confession that has become customary throughout Israel is, "But we have sinned." And this is the essence of the confession.

Those sins to which one has confessed on this year's Yom Kippur, he should repent in his confession on next year's Yom Kippur, even though he has maintained his repentance, as it says: *For I recognize my wantonness, and my sin is before me always (Psalms* 51:5).

☐ **2:9** — *Teshuvah* and Yom Kippur atone only for sins between man and God, for example, one who ate forbidden food or had an illicit relation, and other such sins. But sins between one man and another — such as one who injured or cursed another person, or stole from him — are not forgiven at any time until one gives the other his due and appeases him. Although one repays the money he owes, he must nevertheless also appease the other and ask that person to forgive him.

Even if one has injured another with mere words, he must appease him and plead with him until his forgives him.

If the other party refuses to forgive him, the penitent should gather a group of three of his close friends. They should approach the injured party and request that he grant forgiveness. If he is still unwilling, the penitent should try a second time and a third. If he still refuses to forgive, the penitent should leave him and go on his way. And the one who does not forgive, he is the sinner.

But if the injured party was his teacher, the penitent must approach him even a thousand times, until he forgives him.

☐ **2:10** — It is forbidden for a person to be stubborn and refuse to be appeased. Rather, he should be readily pacified and difficult to anger. When the sinner asks for forgiveness, one should forgive wholeheartedly and with a willing spirit. Even if the other has oppressed him and sinned against him numerous times, one should neither seek revenge nor retain inner hatred for that person. This is the way of the offspring of Jacob and their proper heart.

But the idolaters who are of stuffed heart are different — "they retain their anger forever" (cf. *Amos* 1:11). And so it is said regarding the Gibeonites who would not forgive nor be appeased: *And the Gibeonites are not from the Children of Israel (II Samuel* 21:2).

☐ **2:11** — If one sins against another and the injured party dies before the sinner has asked for his forgiveness, the sinner should gather ten people and stand at his grave site. He should say to them, "I have sinned to Hashem, God of Israel, and to this man. Such and such have I done."

If he owed the injured party money, he should return it to the heirs. If he has no known heirs, the penitent should place the money in trust with the *beis din* and confess his sin.

☐ **4:1** — There are twenty-four things that hamper *teshuvah*.

Four of these are such great sins that God does not vouchsafe the sinner an opportunity to repent. They are: (a) one who causes the public to sin; included in this category is one who prevents the public from performing a *mitzvah*; (b) one who influences another to turn from the good way to the bad, for example, the *meisis* and *meidiach* (see *Deuteronomy* 13:7-12); (c) one who sees his son going out to evil ways and does not admonish him — since his son is under his power, had he admonished him, his son would have abandoned his evil ways, thus he is considered as having caused him to sin; included in this sin is anyone who has the power to admonish others — whether individuals or the masses — and instead of doing so, leaves them to their misdeeds; and (d) one who says, "I shall sin and I shall repent," included is one who says, "I shall sin and Yom Kippur will atone."

☐ **4:2** — Of these [twenty-four] are five things which block the ways of *teshuvah* before those who commit them. They are: (a) one who separates himself from the congregation, for when they repent, he will not be among them, and so he will not merit that which they merit; (b) one who disputes the words of the sages, for his dispute will cause him to separate himself from them, and he will remain ignorant of the ways to *teshuvah*; (c) one who laughs at the *mitzvos*, for since he degrades them, he will not pursue them nor perform them, and if he does not perform them, he will have no merit; (d) one who insults his teachers, for this causes him to be pushed aside and removed as was Gehazi (see *Sanhedrin* 107b), and in this state he will not find anyone to teach him and to show him the true road; and (e) one who hates admonition, for he will not be led on the road to *teshuvah*, for admonition brings about *teshuvah*. When a person is made aware of his sins and is embarrassed by them, he repents . . . in this manner did all the prophets admonish Israel.

Therefore it is incumbent upon each and every Jewish congregation to appoint a great sage and elder — one who fears heaven from his youth and is beloved to them — to admonish the public and bring them to *teshuvah*. But one who hates admonition will not come to the admonisher and will not listen to his words; thus he will remain with his sins which in his eyes are good deeds.

☐ **4:3** — Of these [twenty-four] are five things that make it impossible for the one who does them to do complete *teshuvah*, for they are sins between one man and another, yet the sinner does not know against whom he has sinned, to whom he must make restitution, and to whom he must ask forgiveness. They are: (a) one who curses the public; had he cursed an individual, he would have known from whom to ask atonement; (b) one who shares stolen property with a thief, for he knows not from whom among the masses the thief stole the property that he takes, moreover, he encourages the thief and thus causes him to sin; (c) one who finds an identifiable object and does not announce it so that it may be returned to its owner; after a period of time, if he seeks to repent, he will not know to whom to return it; (d) one who [unlawfully takes and] eats an animal belonging to paupers, orphans or widows; since these unfortunate people are not well known and constantly travel from city to city, no one can recognize them readily and thus the thief will never know to whom he must make restitution; (e) one who accepts bribery to bend the law, for one can never appraise the ramifications and loss caused by bribery and will therefore not be able to return it, for the matter spreads; additionally, he encourages the one who gives the bribe and thus causes him to sin.

☐ **4:4** — Of the [twenty-four] are five things which the one who commits will most likely not repent, for most people do not consider them wrong. Thus, one sins and does not even know that he has sinned. They are: (a) one who eats from a meal that is insufficient for its owner, for this is a small degree of thievery, and the perpetrator thinks that he has not stolen, for he says, "Have I eaten anything without permission?" (b) one who uses a poor man's tools, such as an axe or a plow, that he holds as a pledge, for he will say, "They are missing nothing; I have not stolen them"; (c) one who gazes lustfully at women, for he thinks he has done nothing wrong, and he says to himself, "Have I had relations with her or even touched her?" and he is unaware of the great sin committed with the eyes, for this leads to adultery itself, as it says: *Do not explore after your heart and after your eyes* (*Numbers* 15:39); (d) one who glories in another's degradation thinks that he has not sinned, for the other is not standing before him and therefore is not embarrassed; nor did the sinner embarrass him, rather he merely compared his own good deeds and wisdom to the other's deeds and wisdom in order to glorify himself over the other; and (e) one who is suspicious of innocent people, for he thinks that such suspicion is not sinful, and he says, "What have I done wrong? Have I done anything more than raise a possibility — maybe he did it, maybe he didn't?" But he does not realize that this is a sin, for it takes an innocent person and turns him, albeit only in the other's mind, into a sinner.

☐ **4:5** — Of these [twenty-four] are five things that whoever does them is drawn after them habitually and they are difficult to separate from. A person must be especially scrupulous to avoid them, lest he become attached to them, for they are all extremely bad traits. They are: gossip; slander; anger; thinking evil; and friendship with the wicked with whose deeds he will become familiar and they will become impressed in his heart . . .

☐ **4:6** — All of these [twenty-four] things and their like, despite the fact that they hamper *teshuvah*, do not prevent it. Rather, if one repents from them, he is a penitent and he has a share in the World to Come.

The Goal of Repentance

⊷§Many and varied are the volumes that have been written about repentance. All of them list the steps necessary to attain total *teshuvah*. Yet, we are taught (*Avodah Zarah* 10a) that one can gain his portion in the World to Come in a single moment. What has happened to all the steps? How has he fulfilled all aspects of *teshuvah* in but a trice? The answer lies in the goal of repentance and its achievement.

Teshuvah, return to the ways of Hashem, is essentially achieved by distancing oneself from sin. To the degree that one is successful in this endeavor, does one bring oneself closer to God.

Thus we find (*Berachos* 12b): "If one commits a sin and is embarrassed by it, all his sins are forgiven." His embarrassment is proof of the distance he has placed between himself and his sin (*Mei'imrei Shlomo*).

וְאַל תִּתְיָאֵש מִן הַפֻּרְעָנוּת / Do not Despair of Retribution

⊷§The doctrine of Divine Retribution — that God eventually punishes the wicked — is one of the fundamentals of the faith. Even though it seems long in coming, one should always remember that the time of reckoning will arrive, and justice will be done. As the Mishnah (*Avos* 1:7) states: "Do not despair of retribution!"

A man must never think, "For so many years I've repeated the same sins; so many Yom Kippurs have passed by; and still I'm living and breathing. God does not seek retribution." Instead, take a lesson from the Talmudic dictum (*Shabbos* 10b):

> A man should always seek to dwell in a city which was but recently populated. Its sins are few — as it is stated by Lot when the angel saved him from the destruction of Sodom: *Behold this city is near and small, let me escape there* (*Genesis* 19:20). Now could Lot have been speaking of the city's geographical location and physical size? The angels could see that for themselves! Rather he meant, because it is near in time, that is, recently populated, thus its sins are few.

Now the city in question, Tzoar, had been established fifty-one years earlier, while Sodom had been built only one year before that time. The Tzoarites committed the same sins as the Sodomites, but for one year less. And so Sodom was destroyed while Tzoar was granted a reprieve.

Thus no man should think that because he has escaped retribution in the past, he will continue to do so in the future. Last year he was one year younger and, like Tzoar, he was granted a reprieve. But this year he is a year older, and perhaps as old as Sodom (*Mei'imrei Shlomo*).

סְלִיחָה וּמְחִילָה / Pardon and Forgiveness

You Are Wont to Forgive

◆§A penitent once approached the chassidic master R' Yisrael of Rizhin with a broken heart. For as many times as he did penance for his sins and declared his intention to remain righteous in the future, just as many times did he backslide and revert to his sinful ways.

The rebbe appeased him by explaining the different noun forms found in the Yom Kippur *Amidah* in reference to God as the one Who forgives sin. Sometimes, He is called מוחֵל וְסוֹלֵחַ, *He Who pardons and forgives;* at other times, סָלְחָן וּמָחֳלָן, *Forgiver and Pardoner.*

R' Yisrael explained that the word סוֹלֵחַ refers to a person who forgives because he happens to be in a forgiving mood or for some other reason external to his nature. In other words, sometimes he forgives, sometimes he does not. A סָלְחָן, however, is one who is wont to forgive, time after time. [We learn this from the distinction the Talmud (*Bava Metzia* 33a) makes between רוֹבֵץ, *an animal lying under its burden,* and רַבְצָן, *an animal that lays down every time a burden is placed on its back.*

"And so," said the Rebbe, "even if after Hashem has forgiven you, you once more commit the same sin, He will forgive you again and again, as long as your *teshuvah* is sincere. That is why we call Him סָלְחָן, *the Forgiver.*"

□ Someone asked R' Elimelech of Rudnik why we recite the blessing, ‏ ... מֶלֶךְ מוֹחֵל וְסוֹלֵחַ לַעֲוֹנוֹתֵינוּ, *King Who pardons and forgives our iniquities . . .,* when we do not even know whether or not he will forgive us. R' Elimelech answered with a parable:

> A man once brought home a sack of just-picked apples. The delicious aroma of the fresh fruit tantalized his young son's taste buds. If he could only have an apple for himself! But he knew that his father had brought the apples for some guests who would be arriving shortly. Nevertheless, the boy so desired an apple that he devised a scheme to get one.
>
> Drawing his father's attention, the youngster began to recite the blessing over fruit in a loud, clear voice. Not wishing to let his son's blessing be in vain, the father immediately handed him an apple.

"We are in the same situation as this boy," the Rebbe explained. "When we recite the words, 'Blessed are You, HASHEM, King Who pardons and forgives our iniquities . . .,' God, our Father, does not want our blessing to be in vain. So He forgives us."

Viduy / Confession

One of the highlights of the Yom Kippur prayer services is *Viduy*, Confession. The full version of *viduy* is recited at least nine times (once at *Minchah* of Erev Yom Kippur, and twice each at *Maariv*, *Shacharis*, *Mussaf* and *Minchah* of Yom Kippur). Some recite it one more time, before *Kol Nidrei*.

Viduy and Teshuvah

৵§*Viduy* is inseparable from *teshuvah* [repentance]. According to the oft-quoted *Rambam* (*Hilchos Teshuvah* 1:1), the Torah's commandment to repent makes explicit mention of confession, not of repentance (*Numbers* 5:6,7). Clearly, according to *Rambam*, there can be no repentance unless it is accompanied by a verbal confession. According to *Ramban*, the explicit commandment specifies repentance, but he too agrees that confession is an essential component (*Deuteronomy* 30:2,11). *Rabbeinu Yonah* maintains that both *teshuvah* and *viduy* are separate commandments. According to all opinions, however, confession is necessary before repentance can be regarded as complete. But, we may ask, since repentance is essentially based on heart and mind, emotion and intellect, remorse over the past and resolution for the future, why is a verbal declaration necessary?

R' S.R. Hirsch (*Horeb* §514) declares:

> If you have recognized that you have sinned, then step into the presence of God and say: "O God, I have erred and sinned, I have been disobedient before You, I have done so-and-so (I am sorry and I am ashamed of what I have done, and will never do it again)" . . . Feel in yourself how every sin you have committed, however small, even in the mind and heart, immediately brings with it a curse, namely, that it makes you less capable of doing good, and further inclined to sin; and when you have recognized this, then you can lay the future of your inner and outer life in the just and forgiving hand of God. And as you see yourself in spirit, so confess in word, in order that the picture of your self-abasement may become external to you and stand before you, making it not a passing emotion but a permanent mood and frame of mind which can bear fruit in practical conduct.

☐ As an intelligent, thinking, imaginative being, man has all sorts of thoughts flashing constantly through his mind. Even sublime thoughts of remorse and self-improvement are not strange to him, but they do not last. For his thoughts to have lasting meaning, he must distill them into words, because the process of thought culminates when ideas are expressed and clarified. That is not as easy as it sounds. It is usually excruciatingly difficult for people to admit explicitly that they have done wrong. We excuse ourselves. We refuse to admit the truth. We shift the blame. We deny the obvious. We excel at rationalizing. But the person who pauses, thinks, and wrenches from himself the unpleasant truth, "I have sinned," has performed a great, meaningful act.

☐ When King David sinned with Bathsheba, God sent the prophet Nathan to rebuke him. The prophet spared no words. Without tact or delicacy he admonished his king (*II Samuel* 12:1-12). After Nathan's verbal onslaught ends, there is a blank space in the written text. Then David replies with just two words חָטָאתִי לַה׳, "*I have sinned to* HASHEM." Nathan answers, "[If so] God has removed your sins and you will not die."

The *Vilna Gaon* explains the significance of the blank space before David's response. There was a silence after Nathan's stern words. David was engaged in an inner struggle. He could have justified his deed because, as the Talmud explains, technically he had not sinned (*Shabbos* 56a). He had a right to punish Uriah for his insolence (ibid.). And he knew that Bathsheba always had been his intended queen (*Sanhedrin* 107a). As he silently contemplated Nathan's accusation, he was consumed by emotional turmoil — should he ignore his royal status and admit that the prophet was right? Finally he made his decision: "I have sinned."

David's response remains a prototype of confession and repentance — both his terse answer to Nathan and his lengthy confession and prayer to God (*Psalms* 51) — that is cited by such classic works as *Shaarei Teshuvah* as the very model of repentance: serious thought, frank admission, and the verbal expression of how we have strayed and where we hope to go. This is *viduy*.

Some Elements of the Viduy

◆§A disagreement among the *Tannaim* about the *viduy* recited by the *Kohen Gadol* in the *Beis HaMikdash* has consequences for the wording of our own *viduy*. The disagreement is over the order of the three verbs which mean "to sin." According to R' Meir, the *Kohen Gadol* said, עָוִיתִי, *I have been iniquitous*, פָּשַׁעְתִּי, *I have willfully sinned*, וְחָטָאתִי, *and I have erred*. According to the other Sages, he said, חָטָאתִי עָוִיתִי וּפָשַׁעְתִּי. Each voice in this dispute supports its opinion with relevant verses (*Yoma* 35b). The *Halachah* rules in accordance with the "other Sages," who hold that חָטָאתִי, (from חָטָא) *I have erred*, refers to שׁוֹגֵג, *unintentional sin;* עָוִיתִי (from עָוֹן) refers to (מֵזִיד) *intentional sin;* and פָּשַׁעְתִּי (from פֶּשַׁע) refers to מוֹרֵד, *rebelliousness*, and that in requesting forgiveness it is proper to proceed from the lightest offense to the gravest.

אֲנַחְנוּ וַאֲבוֹתֵינוּ / We and Our Forefathers

•§During the Yom Kippur confessions, we make numerous references to the sins of our ancestors. Why do we mention the sins of earlier generations, sins we did not commit? Many reasons have been advanced.

□ The Torah teaches that one can be punished — and must therefore confess — for the sins of his forefathers as well as for his own (*Leviticus* 26:39,40). Our Sages explain why this is just: We are punished for the sins of previous generations only if we approve of their way of life. By adopting their practices we prove that we are as guilty as they were (*Sanhedrin* 27b).

□ *Or Hachaim* (*Leviticus* 26:40) notes that a proper understanding of our ancestors' sins is often a prerequisite of repentance. Sometimes we accept family or community "traditions" as a proper way of life simply because they have "always been done and no one was ever punished." Thus we must confess — i.e., acknowledge — such sins of the past.

□ Since all Jews are responsible for each other's conduct, we must confess even those sins that we may not have committed individually. For this reason the confession is recited in the plural.

□ *Leket Yosher* cites the Talmudic passage (*Yoma* 86b) that describes the effects of sincere *teshuvah*. There we are taught that when one repents out of fear, one's premeditated iniquities are reckoned as inadvertent errors; but when one does *teshuvah* out of love, all of one's sins, even those that were premeditated, are accounted as merits.

Now it is inconceivable to us that our illustrious forebears could have failed to repent any sins they may have committed. Thus, just as they have atoned for their errors, and their sins have been considered as merits, so may it be with us.

וְעַכְשָׁו שֶׁנּוֹצַרְתִּי / And Now That I Have Been Formed

•§The *Viduy*/Confession ends with a heartbreaking admission of our inadequacy and a plea for mercy. Although we acknowledge that God's master plan for the universe demands the existence of the human race, yet each individual declares himself unworthy of that exalted fast. Moreover, having been created, we have done little to justify our continued existence. Therefore, shamefacedly, we beg that we be enabled to fulfill the purpose of our creation, no longer to be tempted into sinful ways, and that our past misdeeds be wiped away.

אֱלֹהַי, עַד שֶׁלֹּא נוֹצַרְתִּי אֵינִי כְדַאי, וְעַכְשָׁו שֶׁנּוֹצַרְתִּי כְּאִלּוּ לֹא נוֹצַרְתִּי, עָפָר אֲנִי בְּחַיָּי, קַל וָחֹמֶר בְּמִיתָתִי. הֲרֵי אֲנִי לְפָנֶיךָ כִּכְלִי מָלֵא בוּשָׁה וּכְלִמָּה.

My God, before I was formed I was unworthy, and now that I have been formed, it is as if I had not been formed. I am dust in my life and will surely be so in my death. Behold — before You I am like a vessel filled with shame and humiliation.

☐ *Maharsha* (*Berachos* 17a) explains this passage in connection with another dictum of the Talmud (*Eruvin* 13b): The academies of Shammai and Hillel debated whether man would have been better off had he never been created. After years of dispute, נִמְנוּ, they took a count, and it was decided that it would have been better for man not to have been created.

Maharsha explains that the term נִמְנוּ, *they took a count,* does not apply to a census of the students or to a vote. Rather, it refers to the 613 *mitzvos*. He asserts that the question under study was whether it would have been better for man had he not been created, for then it would have been impossible for him to transgress any of the negative *mitzvos*. Or, is it better for him now that he was created, for now he is capable of fulfilling the positive *mitzvos*? Thus, each side in the debate was aware of the advantages and disadvantages of man's being created or not. Yet they could not agree on whether it is better that man has been created and given the opportunity to perform positive *mitzvos* despite the chance that he might transgress the negative *mitzvos,* or whether it would have been preferable that he had never been born and thus would be guaranteed of never transgressing, despite the lost opportunity for performing the positive *mitzvos*. Finally, נִמְנוּ, *they took a count,* of the number of positive *mitzvos,* 248, and the number of negative *mitzvos,* 365, and it was decided that it would have been better for man not to have been created. For his creation could result in the transgression of 365 *mitzvos* while only enabling him to perform 248 *mitzvos*.

Thus, we say, "Before I was formed I was unworthy [of being formed — for it would have been better had I never been afforded the opportunity to transgress], and even now that I have been formed [and am able to perform positive *mitzvos*] it is as if I have not been formed [for I do not fulfill them properly]."

☐ This passage has also been interpreted homiletically:

Before I was formed I was unworthy [for I had performed no *mitzvos*], and now that I have been formed and it is as if I had not been formed [for I have still not performed the *mitzvos* properly], then I am certainly dust in my life and will surely be so after my death.

☐ The *viduy* continues, "Behold — before You I am like a vessel filled with shame and humiliation."

Why do we compare ourselves to a vessel? Shouldn't we say simply, "I am filled with shame and humiliation"?

R' Shalom of Belz gave the answer. When we compare ourselves to a vessel, we are in effect saying: Our shameful and humiliating sinfulness is not really an essential part of our being. Rather, we are like vessels that have been filled. We can be emptied of the shame and humiliation that fills us, just as a vessel can be emptied of its contents.

The Five Afflictions

The Talmud (*Yoma* ch. 8) teaches that the afflictions of Yom Kippur comprise five prohibitions (not counting the prohibition against labor, a restriction which is not considered affliction). The five are: eating and drinking (together considered as one prohibition), washing, anointing, wearing shoes, and marital relations.

☐ According to *Baal HaTurim* (*Leviticus* 23:27), these five afflictions correspond to: (a) the five times the word נֶפֶשׁ, *soul*, is mentioned in the *parashah* of Yom Kippur (*Leviticus* 23:26-32); (b) the five names by which the soul is known — נֶפֶשׁ, *soul*; רוּחַ, *wind*; נְשָׁמָה, *spirit*; חַיָּה, *living one*; יְחִידָה, *unique one* (see below); (c) the five times the *Kohen Gadol* immersed himself in the *mikveh* on Yom Kippur (see Mishnah *Yoma* 3:3); and (d) the five prayer services of the day — *Maariv, Shacharis, Mussaf, Minchah* and *Neilah*.

According to *Maharil* (cited in *Eliyahu Zuta*), the five afflictions correspond to: (a) the Five Books of Moses which were completed on the day of Yom Kippur; and (b) the five senses through which we perform *mitzvos* and commit sins.

☐ *Maharal of Prague* expounds on the connection between the five afflictions and the five names of the soul. Each affliction is intended to reduce the soul's feeling of comfort in its corporeal environment. Only then can the soul be released and separated from the physicality of the body.

(a) חַיָּה, *living one,* alludes to the soul as the life force of the body. Refraining from food and drink lessens the body's life force so that the soul is not comfortable in the body.

(b) יְחִידָה, *unique one,* is a description of the oneness of the soul, for the soul is comfortable in the body only when it forms a unity with the body. This unity of the body can only come about through the joining of man and woman into what Scripture terms "one flesh" (*Genesis* 2:24). Abstaining from marital relations lessens this unity so that the soul is not comfortable in the body.

(c) נְשָׁמָה, *spirit,* refers to man's soul which is *the lamp of HASHEM* (*Proverbs* 20:27). The soul shines with the Godly light, and washing beautifies the body, affording it a shine which makes the soul comfortable. Abstention from washing lets that shine fade so that the soul is not comfortable in the body.

(d) נֶפֶשׁ, *soul,* describes the immutability of the soul. The soul cannot contract *tumah*-impurity, but remains pure, as the Sages have stated (*Berachos* 60b) [and as we recite each morning]: *The soul You placed within me is pure.* This purity corresponds to anointing the body in order to remove its filth and make it pure. Such cleanliness makes the soul comfortable in the body. When the body is afflicted by not being anointed and cleansed, the soul is not comfortable in the body.

(e) רוּחַ, wind, alludes to the quality of lightness, a lack of physicality. Thus, since the wind is lifted from the ground, it can also lift things off the ground. Man is also raised off the ground by his shoes, and this makes his soul comfortable within him. When the feet are bare, however, they touch the ground, and the soul is not comfortable in the body.

אֲכִילָה וּשְׁתִיָה / Eating and Drinking

⦿§The main component of the fast of Yom Kippur is the affliction of refraining from eating and drinking. That this is the nature of affliction of Yom Kippur is not stated explicitly by the Torah, but is derived from the verse, וְהַאֲבַדְתִּי אֶת הַנֶּפֶשׁ הַהִוא, and I shall destroy that soul (Leviticus 23:30). This implies affliction which can lead to destruction of the soul; and which kind of affliction is that? — Abstention from eating and drinking (Yoma 74b). A different derivation refers to the passage where Moshe Rabbeinu reminds the Children of Israel how God tested them by afflicting them in the wilderness. The Talmud (ibid.) points out, "Here (concerning Yom Kippur) the Torah mentions עִנּוּי, affliction, and further on it mentions עִנּוּי again: וַיְעַנְּךָ וַיַּרְעִבֶךָ, And He afflicted you and made you hungry (Deuteronomy 8:3) — just as, further on, affliction means hunger, here, too, affliction means hunger."

Time-Range of the Commandment

⦿§A problem has been raised concerning the fundamental nature of the fast. Is it a general commandment for the entire day of Yom Kippur, from evening to evening — i.e., on this day as a whole, one should be in a state of affliction? Or does the commandment of affliction apply separately to each moment? This is not an abstract speculation, but a very practical question. For if one has transgressed and eaten on Yom Kippur, are we to say that he is still obligated to fast at each subsequent moment? Or should we say that since he has already broken the state of affliction on this day as a whole, he has no further obligation to fast?

Another practical consequence concerns one who is seriously ill and is required to eat. If he became well during the day, would he be forbidden to eat for the remainder of the day? Or do we consider the day as a whole, in which case, once the state of affliction has been broken, it no longer makes a difference whether one eats or not?

This problem is investigated by Rav Yaakov Ettlinger (Bnei Zion 1:34) who discusses the matter at length, basing himself on a number of sources. The Acharonim are in agreement that the mitzvah of affliction applies separately to each moment of the day.

The Decision to Break the Fast

᪣Two sections (*Orach Chaim* 617 and 618) in *Shulchan Aruch* are devoted to the laws concerning מְעוּבֶּרֶת, *a pregnant woman*; מֵנִיקָה, *a nursing woman*; יוֹלֶדֶת, *one who has just given birth*; and חוֹלֶה, *a sick person*, on Yom Kippur. When does the *halachah* require a person in one of these situations to eat, and when do we rely on the opinion of a doctor?

The basic principles are as follows. (a) We always rely on the opinion of the patient when he says that he needs to eat, even if a hundred doctors contradict him. (b) If the doctor says that the patient needs to eat, we rely on the doctor's word even if the patient says that he does not need to eat. And (c) even though generally the testimony of a woman or a non-Jew is not legally valid, *Shulchan Aruch HaRav,* following *Rosh,* tells us that "even if the doctor is a woman or a non-Jew, the doctor is regarded for this purpose just as the most valid witness of Israel, no matter whether his testimony supports a decision in the direction of leniency or of strictness; [moreover:] his or her testimony can stand against that of the most observant Jewish doctor (רוֹפֵא הַכָּשֵׁר בְּיִשְׂרָאֵל)." In *Shulchan Aruch,* additional details of the law are given for cases where there is a disagreement among the doctors.

In Times of Epidemic

᪣The *Acharonim* discuss the question of a cholera epidemic (God forbid), when doctors testify that fasting could be life threatening even for healthy people: Are such people permitted to eat on Yom Kippur? *Chasam Sofer* is of the opinion that such a threat must be considered סַכָּנַת נְפָשׁוֹת, *a life and death situation,* and all the dispensations that apply to פִּקּוּחַ נֶפֶשׁ, *saving a life,* apply here too. Thus he permits eating in these circumstances.

R' Yisrael of Salant, the father of the *Mussar* Movement, held a similar view. In fact, it is related that before Yom Kippur of the year of 1848, R' Yisrael had notices distributed throughout Vilna stating that due to the outbreak of cholera no one should fast. However, his decision was opposed by the *beis din* of Vilna (see below). To emphasize the gravity of the matter, R' Yisrael took the platform in the synagogue on Yom Kippur and delivered a talk to the effect that the congregation should not fast in such a situation. According to some eyewitness reports, in order to underscore the gravity of the situation, R' Yisrael then took a piece of cake, recited the proper blessing and ate it in full view of the congregation.

On the other hand, there is the responsa *Reishis Bikkurim,* by Rav Betzalel HaKohen, a member of the Vilna *beis din,* in which the author writes:

It is our duty to make this great matter known for all generations — for [it is a principle of the Torah that] when an event happens three times it establishes legal validity and thousands and tens of thousands of men and women fasted, thank God, on the Fast of Yom Kippur in the years 5599, 5609, and 5627 [1838, 1848, and 1866 — years of virulent cholera epidemics] throughout our entire land, and no evil (God forbid) befell them; and these events became known throughout almost the entire world at that time.

Angelic Israel

⋙The affliction of fasting gives the Jew a semblance of the angels, for he goes through the day full of humility, with head bowed, standing or kneeling, chanting hymns and praise. All this causing him to forsake his physical powers and natural functions, to engage only in spirituality, as if he had no animal nature within him (*Kuzari* 3:5).

☐ God set aside one day each year on which Israel's repentance will be readily accepted and on which their sins will easily be erased. This day rectifies the damage wrought by their sins and removes the darkness engendered by them. This day returns penitents to higher degrees of sanctity and enables them to approach near to Hashem from Whose Presence they were driven by their sins. On this day a light shines forth with the power to accomplish all of the aforesaid.

But in order to receive that light, Israel must observe all of the *mitzvos* of the day, particularly the fast. For fasting divorces a person from his physical state and elevates him, in some measure, to the level of the angels (*Derech Hashem*).

Fasting and Teshuvah

⋙Another reason for fasting on Yom Kippur is that fasting encourages *teshuvah*. Since it was on Yom Kippur that Moses descended with the second Tablets of the Ten Commandments and informed the nation that it would be forgiven for the grievous sin of the Golden Calf, this day has been eternalized as a day of repentance, totally dedicated to God's service. Therefore, all physical pleasure and all labor for the body's sake have been prohibited on it (*Moreh Nevuchim* 3:43).

Fasting on Shabbos

⋙When Yom Kippur falls on the Sabbath, the *mitzvah* of eating שָׁלֹשׁ סְעוּדוֹת, *three Shabbos meals*, is superseded by the fast.

☐ R' Leib "*Shomer Shabbos*" (lit., the Sabbath observer) would go to the marketplace every Friday to make his purchase for the Sabbath meals. He would approach the flour merchant, "Please sell Leib your finest flour in honor of the holy *Shabbos.*" Then he would enter the butcher's shop.

"Please sell Leib the finest meat for the holy *Shabbos.*" Similar requests were made at the fishmonger's stall, the vintner's shop, and at all the other stores that sold the necessities for *Shabbos.*

When Yom Kippur would fall on *Shabbos,* R' Leib would prepare as if for any other *Shabbos.* His table would be laden with the finest foods. Arriving home after *Kol Nidrei,* he would sit at the set table and declare, "Master of the World, from my side there is no obstacle. I truly desire to delight in the *Shabbos* as You have commanded us to. However, since it is Your will that we afflict ourselves on Yom Kippur, therefore Leib shall leave everything untouched in fulfillment of Your will."

רְחִיצָה וְסִיכָה / Washing and Anointing

Washing on Yom Kippur is prohibited only when done for pleasure. The *poskim* provide a number of details as to what kind of washing is considered "not for pleasure." Thus it is permissible to wash if one is soiled with mud; or upon rising in the morning; or before prayer. A bride, if Yom Kippur falls within the first thirty days of marriage, is allowed to wash. One is permitted to wade through a river while traveling on foot to perform a *mitzvah.* And other examples are given (*Orach Chaim* 613).

Anointing oneself, however, is forbidden both for pleasure and for other purposes (such as removing dirt). Only anointing for medical purposes is permitted.

נְעִילַת הַסַּנְדָל / Wearing Shoes

◆§Wearing shoes is forbidden, whether on one or on both feet. The prohibition applies only to shoes or sandals made of leather, or covered with leather. Footwear made of all other materials is permissible. *Rambam* explains why: " . . . since the hardness of the ground reaches the feet and one feels barefoot." In *Shulchan Aruch HaRav* an additional reason is given: "And further, the Sages forbade only 'shoes', and footwear not made of leather is not classified as a shoe."

☐ Various reasons have been advanced for the prohibition against wearing leather shoes, some esoteric, some ingenious:

The prohibition is related to two laws cited by *Rama:*

It is customary to tell a person wearing a new article of clothing, "תִּבְלֶה וְתִתְחַדֵשׁ, *May you wear it out and get a new one!*" However, some authorities (e.g., R' Yaakov Weil) write that this should not be said to a person wearing new shoes or any other garment made of animal skins. For, in order to produce another such garment to replace the worn-out one, another animal would have to be killed — and it is written: *His mercies are on all His works* (*Psalms* 145:9). Although this reasoning is extremely weak and appears unacceptable, nevertheless, many are careful not to use this formula [for animal-skin garments] (*Rama, Orach Chaim* 223:6).

[One who slaughters a beast or a fowl must cover its blood.] The first time a person performs the mitzvah of slaughtering he should recite the שֶׁהֶחֱיָנוּ, *Shehecheyanu*, blessing when covering the blood, but not upon the slaughter, since he is harming a creature (*Rama, Yoreh Deah* 28:2).[1]

Following the logic of these two rulings, it stands to reason that on Yom Kippur, a day of exceptional compassion and kindness, one should refrain from wearing an article that necessitated killing a living creature (*Siddur HaMinhagim*).

□ At first glance it would appear that wearing shoes is a device invented to protect the soles of the feet. This logic may be refuted, however. Many animals have skin that is as delicate as man's, yet those creatures get around quite well without ever wearing shoes.

R' Moshe Chagiz offer a deeper reason for wearing shoes. Man does not want to touch the ground directly because the ground was cursed as a result of Adam's sin — as it is written: *Accursed is the earth on account of you* (Genesis 3:17). Thus, man took to wearing shoes. This reasoning also explains why God ordered Moses to remove his shoes at the Burning Bush: *For the place where you are standing is holy ground* (Exodus 3:5). Shoes are only worn on accursed ground; on holy ground, one goes barefoot, making contact with the ground.

On Yom Kippur, when Israel stands before God in perfect repentance, the entire world is elevated. Adam's sin is atoned for, to a degree, and the very earth is transformed from "cursed ground" to "holy ground." Therefore we must remove our shoes (*R' Mendel of Rimanov*).[2]

One Hundred Blessings Each Day

◆§According to the Talmud (*Menachos* 43b), each person should strive to recite at least one hundred *berachos* each day. Now on weekdays when

---

1. Animal rights' advocates should not find support for their beliefs in these two decisions. Regarding the case of "May you wear it out and get a new one," *Rama* himself states that the "reasoning is extremely weak and appears unacceptable." And about the *Shehecheyanu* blessing, *Sifsei Kohen* replies: "This reasoning is forced" (*Shach,* ibid. 6). He proceeds to offer a more acceptable reason for this rule.

2. The principle set forth by R' Moshe Chagiz is used by R' Tzvi Elimelech of Dinov (*Agra Depirka*) to explain two Talmudic teachings: (a) In truth, a person should sell even the ceiling beams of his home to buy a pair of shoes for his feet (*Shabbos* 129a); and (b) upon putting on shoes, one recites the blessing שֶׁעָשָׂה לִי כָּל צָרְכִּי, *He has provided me my every need* (*Berachos* 60b). Man's most important function is to elevate himself to a life of blessing and holiness. To achieve this end, he must separate himself from the accursed earth. Thus, his shoes serve a more exalted purpose than his roof beams. Indeed, they serve his "every need."

The prohibition against wearing shoes on Tishah B'Av, the day of mourning for the destroyed *Beis HaMikdash* and our extended *galus,* exile, may be similarly explained. According to tradition, Tishah B'Av is the birthday of Mashiach. And it will be Mashiach's role to elevate the world, to transform the "cursed ground" to "blessed ground." By not wearing shoes, we anticipate his coming.

each *Shemoneh Esrei* contains nineteen *berachos,* this total is readily attainable. Even on the Sabbath and Festivals when all four *Amidah* prayers contain only twenty-eight *berachos,* the minimum is not difficult to reach, thanks to the three meals, *Kiddush,* snacks, etc. However, on Yom Kippur, the hundred seem out of reach. Therefore, many people are accustomed to bringing sweet-smelling spices to the synagogue on Yom Kippur. They recite the *besamim* blessing over these spices every once in a while. This helps complete the hundred *berachos.*

The Permitted Pleasure — the Sense of Smell

❧Why, on a day when we refrain from all bodily pleasures, are we permitted to enjoy the sense of smell? A reading of the third chapter of *Genesis* will show that four of the five senses are mentioned in the story of Adam and Eve's sin when they ate the forbidden fruit: וַתֵּרֶא הָאִשָּׁה, *and the woman saw* (v. 6) — the sense of sight; וַתִּקַּח מִפִּרְיוֹ, *and she took of its fruit* (ibid.) — the sense of touch; וַתֹּאכַל, *and she ate* (ibid.) — the sense of taste; וַיִּשְׁמְעוּ, *and they heard* (v. 8) — the sense of hearing. However, the sense of smell is not mentioned in that passage. It is for this reason that the sense of smell remains a spiritual pleasure [as the Talmud (*Berachos* 43b) states: Which pleasure does the spirit, but not the body, enjoy? We must say that it is the pleasure of sweet smells]. And it is for this reason that it is not counted among the afflictions of Yom Kippur (*Bnei Yisaschar*).

Some Aspects of the Prayer Services

וְגִילוּ בִּרְעָדָה / Rejoice with Trembling

❧It is customary not to begin *Maariv* until night has fallen. Many congregations prolong the *Kol Nidrei* recitation until night so that they can begin *Maariv* immediately. Others pause after *Kol Nidrei* until nightfall. In the interim, one should recite *Tehillim, Tefillah Zakkah,* review the prayers, or engage in some other study or supplication appropriate to the day. Under no circumstances should these awesome moments be frittered away with idle chatter or frivolous activity.

The Yom Kippur prayers express a combination of two attitudes:

On the one hand, we are overcome with awe and fright as we stand before the bar of Heavenly justice, for we know our shortcomings, and our sins are more than we can confess or atone for in a single day or in countless days. On the other hand, we are optimistic that God will be merciful. Thus, with joy in the knowledge that God waits benevolently for our repentance and with trembling at the prospect that our merits are unspeakably meager, we prepare to inaugurate our supplications.

Rabbi Levi Yitzchak of Berditchev epitomized this duality of feeling. While the awe with which he prayed was legendary, he expressed unyielding confidence that God would be merciful. And he was the consummate protagonist of his people. One of his impassioned pleas for God's mercy is preserved in a chassidic song. In it, the Berditchever Rebbe demands God's forgiveness and blessing, as follows:

Master of the universe, I will make a trade with You. I will give You errors, iniquities, and transgressions — O Father!

And if You ask me what You should give in return? You should give forgiveness, pardon, and atonement — O Father!

If You think that that will be an even trade — "No!" I tell You.

I want You to add children, life, and a livelihood — O Father!

If You ask me what I mean by children, I will tell You: children and grandchildren who engage in Torah and *mitzvos* — O Father!

If You ask me what I mean by life, I will tell You: only the living can thank You and praise You — O Father!

If You ask me what I mean by livelihood, I will tell You: you shall eat and you shall be satisfied and you shall bless HASHEM, your God — O Father!

The Egyptians say that their god is a god — "No!" I tell You.

The Persians say that their god is a god — "No!" I tell You.

The atheists say there is no God — "There is!" I tell You.

And I, Levi Yitzchak ben Sarah Sosha, say, יִתְגַּדַּל וְיִתְקַדַּשׁ שְׁמֵהּ רַבָּא — *May His great Name grow exalted and sanctified!*

בָּרוּךְ שֵׁם / Blessed Is the Name . . .

All year, except on Yom Kippur, the second verse of *Krias Shema* — בָּרוּךְ שֵׁם כְּבוֹד מַלְכוּתוֹ לְעוֹלָם וָעֶד, *Blessed is the Name of His glorious kingdom for all eternity* — is recited in an undertone. The Sages give two reasons for this custom:

(A) *Our Father Jacob and His Twelve Sons*

At Jacob's deathbed, his children affirmed their loyalty to God by proclaiming the verse *Shema* [the word 'Israel' in that context refers to Jacob]. Jacob responded with the words *'Blessed is the Name . . .'* The Sages taught: Should we say these words in our prayers because Jacob said them? Yes. But on the other hand, Moses did not transmit them to us, for they are not found in the Torah. Therefore, let us say them silently (*Pesachim* 56a).

(B) *Likened to the Angels*

Moses heard this beautiful prayer from the angels, and taught it to Israel. We dare not say it aloud, because we are sinful and therefore unworthy of using an angelic formula. On Yom Kippur, however, when Israel elevates itself to the sin-free level of angels, we proclaim it aloud as do the angels (*Devarim Rabbah* 2:36).

☐ *Ramchal's Synthesis*

R' Moshe Chayim Luzzatto (known by the acronym *Ramchal*), in his *Derech Hashem* — a fundamental work on the basic beliefs of Judaism regarding God and His purpose for creating the world — synthesizes the two reason given by the Sages:

Man comprises two opposites — body and soul. The body is finite by its very nature. The soul is by nature eternal, yet is limited by the physicality of the body into which it has been placed. Moreover, God's wisdom decreed that the soul be restricted in certain other ways as well.

Nevertheless, God desired that man be able to rid himself, to some degree, of these binds and chains. Then, he would be capable of arriving at his ends in accordance with spiritual, rather than physical, law. In this way he could achieve an otherwise unattainable grasp of spiritual matters. Thus, God established means to enable man to reach this higher plane, but man must make the effort to elevate himself through these means. [In a long, complicated discussion beyond the scope of this book, *Ramchal* describes the metaphysics of these means. Suffice it for us to know that spiritual perfection can be attained only through these means, and that these means ultimately depend upon God's Oneness.]

The intent of the first verse of *Shema* is to declare that everything depends on this Oneness, and will eventually return to its true perfection.

With respect to human beings, true perfection means that God will rest His Name upon them, and His sanctity will attach itself to them. He will rule over mankind and draw them after Him. All will depend upon Him and become perfected through His perfection. This is God's crowning glory which comes from His creation and, so to speak, through which He makes Himself great.

Today, this perfection is fulfilled only by spiritual beings, for they are pure and holy and His Name rests upon and is bound to them with strong ties. They are drawn after Him at all times and His glory magnifies itself through them. But among the terrestrial beings this is not the case. They have not yet reached this measure of perfection. They have not yet rid themselves of evil. As a result, God's glory, so to speak, is not magnified properly through them.

Having reached a state of perfection the angels are permitted to praise God with the verse, בָּרוּךְ שֵׁם, *Blessed is the Name. . .* Mankind, which has not achieved perfection, cannot. The Name does not rest upon them; His glory is not magnified through them.

Yet there are two exceptions to this rule: Jacob, just before he died; and Israel on Yom Kippur.

Jacob, on his deathbed, was surrounded by his twelve righteous and holy sons, all free of blemish, all crowned with God's Oneness, all declaring as one, "שְׁמַע יִשְׂרָאֵל", *Hear, our father Israel, HASHEM is our God,*

HASHEM *the One and Only.''* Then he was able to reply, in a loud voice, like the angels, ''. . . בָּרוּךְ שֵׁם, *Blessed is the Name of His glorious kingdom for all eternity.''*

We have not yet reached this level. Nevertheless, in the merit of the Patriarch Jacob, we are permitted to recite this verse, but only in a whisper. On Yom Kippur, however, when all of Israel elevate themselves to the level of the angels, then they may recite the verse aloud.

שֹׁמֵעַ תְּפִלָּה / He Who Hears Prayer

◆§A series of forty-five verses, mostly from *Psalms,* forms the introductory prayer to the daily *Selichos* (penitential prayers) as well as to the *Selichos* of Yom Kippur night. The first verse of this series is: שֹׁמֵעַ תְּפִלָּה עָדֶיךָ כָּל בָּשָׂר יָבֹאוּ, *He Who hears prayers, unto You shall all flesh come* (*Psalms* 65:3).

But why do we say the word תְּפִלָּה, *prayer,* in the singular, when, in reality, God hears all prayers?

Noam Megadim suggests that the prayer of our verse does not refer to our prayers but to the prayer of the angels. For one may ask: By what right do we come to praise and exalt the great King of Kings? Indeed, it is even incomprehensible that the angels, lofty as they may be, can sing God's praises. They and we are so much lower than God; we do not even begin to understand His majesty and His glory. Regarding the angels it is written: *In His angels he placed falseness* (*Job* 4:18). Nevertheless we find that the heavenly beings were permitted to utter His praise [e.g., *Isaiah* 6:3; *Ezekiel* 3:12]. It is to this angelic prayer that we refer when we say, ''He Who [has granted the angels the right to utter prayer, and Who] hears [that] prayer, [as a result of that permission] unto You shall all flesh come.''

מַעֲבִיר רִאשׁוֹן רִאשׁוֹן / He Removes Sins One by One

◆§The Talmud (*Rosh Hashanah* 17a) discusses the workings of God's kindness in judgment:

> According to the teachings of the Academy of Hillel, God, Who is רַב חֶסֶד, *Abundant in Kindness,* מַטֶּה כְּלַפֵּי חֶסֶד, *tips [the scales of justice] toward kindness* . . . The Academy of R' Yishmael explains that God accomplishes this by removing sins one by one.

The *Rishonim* interpret this passage in various ways:

— According to *Rashi,* if one's good deeds are equivalent to his sins, God removes a sin from the balance so that the side of virtue outweighs the side of sin.

— *Rif* interprets that if someone has committed a particular sin for the first time, God holds it in abeyance and does not include it in the calculation, as long as it has not yet become habitual.

— *Rambam*, based on *Yoma* 86b, writes that the first *two* sins are removed (*Hilchos Teshuvah* 3:5).

☐ Why does God remove the sins instead of destroying them entirely?

Since *teshuvah* done out of love for Hashem causes one's sins to be reckoned as merits (*Yoma* 86b), therefore, God merely removes the sins and sets them aside, waiting until the sinner repents (*R' Avraham of Slonim*).

מוֹל אֶת לְבָבֵנוּ / Expose Our Hearts

⇥§We pray that God expose our hearts that they become filled with love for Hashem, as it is written: וּמָל ה׳ אֱלֹהֶיךָ אֶת לְבָבְךָ וְאֶת לְבַב זַרְעֶךָ, *May HASHEM, your God, expose* [lit. circumcise] *your heart and the heart of your offspring,* לְאַהֲבָה אֶת ה׳ אֱלֹהֶיךָ בְּכָל לְבָבְךָ וּבְכָל נַפְשֶׁךָ, [so that you will be able] *to love HASHEM, your God, with all your heart and with all your soul,* לְמַעַן חַיֶּיךָ, *that you may live* (*Deuteronomy* 30:6).

Exposing, or circumcising, the heart allows spirituality to enter it. A person's accumulation of sins builds a barrier of habits, self-justification, and materialism over his heart, making it extremely difficult for him to experience love for God and Torah. When he attempts to repent, God helps by cutting away this barrier, thereby exposing the true inner yearnings of his heart, and allowing love to enter.

☐ A simple reading of this verse seems to indicate that we should love Hashem in order that we may live. But is this not a direct contradiction to the dictum in *Pirkei Avos* (1:3): "Do not be like servants who serve their masters in order to receive a reward"?

To answer this question, *Noam Megadim* explains the verse as a supplication to God to remove from our hearts the improper attitude describe in *Pirkei Avos,* that of serving one's master in order to receive reward. "May Hashem, your God, circumcise [from] your heart [the improper manner of service that allows you] to love Hashem, your God . . . [only] that you may live."

☐ The Talmud (*Berachos* 33b) states: "Everything is in the hands of Heaven, except for fear of Heaven." This means that all aspects of man's life are out of his control, except for matters that pertain to his *mitzvah* observance, both *mitzvos* between man and God, and *mitzvos* between man and his fellow. Included in this are all of his character traits. If so, how can we ask God to expose our heart. That must come from within ourselves for it involves "fear of Heaven."

R' Yissachar Dov of Belz explains that when a righteous person realizes that he has sinned, he may become so upset by his lapse that he will begin to neglect all his physical needs and devote himself, heart and soul, to *teshuvah*. But these bodily needs fall into the category of "everything is from Heaven." Therefore, we ask God to assist us in getting on with our repentance so that we will no longer neglect our physical needs.

The Temple Service Recalled

⋖§The verse, . . . *so we will offer the words of our lips instead of bulls* (וּנְשַׁלְּמָה פָרִים שְׂפָתֵינוּ; *Hosea* 14:3), tells us that when the sacrificial services are impossible, our prayers take the place of the sacrifices. Accordingly, all Israel have followed the custom of including a recital, during the Yom Kippur prayers, of the Order of Service performed by the *Kohen Gadol* (High Priest) in the *Beis HaMikdash*. This is in commemoration of the atonement which came about through the sacrifices performed by the *Kohen Gadol*. This custom was already in force in Talmudic times (see *Yoma* 36b and 56b). The *seder haavodah* (order of the *Kohen Gadol's* service) is found in various versions, of which two, both of ancient lineage, are prevalent. The more ancient one, beginning, אַתָּה כּוֹנַנְתָּ עוֹלָם מֵרֹאשׁ, *You established the universe from the start . . .*, and ascribed to the fourth-(or fifth-)century sage Yose ben Yose, is recited by *Sephardim* and *chassidim*. Most *Ashkenazi* congregations, on the other hand, recite the one that begins, אַמִּיץ כֹּחַ, *Vigorous in strength, mighty, and great in power*. This latter version was composed by R' Meshullam ben Klonimos of tenth-century Lucca, Italy, and Mainz, Germany.

The Kohen Gadol's Preparation for the Service

⋖§*Shevet Yehudah* cites an eyewitness account by Marcus, a Roman consul in Jerusalem, during the days of the Second Temple:

Seven days before the special day that the Jews call Yom Kippur, the most important of their calendar, they would prepare — in the home of the *Kohen Gadol* — chairs for the head of the Court, the *Nassi*, the *Kohen Gadol*, the Deputy *Kohen Gadol*, and the king, besides seventy silver chairs for the seventy members of the Sanhedrin. Then the senior *Kohen* would stand up and say [to the *Kohen Gadol*] the following words of admonition:

"Look before Whom you will enter, and know that if you fail to concentrate on what you will do, you will immediately fall dead and the atonement of Israel will be lost. Behold, the eyes of all Israel depend on you. Examine your ways; perhaps you have committed a sin, even a minor one, for sometimes a transgression can be equal to many good deeds, and the measure is in the hands of the God of knowledge. Also investigate your fellow *Kohanim* and purify them. Bear in mind that you come before the King of all kings, Who sits on a throne of justice and scatters all evil with His eyes. How can you come before Him in the company of the enemy?"

The *Kohen Gadol* would reply that he had already examined his deeds and repented for every sin that was known to him. He also had brought his fellow *Kohanim* to the Temple Courtyard and had adjured them by the One Who rested his Name there, that each of them was to declare what he knew about his fellow, or himself, in order that the High Priest might prescribe for them the proper repentance for each sin.

The king too would speak approvingly to the *Kohen Gadol*, and promise to honor him when he came out of the Sanctuary in peace. Then they would announce that the *Kohen Gadol* would leave for his chamber in the Sanctuary, and then all the people would go out to escort him, and walk before him in the proper order.

I saw this with my own eyes. The first to walk before him were the members of the royal family — for the closer one was to him, the more worthy he was; after them were the descendants of the kings of the House of David, all in their proper order, one following another. A herald would walk before them, crying, "Give honor to the house of David!"

Then came the house of Levi, and a herald crying, "Give honor to the house of Levi!" There were thirty-six thousand of them, and their deputies dressed in clothing of blue satin, and the priests, twenty-four thousand of them, dressed in white satin. After them came the singers, then the musicians and then the trumpeters, then the gatekeepers, then the incense-makers, then the curtain-makers, then the watchmen, then the treasurers, then the group called *kartofilor* (the chair-bearers), then those who worked in the Sanctuary, then the seventy members of the Sanhedrin, then a hundred *Kohanim* with silver rods in their hands to clear the way, then the *Kohen Gadol*, and after him all the elders of the priesthood, two by two. At the main intersections, the heads of the academies stood and declared, "O master, *Kohen Gadol*, come in peace! Pray to our Creator that He grant us long life that we may engage in His Torah."

When they reached the entrance of the Temple Mount, they would pray for the continuation of the kingship of the Davidic dynasty, and then for the *Kohanim*, and then for the Temple, and the noise was so great from the multitudes of people crying Amen, that the birds flying overhead fell to the ground. Then the *Kohen Gadol* would bow to the entire people and take leave in tears and awe. The two deputies of the priesthood would lead him to his chamber, and there he would seclude himself from all his priests.

All that I have just described occurred when he entered. But when he left the honor was multiplied, for all the people in Jerusalem passed before him, most of them carrying torches of white wax, and all of them dressed in white clothing. All the windows were adorned with embroidery, and filled with candles. *Kohanim* have told me that often the High Priest could not get home before midnight, because of the press of people passing by and because of the great numbers. For even though all of them were fasting, they did not go home until they had attempted to approach the *Kohen Gadol* and kiss his hand. The next day he would make a great feast and invite his friends and relatives, and make it a holiday because he had emerged from the Sanctuary in peace.

Then the *Kohen Gadol* would order a smith to make a gold tablet, and engrave upon it these words: "I, so-and-so the *Kohen Gadol,* son of so-and-so, the *Kohen Gadol,* have served in the high priesthood in the great and holy Temple in the service of Him Who rested His Name there, and it was such and such a year from Creation. May He Who found me worthy for this service find my son after me worthy to stand in service before Him."

Minchah

The Torah Reading

◄§The Torah reading for *Minchah*, *Leviticus* 18, is a chapter that details the forbidden sexual relationships. Several reasons are offered for this seemingly strange selection for the afternoon Torah reading:

— Since all people are subject to strong passions from time to time, they should hear this chapter and repent in case they have sinned in this manner (*Rashi*, *Megillah* 31a).

— The women adorn themselves and attend the synagogue on Yom Kippur, therefore this chapter is intended to caution against frivolity (*Tosafos* ibid.)

The Haftarah

◄§The Book of *Jonah*, one of the books of תְּרֵי עָשָׂר, *The Twelve Prophets,* is read at *Minchah* on Yom Kippur. It is particularly appropriate for the Yom Kippur *Haftarah* because:

— The story of Jonah teaches that sincere repentance can reverse even the harshest Heavenly decree (*Levush*).

— The repentance of Ninveh's inhabitants is to serve as an example to us to repent our sins (*Shelah*).

— The miraculous manner in which Jonah's flight was prevented shows that no one can escape from God (*Abudraham*).

Because the lessons of *Yonah* are so pivotal to the meaning of Yom Kippur, it is considered a special merit to be called to the Torah for the *aliyah*.

Ne'ilah

The Moment of Atonement

⋅§The moment of atonement is at the end of the day — עִם חֲשֵׁכָה, at nightfall — the time of the Ne'ilah service. Tur tells us that after Minchah the congregation "multiply requests for forgiveness and mercy until the time arrives to recite the Ne'ilah Prayer." In the Talmud Yerushalmi there are two opinions as to the significance here of the word ne'ilah, which means "locking." It may refer to the locking of the שַׁעֲרֵי הֵיכָל, gates of the Sanctuary, in Temple times. As Levush puts it, "Like a servant who, before taking leave of the king, requests a reward and a royal gift, and then, as he leaves, locks the gate behind him." Or it may refer to the locking of the שַׁעֲרֵי שְׁמַיָּא, gates of heaven, at the conclusion of the prayer. The gates of the Beis HaMikdash were locked before sunset, soon after the second daily Tamid sacrifice — which would be well before nightfall, the time of the locking of the gates of heaven. In actual practice, most congregations begin Ne'ilah shortly before sunset.

חָתְמֵנוּ / Seal Us

⋅§The Ne'ilah Prayer reflects in a number of ways the fact that the atonement of the day is being "sealed" at the time of this prayer. For the word, כָּתְבֵנוּ, inscribe us, in Avinu Malkeinu, we substitute, חָתְמֵנוּ, seal us. Those interpolated sentences in the Amidah prayer which read וּכְתוֹב, and inscribe, and וְנִכָּתֵב, may we be inscribed, during the Ten Days of Repentance, now read instead, וַחֲתוֹם, and seal, and, וְנֵחָתֵם, may we be sealed.

The Shechinah Departs

⋅§At the end of the Ne'ilah Service, Shema Yisrael is recited once, Baruch Shem . . . three times; and ה' הוּא הָאֱלֹהִים, HASHEM is God, seven times. The purpose of these recitals is to accompany the Shechinah, the Divine Presence, as it departs and rises heavenward. Beis Yosef, in the name of the Rishonim, gives several other reasons for the shofar blast (as a commemoration of the shofar blown on the Yom Kippur of Yovel to announce the emancipation of all Jewish servants and the return of ancestral estates to those who sold them during the past fifty years; to announce the night and the end of the fast; to confuse the Accuser). Nevertheless, according to Taz, the reason having to do with the withdrawal of the Shechinah is the "preferred reason."

Finally, the blast of the shofar, after Ne'ilah is over, is a sign that the Shechinah has departed upward.

The Night After Yom Kippur

Maariv

⋅≶During the *Shemoneh Esrei* after Yom Kippur, we pray, "Forgive us" — but hasn't Yom Kippur atoned for our sins?

Rabbi Yitzchok of Vorki explained with a parable of a king who walked through a field. A peasant saw him and kicked him. The king's bodyguards wanted to kill the peasant, but the king said, "Don't harm him. He does not know who I am, or he would not have done such a thing. Put him in a school and teach him how to behave. Then he will become a new man." They put the man in a school and he truly changed. When he understood how great the king was, he was overcome with shame and began to cry, "Forgive me!" When he was an ignoramus, he had not known how great his sin was, but now that he understood, he was overcome with grief.

So it is with us. All year, we didn't realize how terrible our sins were against the King Who is over all kings, the Holy One, Blessed is He. Now that we have cleansed ourselves, and He has forgiven our transgressions, we are ashamed and we beg: "Forgive us, our Father, for we have erred; pardon us, our King, for we have willfully sinned."

After the Fast

⋅≶And as a sign of confidence that complete atonement has taken place, "we eat and are joyous on the night on which Yom Kippur ends, for it partakes somewhat of the quality of *Yom Tov.*" The source of this *halachah* is a *Midrash* : On the departure of Yom Kippur a בַּת קוֹל, *heavenly voice*, is heard declaring (in the words of *Ecclesiastes* 9:7): לֵךְ אֱכֹל" בְּשִׂמְחָה לַחְמֶךָ וּשְׁתֵה בְלֶב טוֹב יֵינֶךָ כִּי כְבָר רָצָה הָאֱלֹהִים אֶת מַעֲשֶׂיךָ, *Go, eat your bread in joy and drink your wine with a good heart, for your deeds have already found favor with God!"*

Maintaining the Level

⋅≶True, one can scale to the greatest heights of spirituality on Yom Kippur, to the level of the very angels, to a place that is a foretaste of the World to Come. But how does one retain this sanctity, or at least a portion of it, for the future? What can one do not to lose the lofty achievements and status of the day? The answer, according to *Mei'imrei Shlomo*, is prayer.

The purpose of the day is nearness to God. All the preparations of the Ten Days of Repentance were to this end. And this can be attained through prayer. For what is prayer but a drawing closer to God. This is why one may not recite the *Amidah* aloud. When the petitioner is in close proximity to the one he is petitioning, there is no need to shout. Up close, even a whisper is audible.

This is also why the Talmud (*Berachos* 30b) states that the early *chassidim*, that is, the righteous of old, would wait a full hour before beginning to pray. During this time they would direct their thoughts and their hearts to Hashem. Rabbeinu Yonah explains that this does not mean that they studied the meanings of the words they were about to recite. Rather, they directed their hearts to draw closer, with great cleaving, to Him, until they were actually touching Him, so to speak. With such closeness, there is no need for loud voices, the softest whisper is sufficient.

❧ Yom Kippur Stories

Haazinu — A Concise History of the World

R' Moshe ben Nachman (better known as *Ramban* or Nachmanides) had a disciple named R' Avner. Despite his obvious reverence for his mentor, this Avner left the path of Hashem and became a disbeliever. After a period of time, it was his fortune to be appointed to high office and he became both well known and feared throughout the land.

One Yom Kippur he had the *Ramban* brought before him. With his former teacher standing before him, this renegade butchered a pig, cooked and ate it. After completing his meal, Avner asked the *Ramban*, "How many times does the Torah hold me liable for *kares* (spiritual excision) for what I have just done?"

The *Ramban* replied, "Four."

As if his brazenness was yet insufficient, Avner attempted to refute *Ramban's* reply, "No, I committed five sins for which the penalty is *kares*, not four!"

At this, *Ramban* no longer tried to contain his feelings. He gazed upon his opponent with such intense anger, that the former disciple's reverence for his master returned and he was speechless. After a while, *Ramban* asked Avner what had caused him to turn away from his faith.

"You once taught us that all the *mitzvos* of the Torah and all the events of history can be found alluded to in the Song of *Haazinu* (*Deuteronomy*, 32:1-43). But knowing this to be impossible, I dismissed the idea along with all your other teachings and became a new person."

"I still maintain that this is so," said the *Ramban*. "Test me with anything you desire to know."

The man stood astonished. "All right! Where is my fate mentioned in *Haazinu*?"

Ramban answered, "You have asked well. In a moment I will show you." He then stepped into a corner of the room and prayed for Divine guidance. When he returned, the *Ramban* pointed to the five-word verse, אָמַרְתִּי אַפְאֵיהֶם אַשְׁבִּיתָה מֵאֱנוֹשׁ זִכְרָם, *I said I would scatter them, I would erase their remembrance from mankind* (ibid. 32:26). "Taking the third letter of each word will spell your name, ר׳ אַבְנֵר, *R' Avner.*"

Upon hearing this, Avner paled. "Is there any cure for my condition?" he pleaded.

Ramban responded, "You understand the meaning of the verse." And he departed.

Avner immediately set out on a sea journey in a boat with neither oarsman nor oar. He would drift wherever the wind would take him. And nothing was ever heard from him again (*Seder HaDoros*).

The Sincerity of the Flute

Once there was a villager who used to pray on the Days of Awe in the Baal Shem Tov's *shul*. Unfortunately, he had a retarded son who could not even be taught to read or recite a holy word. His father never brought him along to the city, but when the boy became a *bar mitzvah*, his father took him along to the city on Yom Kippur, so that he could make sure the boy would fast.

The boy had a little flute that he used to play when he sat in the field tending the sheep. Without his father's knowledge, he took the flute with him when they went to pray with the Baal Shem Tov. The boy sat in *shul* without praying, because he did not know how to read. During *Mussaf* he said to his father: "Father I want to play my flute." His father shuddered and angrily told the boy that it was forbidden to do so on Yom Kippur. The boy had to restrain himself.

During *Minchah*, the boy spoke up again: "Please Father — let me play on my flute." Again the father warned him that it was strictly forbidden to do such a thing. He couldn't take the flute away from the boy because it was *muktzah* [something that is forbidden to handle].

After *Minchah*, the boy asked again: "Please let me play my flute."

Seeing how badly he wanted to play, his father said: "Where is it?" When the boy said it was in his pocket, the father held his hand on the pocket to keep his son from taking the flute out. The man stood and recited *Ne'ilah* with his hand on the pocket.

But in the middle of *Ne'ilah*, the boy wrested the flute from his father and played it so loud that everyone in the *shul* was shocked. When the Baal Shem Tov heard the blast, he finished *Ne'ilah* more quickly than usual.

After Yom Kippur the Baal Shem Tov said, "With the sound of his flute, the little boy elevated all the prayers and made it easier for me. He is completely unlearned, but all day he saw and heard Jews praying, and these prayers made the holy spark inside him grow into a great fire. The flame of his longing for Hashem burned more and more until his soul nearly left him. He had such longing that he played from his heart with complete sincerity and no selfish motives — purely for the sake of God's Name. This boy's pure breath was so acceptable to God that it was able to elevate all the prayers."

The Cantonist

During the reign of Czar Nikolai I, the Russian government decreed that Jewish boys between the ages of seven and ten would be drafted into the army and forced to serve for twenty-five years. The purpose of the law was not military in nature; the czar and his ministers wanted to force these children to convert to Christianity. They would be stationed far from home and severely persecuted. There only hope for decent treatment was conversion. Otherwise they could look forward to hunger, beatings, and curses for the full term of their service. Tragically, but not surprisingly, there were many who were weaned away from their religion — but many others survived the pain and loneliness, and sanctified Hashem's Name by refusing to surrender. There were many synagogues founded by these so-called Cantonists after their discharge from the hated army. Few of them were able to marry and have children — so old and worn were they upon gaining their freedom — and hardly any were able to earn more than subsistence wages, but they were genuine heroes, living testimony to the greatness of the Jewish soul.

Once a delegation of prominent rabbis was in St. Petersburg, the capital, to plead before Czar Nikolai for the Jewish people. Since Jews could not live in the city without special permission, the only synagogue was that of the Jewish soldiers stationed in St. Petersburg, and it was there that the distinguished rabbis were forced to pray on Yom Kippur.

When the time came for *Ne'ilah*, the rabbis turned to one of their number, who combined Torah, piety, and a pleasant voice. He was their logical choice to serve as *chazzan* for the holiest prayer of the year. But the soldiers thought otherwise.

"There is no doubt that the rabbi is a very great man, but there is one man among us who has sanctified God's Name as have few others. He withstood countless tests and excruciating pain to remain true to God. Look at his body, crippled and scarred. No one has endured more torture to glorify the Name. We beg you to let him pray for us now. Whose prayers could be more acceptable before the Heavenly Throne?"

The rabbis shuddered with awe and respect for the humble soldier who had achieved such greatness. They agreed that it would be their honor for him to be the *chazzan*.

Before the Cantonist began the *Kaddish*, he said aloud, "Normally a Jew prays for children, life, and livelihood. But for what can we pray? For children? — we are unmarried. For life? — our lives are so painful that we would rather be dead. For livelihood? — the czar feeds us.

"For what do we pray? יִתְגַּדַּל וְיִתְקַדַּשׁ שְׁמֵהּ רַבָּא, *May His great Name grow exalted and sanctified!*"

Yom Kippur During World War II

In a D.P. [Displaced Persons] camp, in the first year of liberation after the defeat of the Nazis, a few remnants of European Jewry got together shortly before Yom Kippur. Each reminisced on his Days of Atonement during the years of horror. Moshe Prager, chronicler of the Holocaust, recorded their stories in *Sparks of Glory*.

The Oldest Partisan's Story

It was during the last manhunt conducted against the Jewish fugitives who were still hiding out. In my region, in Eastern Galicia, the few Jews who had escaped deportation were getting caught. The number of survivors had dwindled, yet the murderers' lust for blood kept growing. They searched everywhere for hidden Jews. The deathtrap was spread everywhere. High ransoms were offered for every Jew caught alive, and many local peasants joined in the hunt. If there was still a chance to hide from the Germans, it had become almost impossible to escape the insidious look of the peasants who knew everyone in their neighborhood and who did not leave a single stone unturned.

When I realized that I was the only Jew left in the entire region, I decided to walk right into the lion's den. It occurred to me that the safest place to hide was at the home of the village priest, who was at the head of all the hoodlums and murderers. I disguised myself as an old peasant, a wayfarer who walked with a limp, and I hired myself out as a day laborer at the priest's house. What helped me in lending credence to my new role was my full-grown beard, streaked with grey. From time to time the Nazi pursuers searched the entire neighborhood, but it never occurred to them to search the house of their accomplice, the priest. And even the people who worked for the priest never suspected me. One time the priest's elderly maid said with a sigh, "Ah, my old man, you are a little different from all the rest of those poor peasants, you never swear the way they do. You never curse the way they do. It's strange . . ." After that I began to force myself to swear and curse like the rest of them.

One time the regional head of the Gestapo came to the priest's house. I was cleaning the priest's room when that murderer walked in. I knew his face from the ghetto, and I began to shake. I shook for only a moment. I knew that any suspicious move might reveal my true identity, and I stood like a dummy with the broom in my hand. "Father," the Nazi said to the priest as he came in, "I came to enlist your help in an urgent matter. Tomorrow is the Day of Atonement for Jews. I must find myself a living Jew in honor of the occasion. Last year and the year before I had Jewish men, women, children, and even rabbis at my disposal, but this year, not even one living Jew . . ." I listened to his words and I noted that his eyes turned toward me, either intentionally or by chance. At that moment I started laughing, loudly and stupidly — and that laughter removed all suspicion from me.

When I heard that the next day was Yom Kippur I made a vow to fast, come what may. I took my food ration to the stable where I had my bed, gave my food to the horses, and hummed the *Kol Nidrei* chant to myself. There was a great deal of work at the field in the morning. They were gathering potatoes, and I was sent out to help. Several workers sat around me and chewed their bread. Since I could not afford to arouse the smallest suspicion, I did what the angels did at the house of our patriarch Abraham: I pretended to swallow the bread, while in reality I slipped the slices into my sleeve.

Lunch made things even more difficult. Each worker was served a bowl of stew daily, and the last thing I would dare do was refuse it. I suddenly had an idea. Before lunch was served, I went to the other end of the field to work, and when the food distributor called my name, I pretended I did not hear him — I was too absorbed in my work. Suddenly the workers began to call out from all sides, "Hey, old man, you missed your lunch. Your food is cold!"

I came back and looked into the pot and I let out a bitter cry, "You expect me to eat this cold garbage? I won't eat it! I am going to tell the father about this! You shameless people, taking a poor old man's food away from him!" Of course I peppered my words with a few sharp expletives which I do not care to repeat.

I didn't touch the stew. I returned to my work with great gusto, cursing and swearing and working till sundown. As soon as I finished my work I hurried back to the priest and presented my complaint. I finally let myself be calmed down and agreed to receive a double portion for supper. This is how I successfully completed my Yom Kippur fast, under the protection of the priest . . .

❧ ❧ ❧

The Young Girl's Story

❧We too, in Auschwitz, saw to it that we observed Yom Kippur properly. We had to fight a tough battle for the privilege of fasting on Yom Kippur. But that was one battle which we Jewish girls, the weakest of all, did win.

I must add that the story of our victory ends with a bitter disappointment. And when you hear about our victory and also about our disappointment, you will realize what we had to go through in that hellish extermination camp.

Each section in the camp was separated from the others by a maze of electrified barbed wire fences. To touch the wire meant instant death. Those fences were used more than once as tools of suicide. Anyone who was tired of living would approach the fence, throw himself against it, and that was all.

But in spite of the lethal fence surrounding us, a good word did reach our section, the section for girls doing forced labor. The word came from a neighboring camp inhabited by Hungarian Jews slated for quick extermination. They had arranged a public prayer in their camp for Rosh Hashanah, and were not stopped by the guards. That bit of news cheered us up. We discussed it and decided to determine the date of Yom Kippur according to that information and fast on that day as we were accustomed to do in the past.

We worked out a complete plan. A few days before Yom Kippur we started working as hard as we could, without giving respite to our frail bodies. We wanted to placate our ruthless S.S. lady supervisor. Indeed, because of that effort we received a compliment from her for the first time, something to the effect of "those industrious Jewesses." Then, when the accursed witch was in a good mood, one of the girls, who spoke perfect German, presented with great tact and discretion a request on behalf of all the girls:

"Please, may we bring forth an extraordinary request: This week we Jews will observe our most important holiday. It is a fast day. Our request is that we be permitted work only half a day, to enable the girls to fast. The remaining work hours the girls will give in advance before the holiday."

"Such Jewish impudence," the Nazi, following in the footsteps of the Biblical Pharaoh, exploded. "I am too good to you, you despicable Jewesses, so you dare to come to me with such requests. From here on you will work longer hours, and in honor of your holiday you will work overtime. And don't dare fast on that day. If any of you gets too weak on that day she will be immediately sent to the crematorium. It's an order!"

None of us was discouraged from fasting. We had decided to do it, and so we did. Some of us had come from non-observant homes and had not paid much attention to fasts. But here, in the camp, they did not hesitate for a moment and were ready to join in the fast despite the danger involved. We had decided that on the day of the fast none of us would complain or show any outward sign of weakness. We would all work hard so as not to give the witch any reason to complain.

And so it was. On that day she watched us constantly. She inspected every girl's work, making sure each of us completed her quota. And we, the young girls, passed the test. We were physically weak, but our spirits were strong. The thought that we were joined by all the Jews in the world in our fast gave us more strength than the measly food ration apportioned to us by our enemies.

When the fast ended, as each of us tasted her piece of black bread, our satisfaction was full. But the next day our joy was marred when we learned, through a secret contact with the next section, that we had miscalculated the date and missed the Day of Atonement by one day. We had fasted on the day following Yom Kippur. How sad we were when we learned about our mistake of having eaten on Yom Kippur! But not a single girl regretted having fasted and suffered and having withstood the test. After all, our intention was pure and our devotion was total.

❋ ❋ ❋

The Yeshivah Boy's Story

❺§I had to endure a double slavery, one on each side of the fence. At the beginning of the war the Nazis captured me and took me to a labor camp. The purpose of the camp was not just to put Jews to work, but also to torture them and humiliate them and to invent imaginary tasks for them to do. Nevertheless, I escaped the torture camp and found myself on Russian soil.

The Russians decided I was a suspicious person and banished me to the wilderness of Siberia. In the Siberian exile there were many other "suspicious" Jews like myself. We were all made to cut down trees in the primeval forests, in a nearly perpetual snow. I won't dwell on how cold it was in those parts, or on the slave labor, or on the exile's way of life. The important thing is that Jews, wherever they are, can never forget that they are Jews, sons of Abraham, Isaac, and Jacob. If you banish them to the end of the earth, they will soon create Jewish life with all its rules and regulations.

Small wonder, then, that the Jewish exiles in the snowy steppes of Siberia remembered all the Sabbaths and all the Jewish holidays. The Russian oppressors, themselves exiles who were elevated in rank as supervisors of the Jewish slaves, could not understand the recurring demands of the Jews to be off from work because of T.S.—T.P. (Today is *Shabbos,* Today is Pesach.) "We don't have any holidays, except for May Day," the Russian supervisors would say, "and anyone who doesn't show up for work won't get his bread ration, and will be locked up." And they added: "Don't get too smart, Jews. We know all the tricks of your *Pops.*" The title *Pop* (priest in Russian) was attached to any Jew who came to them with any religious demands.

Nevertheless, when the High Holy Days approached, the rebellious mood among the Jewish slaves grew. Again and again the question was asked, "How can we avoid violating Rosh Hashanah and Yom Kippur?"

The observant Jews were the first ones to raise the question. They urged the rest of the slave-laborers not to go to work on the Days of Awe, and their enthusiasm infected the multitudes. The word about the rebellion finally reached the ears of the supervisors.

They started threatening that anyone who did not come to work on the Jew's holiday would be charged with sabotage, and the punishment for sabotage in time of war was well known. Still, many Jews did not show up for work on the first day of Rosh Hashanah. The taskmasters investigated and found a makeshift synagogue in one of the cabins, where some Jews had gathered for public worship. The chief overseer immediately ordered that all those who had gathered illegally for prayer be arrested. The order was carried out, but on the next day, the second day of Rosh Hashanah, not a single Jew showed up for work in the forest. The Jews, observant and non-observant alike, were determined to fight for their rights.

Everything turned out all right. The person in charge was a shrewd Russian peasant. When he realized how determined the Jews were, he gave in. When the Day of Atonement approached, before the Jews had a chance to ask to have the day off, he issued an order proclaiming that day, because of special circumstances, a day off for all the workers, Jews and non-Jews alike. The Jews were delighted. They rejoiced at the opportunity to celebrate Yom Kippur freely and openly among the great multitude of Siberian exiles.

◈§ Observance /
Selected Laws and Customs

– Rabbi Hersh Goldwurm

∞§ Selected Laws and Customs

The following digest of the laws and customs of the Ten Days of Repentance and Yom Kippur have been taken, in the main, from the most widely accepted authorities: *Shulchan Aruch Orach Chaim* [here abbreviated O.C.]; *Mishnah Berurah* [M.B.]; and R' Ephraim Zalman Margulies' classic work on the laws and customs of the period from Rosh Chodesh Elul through Succos — *Matteh Ephraim* [M.E.]. When a particular *halachah* is disputed by the *Poskim*, we have generally followed the rulings of *Mishnah Berurah*. There are of course instances where the custom in a community follows the view of another *Posek*; as a general rule each community should follow its traditions and the rulings of its authorities.

A word of warning: This digest is not meant to be either exhaustive or authoritative; it is meant merely to educate and should be used only as a guide. For matters of practical *halachah*, a competent halachic authority should be consulted.

THE TEN DAYS OF REPENTANCE

∞§ General Laws and Customs

1. The entire week preceding Yom Kippur should be devoted to repentance and the betterment of one's self. The seven days between Rosh Hashanah and Yom Kippur correspond to the seven days of the week. Therefore, one should try to devote each of these seven days to repentance for what he did wrong on all days corresponding to that day - i.e., on Sunday he should repent for what he did wrong on all the Sundays of the year, etc. (*M.B.* 603:2 citing *Yaaros Devash*).

2. It is the universal custom of all Jews to increase their giving of charity and performance of good deeds, and to busy themselves in the performance of *mitzvos*, in the period from Rosh Hashanah to Yom Kippur, beyond that which they do the rest of the year. During this period, it is the common practice for everyone to rise while it is yet dark to pray in the synagogues with supplications and *selichos* [penitential prayers] (*Rambam, Hilchos Teshuvah* 3:4).

3. During these days one should read works which inspire one to repentance and a proper life style — *sifrei mussar* — such as Rabbeinu Yonah's *Epistle of Repentance (Iggeres HaTeshuvah)* —and others (*Rosh* cited by *Ba'er Heitev* 603:1, *M.B.* 603:2). Although *Arizal* and *Vilna Gaon* caution that one should learn *mussar* every day of the year, during this period of repentance one should read specifically *mussar* works of the genre of R' Yonah's Epistle which deal specifically with the topic of *teshuvah* (*M.B.* loc. cit. with *Shaar HaTziyun*).

4. Nevertheless one should not spend the major portion of his learning time studying works of *mussar* since this would be counterproductive; the mind ceases to respond appropriately if it is bombarded with an overabundance of inspirational material. Rather one should read a work of *mussar* for a short while every day until he feels that he has been inspired to better himself and come closer to G-d, and devote the additional time to studying *masseches Yoma* with its commentaries, so that he understand the recital of the *Avodah*, the offering service, which is the focal point of the *Mussaf* prayer on Yom Kippur (*M.E.* 603:4).

5. One should also study the prayers, *piyutim*, and *selichos* which are recited during these days, so as to understand their content. Surely if one is a *chazzan*, he is obligated to do so (ibid.).

6. The repentance for a sin one is not sure he committed should be more intense than for one he surely committed, because it is natural to feel greater remorse for a definite sin than a doubtful one. We see that the Torah requires one to bring a ram worth at least two shekels as a guilt-offering for a doubtful sin (*asham talui*; see *Lev.* 5:17-18), whereas for a definite sin one brings a sin-offering [*chatas*] requiring no minimum worth (*Rama* 603:1).

7. During the days of repentance one should adopt the custom proposed by the *Zohar*, to examine one's deeds, regret one's sins and repent them before lying down to sleep (*M.B. 603:2*).

8. Repentance is called for not only well-known, major, sins. There are little-known aspects to all *mitzvos* which people transgress constantly. For example, in interpersonal affairs we find people who harass others legally, by summoning someone to court knowing full-well that the suit has no merit; their intent is merely to annoy the other person and cause him loss. Such people are guilty of *gezeilah*, unlawful appropriation of property. Similarly, in one's relations with God: One is obligated, for example, to have the proper concentration — *kavanah* — when praying or reciting the blessings, yet very few people do so. A person should set aside time to study the details of the *mitzvos* so that he may avoid these failures (*Eliyah Rabbah* 603:3).

9. One should examine the *mitzvos* he does to ascertain whether he performs them routinely or in an ideal manner. Does he recite the prayers with the proper concentration? Without interjecting idle talk? Does he conduct himself

with the proper decorum while wearing *tefillin*, never becoming oblivious to the *tefillin* [*hesech hadaas*]? Does he observe the Sabbath with all its legal stringencies and safeguard its sacred character? Does he have a fixed schedule for Torah study? Are his contributions to charity given with pure intentions, without ulterior motives? These and numerous similar matters should be evaluated (*Machazik Berachah* and *Kaf Hachaim O.C.* 603).

10. A person should write down his resolutions and review them at the beginning of the following year to see whether he has kept them. One should be careful, however, not to commit himself to them with a vow, lest he add to his sins the transgressions of vows (ibid.)

11. A person should conduct himself with greater circumspection during these days, and observe even non-requisite stringencies of law that he does not follow throughout the year. [This will have the effect of reminding him of the significance of this period (*Levush*).] Hence, one should refrain from eating bread baked by a gentile baker — *pas palter* — during these days, even if he does not observe this stringency the year round (*O.C.* 603).

12. It is customary not to recite the blessing over the new moon until after Yom Kippur (*Rama* 602:1). The recitation of this blessing is likened to 'greeting the countenance of God,' and it should therefore be said in a festive and joyous frame of mind (*Maseches Soferim* ch. 20, *O.C.* 426:2); during these days, because of the impending judgment, it is difficult to put oneself into the proper mood (*Darchei Moshe, O.C.* 426). *Levush* cites the view of an anonymous *gadol* that to the contrary, one should recite the *berachah* as soon as possible so as to add yet another merit to one's credit before the 'Day of Judgment' (see also *Beur HaGra* 603:9). However, *Levush* himself reasons that honoring this blessing by refraining from reciting it before the most appropriate time is in itself a meritorious act. Nevertheless, if one suspects that he will be unable to recite the blessing after Yom Kippur, he should recite it as soon as possible (*M.E.* 602:46).

13. If possible, one should purchase his *esrog* and the rest of the 'Four Species' during these days, so as to have yet another merit in his favor (*M.E.* 603:5).

THE PRAYERS

14. On the days between Rosh Hashanah and Yom Kippur one should pray more and add to his supplications (*O.C.* 602:1). The *Gemara (Rosh Hashanah* 18a) states that prayer during these days is more efficacious than during the rest of the year; the verse, *Seek HASHEM while He is available, call Him while He is near (Isaiah* 55:6), is understood by the Gemara to refer to the ten days from Rosh Hashanah to Yom Kippur (*Beur HaGra O.C.* 603:2). Even a *talmid chacham* may diminish the time he usually devotes to learning in order to allot more time for prayer (*Shaarei Teshuvah* 581:1 citing *Birkei Yosef*).

15. It is customary in many communities to recite the entire book of *Tehillim* during this week, saying either an entire *yom* every day except Shabbos (to finish the entire *Tehillim* on Yom Kippur), or thirty psalms each day (*M.E.* 602:20).

ـ§ Selichos

16. As on the days preceding Rosh Hashanah, *selichos* are said every morning before the regular prayers in the period between Rosh Hashanah and Yom Kippur (see above §2). Ideally the *selichos* should be said before daybreak (in the last quarter of the night; see *O.C.* 581:1), or commencing with dawn (*M.E.* 581:11), but this practice has — for the most part — fallen into disuse in our generation.

17. The recitation of the שְׁלֹשׁ עֶשְׂרֵה מִדּוֹת הָרַחֲמִים, 'Thirteen Attributes of Mercy', is an essential element of the *selichos*. In order to recite the

Thirteen Attributes of Mercy in a manner of supplication, a *minyan* should be present (*O.C.* 565:5). One may, however, say those portions of the *selichos* which merely mention the Thirteen Attributes of Mercy (*M.B.* 565:13), or even the prayers which introduce the recitation of the Thirteen Attributes [אֵל מֶלֶךְ יוֹשֵׁב] and אֵל אֶרֶךְ אַפַּיִם] (*M.E.* 581:21). If an individual wishes to recite the Thirteen Attributes of Mercy in the absence of a *minyan* he may do so by reading them with the traditional cantillation (*trop*) employed for the public reading of the Torah (*O.C.* 565:5 with *M.B.*).

18. At the end of the *selichos* there are a number of passages in Aramaic. These should also not be said if there is no *minyan* (*M.E.* 581:26). The *Gemara (Shabbos* 12b) states that an individual should not pray in Aramaic because the ministering angels (who bring the prayers before the heavenly throne) do not concern themselves with Aramaic prayers. Only in communal prayer (i.e., when a *minyan* is present), where the assistance of the ministering angels is not vital, can Aramaic be used as a language of prayer (see *O.C.* 101:4).

19. Ideally one should stand while saying *selichos*. If this is difficult, one should at least stand for the recitation of the prayers אֵל מֶלֶךְ יוֹשֵׁב and אֵל אֶרֶךְ אַפַּיִם which introduce the recitation of the Thirteen Attributes (and surely for the recitation of the Thirteen Attributes themselves). One should also stand for the וִדּוּי, *confession*, which begins with אָשַׁמְנוּ, *we have become guilty* (*M.E.* 581:18; see below, §87-88).

20. *Tachanun* is said toward the conclusion of the *selichos*. Ideally one should sit when saying *tachanun* (O.C. 131:2). Since one is not usually wearing *tefillin* when saying *selichos*, he should lean his head on his left arm when saying *tachanun* (Rama in O.C. 131:1).

21. If there is to be a *bris* and the *sandak*, *mohel*, or father of the boy is present during the *selichos* service, even though *tachanun* will not be said after the *Shemoneh Esrei*, it is nevertheless said in the *selichos* if it is yet before dawn. Since this time-period is not valid for the performance of a *bris*, the *tachanun* prayer cannot be omitted because of it. If, however, it is already after sunrise when *tachanun* is about to be said, it should be omitted.

A *bris* should not be performed in the period between dawn and sunrise but it is valid *post facto* if performed then (see *Yoreh Deah* 262:1). Hence, it is questionable whether *tachanun* should be omitted in the period between dawn and sunrise (*Pischei Teshuvah* 581:1).

⋐§ Shelosh Esrei Middos

22. The *selichos* service and indeed the entire day preceding the eve of Yom Kippur is called *Shelosh Esrei Middos*. The name derives from the *pizmon* (liturgical poem which is recited responsively) in the *selichos* of the day, which begins with a recitation of the Thirteen Attributes of Mercy. The *selichos* service on this day should be started a little bit earlier than usual. Great importance is attached to this *pizmon*; it should be said tearfully and with great concentration (*M.E.* 603:7; see *Sefer Chassidim* §250).

23. In some communities it is customary to say the *selichos* of *Shelosh Esrei Middos* on the Monday or Thursday closest to Yom Kippur, so that it coincide with reading of the Torah. However, in most communities they are always said on

the day before the eve of Yom Kippur (*Eleph HaMagen* 603:10).

⋐§ Changes in the Regular Prayers

24. In most congregations, psalm 130, שִׁיר הַמַּעֲלוֹת מִמַּעֲמַקִּים, is inserted between יִשְׁתַּבַּח and בָּרְכוּ in the days between Rosh Hashanah and Yom Kippur (see *Eliyah Rabbah* 602:3). It is customary to recite the psalm verse by verse responsively, intoning with the traditional *Yamim Noraim* melody. If one is still saying *Pesukei D'Zimrah* [the part of the daily service which precedes יִשְׁתַּבַּח] when the congregation recites the psalm, he may recite it together with the congregation. He may then repeat the psalm when he finishes יִשְׁתַּבַּח (*Eleph LaMatteh* 584:2).

25. Two changes are made in the *Kaddish*: Instead of לְעֵילָא מִן כָּל בִּרְכָתָא, one says לְעֵלָּא וּלְעֵלָּא מִכָּל בִּרְכָתָא (*M.E.* 582:1). At the conclusion of *Kaddish*, instead of עוֹשֶׂה שָׁלוֹם בִּמְרוֹמָיו, one should say עוֹשֶׂה הַשָּׁלוֹם בִּמְרוֹמָיו. [However, if these changes were not made, the *Kaddish* need not be repeated.]

⋐§ Additions to the Shemoneh Esrei

26. Several passages are inserted into each *Amidah* [i.e., *Shemoneh Esrei*] from the first night of Rosh Hashanah until the end of Yom Kippur. In the first blessing, the supplication זָכְרֵנוּ לְחַיִּים, *Remember us for life*, is added; in the second, מִי כָמוֹךָ, *Who is like You*; in the second to last, וּכְתוֹב לְחַיִּים, *And inscribe for life* [this is changed in the Ne'ilah prayer to וַחֲתוֹם, *And seal*]; and in the last blessing, בְּסֵפֶר חַיִּים, *In the book of life*. If one forgot to say any of these additions he does not repeat the *Shemoneh Esrei*. However, if he became aware of the omission prior to saying the word 'HASHEM' at the conclusion of the respective blessing, he should return to the place where the passage should have been inserted and continue from there (O.C. 582:5 with *M.B.*).

27. The usual ending of the third blessing of the *Amidah* — הָאֵל הַקָּדוֹשׁ, *the holy God* — is changed to הַמֶּלֶךְ הַקָּדוֹשׁ, *the holy King*. This emendation is made to accentuate God's role as Ruler and Judge of the world. If one recited the usual ending, he may correct himself immediately by saying הַמֶּלֶךְ הַקָּדוֹשׁ. ['Immediately' in this regard is defined as the span of time it takes to say the three words שָׁלוֹם עָלֶיךָ רַבִּי (see M.B. 582:7, 206:12, and 487:4 with *Shaar HaTziyun*.] If, however, he did not correct himself in time, he must begin the *Amidah* anew (O.C. 582:1).

28. If one had already begun the next blessing before realizing his mistake (even if the above time span had not elapsed), he must begin the *Amidah* anew (*Shaarei Teshuvah* to O.C. 582:2, *Daas Torah* there, M.E. 582:9, *Beur Halachah* to 487:1 s.v. תוך).

29. If one had merely said the word הָאֵל but had not yet ended the blessing with the word הַקָּדוֹשׁ, then he may correct himself even if he had waited longer than the allotted time (*Daas Torah* and *Eishel Avraham* to O.C. 582).

30. If one is in doubt whether he said the correct version, he must assume that he said the version he customarily recites every day. Consequently, he must begin the *Amidah* anew (O.C. 582:1, M.B. §3).

31. At the conclusion of the tenth benediction the phrase הַמֶּלֶךְ הַמִּשְׁפָּט, *the King of of judgment*, is substituted for מֶלֶךְ אוֹהֵב צְדָקָה וּמִשְׁפָּט, *the King who loves righteousness and judgment*. If one forgot to make this change, he does not repeat the prayer. However, if he realized his error immediately (see above §27), he should rectify his error (O.C. 118:1 with M.B. §3).

32. Many *siddurim* change the ending of the last blessing in the *Amidah* from הַמְּבָרֵךְ אֶת עַמּוֹ יִשְׂרָאֵל

בְּשָׁלוֹם, *Who blesses His people Israel with peace*, to עוֹשֶׂה הַשָּׁלוֹם, *Who makes the peace* (see *Levush* 582:5). R' Seligman Baer in his *Siddur Avodas Yisrael* demonstrates that this version is rooted in ancient traditions.

Many later authorities, however, object to the change and maintain that the ending of this blessing should not be altered (see *Sh'lah* and R' Yaakov Emden in their *siddurim*, *Tosefos Maaseh Rav* citing R' Chaim Volozhiner, *Minhagei Chasam Sofer*, *Matteh Ephraim* 582:22). *Nusach Sefard* congregations follow this latter opinion. However, at the conclusion of *Shemoneh Esrei* and *Kaddish*, instead of עוֹשֶׂה שָׁלוֹם בִּמְרוֹמָיו, one should recite עוֹשֶׂה הַשָּׁלוֹם בִּמְרוֹמָיו. [See also *Kaf HaChaim* 582:22 citing *Pri Etz Chaim*.]

⋙§ Avinu Malkeinu

33. The prayer אָבִינוּ מַלְכֵּנוּ is said twice daily — after the *Shemoneh Esrei* of both the *shacharis* and *minchah* — except on the Sabbath and on Friday afternoon [and Erev Yom Kippur] (O.C. 602:1 with M.B.). [The prayer is said after the *chazzan's* recitation of the *Shemoneh Esrei* — before *tachanun* in *Nusach Ashkenaz*, and after *tachanun* in *Nusach Sefard*.] It is said even when *tachanun* is not said, e.g., when there is a *bris* (O.C. 602:1). [In such a case it is said immediately after the *chazzan's* recitation of the *Shemoneh Esrei* before *Kaddish*.]

⋙§ Bircas HaMazon

34. Many insert in *Bircas HaMazon* the short prayer הָרַחֲמָן הוּא יְחַדֵּשׁ עָלֵינוּ אֶת הַשָּׁנָה הַזֹּאת לְטוֹבָה וְלִבְרָכָה, *The Compassionate One! May He inaugurate this year upon us for goodness and for blessing*, in the period between Rosh Hashanah and Yom Kippur, just as is done on Rosh Hashanah (M.E. 602:1). Some substitute עוֹשֶׂה הַשָּׁלוֹם for עוֹשֶׂה שָׁלוֹם at the conclusion of the next-to-last paragraph of *Bircas HaMazon* (*Minhagei Chasam Sofer*).

35. The Sabbath which occurs in the Ten Days of Repentance is called *Shabbas Shuvah* because the *haftarah* which is read on it begins with the word *shuvah* (שׁוּבָה). Some called it *Shabbas Teshuvah, the Sabbath of Repentance,* because it falls within the Ten Days of Repentance.

36. The changes made in the prayers during the Ten Days of Repentance are also made on *Shabbas Shuvah*. As part of every Friday night service, the *chazzan* recites a summarized repetition of the *Amidah*. When reciting it on *Shabbas Shuvah*, the phrase הָאֵל הַקָּדוֹשׁ שֶׁאֵין כָּמוֹהוּ, *the Holy God Who is unequalled*, is changed to הַמֶּלֶךְ הַקָּדוֹשׁ שֶׁאֵין כָּמוֹהוּ, *the Holy King Who is unequalled* (O.C. 582:3). If the *chazzan* forgot to make this change and has not yet said the word HASHEM at the conclusion of the blessing (בָּרוּךְ אַתָּה ה׳ מְקַדֵּשׁ הַשַּׁבָּת), he must return to that part of the blessing, correct his error and continue from there (M.B. 583:10). However, if he has already concluded the blessing he should not repeat it (*Derech HaChaim, Kitzur Shulchan Aruch* 129:4; see *M.B.* 582:10; cf. *M.E.* 582:5).

37. Various customs are recorded regarding the *haftarah* of this Sabbath. Most customs incorporate the last nine verses in *Hoshea* (14:2-10), beginning with the words שׁוּבָה יִשְׂרָאֵל, *Repent O Israel*, in the *haftarah* (O.C. 428:8). However, since the last verse concludes on a negative note — *and sinners shall stumble in them* — it is customary to add some other verses. In some communities the passage in *Joel* (2:11-27 or 2:15-27), which describes a penitent fast and its acceptance by God, is added, while others also add the last three verses in *Michah* (7:18-20) which speak about God's acceptance of our repentance (*M.E.* 602:40). The prevalent custom, as recorded by *Eliyah Rabbah* (603:2) and printed in most *Chumashim*, is to read the verses in *Hoshea,*

followed by those in *Michah*, and to conclude with the verses from *Joel*. However some argue that the verses from *Joel* should be said before those in *Michah*, because the book of *Joel* precedes the book of *Michah* (see *Ketzeh HaMatteh* 602:31).

38. Though a boy who is not yet *bar mitzvah* may be called to read the *haftarah* most of the year, he should not be called to read this *haftarah* (*M.B.* 602:11). Rather, a distinguished person should be called upon to read it (*M.E.* 602:40).

39. There is a widely practiced custom that the rabbi of the congregation preach a sermon (*derashah*) on this Sabbath. The sermon should be devoted to the theme of *teshuvah* (repentance) and should seek to inspire the people to better themselves (*M.E.* 602:41).

40. *Pirkei Avos* is not said (from this Sabbath forward), because the purpose of the recitation of *Avos* — Torah study and inspiration to self-betterment — is accomplished with the sermon (*Levush* 603:1). Neither are בָּרְכִי נַפְשִׁי (psalm 104) and the accompanying psalms (120-134) said (as they are during the winter). These psalms attest to God's creation of the world; thus the most appropriate Sabbath on which to begin this recitation is the Sabbath on which *Bereishis* is read, the reading which contains the Torah's account of Creation (*Levush* 603:1 and 669; see *M.E.* 602:44).

41. The verses of צִדְקָתְךָ צֶדֶק are said after *Minchah* even if the eve of Yom Kippur occurs on Sunday (*M.E.* 603:44).

42. The passages וִיהִי נוֹעַם and וְאַתָּה קָדוֹשׁ are not said after *Maariv* unless Yom Kippur will be on the following Sabbath (*M.E.* 603:45). However, וְיִתֶּן לְךָ is said in any case.

43. On this Saturday night one should make sure to observe the *melavah malkah* meal — the meal which celebrates the 'departure of the Sabbath queen' — by eating bread or *challah* even if he usually relies on the more lenient views that one may discharge this obligation by eating fruit or cake (*M.E.* 602:47; see above §11).

EREV YOM KIPPUR

44. Erev Yom Kippur [the day before Yom Kippur] is considered a semi-holiday and to accentuate its festive aspect some prayers are abbreviated or deleted, as explained below. Yet another aspect of the day is the *mitzvah* to eat on this day. Because of this, the meals take on a festive mood. There are also a number of customs and laws which are designed to prepare one for the impending fast.

⊷§ כַּפָּרוֹת / Atonement

45. The ancient ritual of *kaparos* literally, atonements, is cited by the early *Geonim* (see *Rosh, Yoma* 8:23; *Tur Orach Chaim* 605). *Rashi* (*Shabbas* 81b) describes a vastly different form of this custom, but that form is no longer practiced.

46. The ritual calls for taking a chicken and moving it in a circular motion around the penitent's head. This procedure is accompanied by the recitation of verses expressing the theme of repentance and a formula communicating the underlying concept of the rite. The verse and prayers should be said with intense concentration. After concluding these prayers, one puts his hand on the chicken's head.

47. The chicken is later slaughtered and either the chicken or its cash value is given to the poor, for charity is an indispensable part of repentance — and the combination of the two can achieve atonement. In giving the *kaparos* chicken to the poor, one must be extremely careful not to embarrass the recipient or to cause him to feel that the donor is ridding himself of his sins and placing them on this poor man's head (*Matteh Ephraim* 605:6,10). The entrails should be left for birds and animals, to exhibit the same kind of compassion that we pray God will show us (*Rama O.C.* 605:1 with *M.B.*).

48. The ritual is designed to imbue people with the feeling that their lives are at stake as Yom Kippur approaches, and that they must repent and seek atonement. The ceremony symbolizes that our sins cry out for atonement, that a sinner deserves to give up his soul for not having used it to do God's will, but that our good deeds and repentance can save us from the punishment we deserve.

While moving the chicken around one's head, one should contemplate that he may have a potential death sentence hanging over his head and that the chicken should take his place when being slaughtered. Of course, no one should be deluded into thinking that the chicken can actually die in his stead. Rather, the rite should awaken in oneself the realization that a fate similar to the chicken's may await him, and thereby should stimulate him to repentance. The early commentators (see *Ramban* to *Lev.* 1:9) explain the offerings in the Holy Temple in this manner (*Matteh Ephraim* 605:5).

49. Because of the strong resemblance between the *kaparos* rite and the Temple-offering service, it is extremely important that one bear in mind that the *kaparos* are not an offering. For this reason, one may not use for *kaparos* a species fit to be offered in the Temple [e.g., doves], even if chickens are not available. Preferably, one should use chickens, because the term used in the Talmud for it — גֶּבֶר, *gever,* — also means *man* in

Hebrew. If chickens are not available, other kosher species, such as ducks, may be used (*Matteh Ephraim* 605:4).

50. Ideally the ritual should be performed on the night before Yom Kippur, with the slaughter taking place after dawn. Rising before dawn, the *selichos* are said first, followed by the *kaparos* ritual (*Matteh Ephraim* 605:1, see O.C. there). Nowadays most people perform the ritual any time during the Ten Days of Repentance (*M.B.* 605:2).

51. It is preferable to take white fowl for the *kaparos* because the color white symbolizes atonement (see *Isaiah* 1:18). Nevertheless, it is forbidden to make strenuous efforts to find birds of such color, lest it appear that one is following the idolaters' practice of using only white birds in their ceremonies (see *Avodah Zarah* 13b-14a). A rooster is used for a male and a hen for a female (*Rama O.C.* 605:1 with *M.B.*).

52. Some use a separate chicken for each person. According to this practice, a pregnant woman uses two hens and one rooster — one hen for herself and the other in case she is carrying a female child, and the rooster in case she is carrying a male. Others perform the ritual for all the males simultaneously using one rooster, and for all the females simultaneously with one hen. A pregnant woman performing the rite alone uses, according to this view, one hen for herself and for her child in case it is female, and one rooster in case she is carrying a male (*Rama O.C.* 605:1 with *M.B.*).

53. Many people use money for this ritual instead of a rooster. The money is then given to the poor (see *M.B.* 605:3).

⋙ Shacharis

54. The *selichos* of Erev Yom Kippur are said, according to the East

European custom, in abbreviated form (*Rama O.C.* 604:2). However, the custom of some communities [most notably among German Jews] is to recite a very lengthy *selichos* (ibid.).

55. In *Pesukei D'Zimrah*, psalm 100, מִזְמוֹר לְתוֹדָה (usually said immediately after בָּרוּךְ שֶׁאָמַר), is omitted (O.C. 604:2). The subject of this psalm is the thanksgiving offering; since in the Temple no thanksgiving offering could be offered on this day, the psalm which commemorates that offering is not said. The reason a thanksgiving offering could not be brought on Erev Yom Kippur is because this offering is to be eaten for a day and a night. Since it can not be eaten on the evening of Yom Kippur, bringing it on Erev Yom Kippur would shorten the time span within which it may be eaten. Whenever this type span is so shortened, the offering may not be brought.

56. Psalm 130 — שִׁיר הַמַּעֲלוֹת מִמַּעֲמַקִים — is recited after יִשְׁתַּבַּח (before *Kaddish*) throughout the Ten Days of Repentance (*M.E.* 584:9), as well as on Erev Yom Kippur and Yom Kippur (see above §24).

57. *Tachanun* is omitted all day (after *selichos*, *Shacharis*, and *Minchah*). However, *tachanun* is recited at *minchah* of the day before Erev Yom Kippur (O.C. 604:2; *M.B.* 131:33).

58. The prayer אָבִינוּ מַלְכֵּנוּ, *Avinu Malkeinu*, too, is omitted after both *Shacharis* and *Minchah*). However, when Yom Kippur falls on the Sabbath, and *Avinu Malkeinu* will be omitted from all Yom Kippur prayers (except *Ne'ilah*), then *Avinu Malkeinu* is said after *Shacharis* of Erev Yom Kippur — but not after *Minchah* (O.C. 604:2, M.B. §5).

59. Also omitted on Erev Yom Kippur is לַמְנַצֵּחַ [psalm 20, said between אַשְׁרֵי and וּבָא לְצִיּוֹן] (O.C. 604:2; 131:1, M.B. there §35).

⊷§ Reconciliation

60. The observance of Yom Kippur (with repentance and confession) is sufficient to cause sins to be forgiven, but only sins against God that do not involve another person. Sins against one's fellow man, however, cannot be forgiven until one mollifies the injured person and gains his forgiveness; only then can his repentance on Yom Kippur be accepted (*O.C.* 6061). [Sins against one's fellow man are two-fold, being sins against God as well. Thus, both human and divine forgiveness are required.] It is customary to ask for this forgiveness on the eve of Yom Kippur (*Rama* in *O.C.* 606:2)

61. Reconciliation involves making monetary restitution where such is due, and arranging for adjudication where there is a question. If the other person does not know that he has been aggrieved, restitution must nevertheless be made to him, and in case of doubt a halachic authority should be consulted. A person should not rely on his own understanding and interpretation in monetary matters because the temptation to favor oneself unfairly and unjustly is very great (*M.B.* 606:1).

62. Even if one has caused another no monetary loss but has caused him pain by abusing him verbally, he must appease him and win his forgiveness (*O.C.* 606:1).

63. When seeking forgiveness one should specify the wrong for which one is seeking forgiveness. If, however, this would cause the wronged person embarrassment or pain, the recountal of the event should be omitted (*M.E.* 606:2, *M.B.* 606:3).

64. Ideally, one should attempt to meet and mollify personally the person he has aggrieved. However, if this is difficult, or if one feels that the reconciliation attempt has more chance to succeed through a third party, an intermediary may be used (*M.B.* 606:2).

65. If the aggrieved person refuses to accept the reconciliation overtures, then the person seeking forgiveness must make another three reconciliation attempts, taking with him each time a committee of three people, using a different approach each time. If all of this is of no avail, he has no further obligation. However, he should get together a quorum of ten people and state in their presence that he has sought forgiveness and been rebuffed (*O.C.* 606:1 with *M.B.* §3 and *Beur Halachah*). The *Midrash* (*Tanchuma Vayera* §30 in the Buber ed., cited by *Beur HaGra O.C.* 606:3) concludes: 'The Holy One, Blessed is He, will see that he has humiliated himself and will have compassion upon him.'

66. The above applies only to ordinary relationships. If the aggrieved person is the *Rebbi*, Torah mentor, of the one seeking forgiveness, even if he is not his רַבּוֹ מֻבְהָק, *primary mentor*, he must seek forgiveness again and again until a reconciliation is reached (*O.C.* 606:1 with *Magen Avraham* §3).

67. The aggrieved person should not act cruelly, and should not withhold his forgiveness. Even if he is the wrongdoer's mentor, he should not withhold his forgiveness, unless he sees that it is necessary to teach the wrongdoer a lesson. In such a case, he should nevertheless forgive him in his heart and expunge any hatred he may harbor. One who overlooks personal slights will have his sins forgiven too (*Yoma* 87b). Conversely, a person who refuses to forgive others will have his own sins treated in the same manner (*O.C.* 606:1 with *M.B.*).

68. If one has been libeled, he is not obligated to forgive, because not everyone who has heard the libel will know that its author has admitted to its falseness. However, it is an act of humility to forgive even in such a case (ibid.).

69. If the person who was wronged has died in the interim, the person seeking forgiveness should go to the deceased's grave with a group of ten people and, standing barefoot, declare in their presence: 'I have sinned toward the God of Israel and toward so-and-so whom I have wronged in such and such manner.' If the grave site is far away, he may send someone else to make the declaration in his stead (O.C. 606:2 with M.B.).

70. Libeling a dead person is not proscribed under Scriptural law. Nevertheless, the rabbis of the post-Talmudic era placed a ban (*cherem*) on such actions (O.C. 606:3). If one spoke in an insulting manner about a dead person, he must repent for having transgressed the ban and also seek the dead man's forgiveness [presumably by making a declaration in front of ten people]; however, it is not necessary to visit the dead man's grave (M.B. §14, 16; c.f. M.E. §6).

⊷§ Visiting the Cemetery

71. In some communities it is customary to visit the cemetery on Erev Yom Kippur to pray there and to distribute substantial amounts for charity (O.C. 605:2).

⊷§ The Seudos

72. There is a *mitzvah* to eat substantial meals on Erev Yom Kippur; it is forbidden to fast on this day (O.C. 604:1). One may reduce the amount of time he devotes to learning in order to fulfill this *mitzvah* properly. This *mitzvah* is a Biblical one. The Sages (*Yoma* 81b) deduce from a verse that, 'One who eats and drinks on the ninth [of Tishrei] is regarded by the Torah as though he had fasted on the ninth and the tenth.' One who fulfills this *mitzvah* is not regarded as if he had performed just a mere *mitzvah*, but as if he had performed a difficult *mitzvah* like fasting (M.B. 604:1).

73. [It is customary to eat two festive meals on this day, one in the morning or early afternoon, and the other after *minchah* just before the fast.] It is customary to dip the *challah* over which one recites the *hamotzi* blessing in honey (M.E. 605:18). One should honor the occasion by eating fish at the first meal. The *Tur* (O.C. 604) cites a *Midrash* which relates how a Jewish tailor went to great trouble and expense, and exposed himself to danger to purchase fish in honor of the festive meal of this day. It is customary to eat fowl, not meat, for this meal [because it is digested with greater ease] (M.E. 604:18; see M.B. 608:16). It is customary to dip the *challah* over which one recites the *hamotzi* blessing in honey (M.E. 605:18).

74. Men should refrain from eating the following foods: garlic, eggs, and dishes whose primary ingredient is hot milk. [These foods are conducive to the production of semen and may thus lead to a spontaneous emission.] One may, however, consume foods which have only a small amount of milk in them. Thus, one may drink coffee or tea with milk. The *Poskim* assert that these strictures be followed for the entire day, but *Rama* testifies that in his day it was customary to have dairy for the first festive meal; the *Poskim* are at a loss to explain the custom satisfactorily. However, nowadays it is customary to have meat even for the first meal (M.B. 608:16-18).

75. One should be careful neither to overeat, nor to eat foods which take long to digest, nor to become intoxicated, so as not to approach Yom Kippur in a mood of arrogance and self-indulgence (O.C. 608:4 with M.B. §18).

76. It is especially meritorious to invite needy and worthy persons to join in these meals. The Sages (*Chagigah*

27a) state that nowadays a person's 'table' serves in lieu of the Temple Altar and atones for him; *Rashi* (there; see *Gem. Berachos* 55a) explains that this refers to the hospitality one extends at one's table. Surely on this day when our thoughts and actions are directed at gaining atonement for ourselves one should make sure to avail himself of this merit (*M.E.* 605:18).

◆§ Mikveh

77. There is a very ancient and universally accepted custom to purify oneself by immersing in a *mikveh* (ritual bath) on the eve of Yom Kippur. Some *Poskim* refer to this custom as an obligation (see *M.E.* 606:8). Some of the *Geonim* (specifically *R' Saadiah Gaon*; see *Tur*) held that a *berachah* be recited for this immersion, but this is not the accepted *halachah* (*O.C.* 606:4).

78. This custom is practiced by all males and by all married women; in some communities young girls also immerse themselves in the *mikveh* (*M.B.* 606:17; see *Ketzeh HaMatteh* §14).

79. One immersion is sufficient but some say that three immersions should be made (*O.C.* 606:4 with *M.B.*).

80. The immersion can be done anytime during the day but it is best to perform it before the *Minchah* prayer (*O.C.* 606:4 with *M.B.* §18).

81. If one finds it difficult to immerse in a *mikveh*, he may instead pour nine *kabin* (appr. 3.5-6.8 gallons) of water over himself, or have someone pour them over him (*M.B.* 606:22; see *M.B.* 88:4 for details about this procedure).

◆§ Minchah

82. One should don his festive Sabbath clothing before going to the synagogue for the *Minchah* prayer (*M.E.* 607:1).

83. The *Minchah* service of Erev Yom Kippur should precede the final meal of the day. In scheduling *Minchah*, one should allow ample time for the festive meal following *Minchah*. He should bear in mind that due to the gravity of the day, *Minchah* will be recited slowly and with much concentration, and that *viduy* (the confession) will be recited (see §86-89 below). Therefore, it is customary to schedule *Minchah* earlier than usual, even as early as the first half of the afternoon (*Minchah Gedolah*), although according to many *Poskim* it is preferable not do so the rest of the year (*M.E.* 607:1; see *O.C.* 233:1).

84. It is a time-honored custom to distribute charity lavishly before the *Minchah* service of Erev Yom Kippur. A practice which enjoys widespread acceptance is to set up plates or boxes in the synagogue for various charities so that everyone can contribute according to his means (see *M.E.* 607:3).

85. The *chazzan* chosen to lead *Minchah* should be worthy of being a *chazzan* on the Holy Day itself. The *chazzan* should don a *tallis* even if the congregation does not do so for a regular *Minchah* (*M.E.* 607:4).

86. One recites the *Shemoneh Esrei* until עוֹשֶׂה הַשָּׁלוֹם (or אֶת הַמְבָרֵךְ), says the verse ... יִהְיוּ (עַמּוֹ יִשְׂרָאֵל בַּשָּׁלוֹם), וְגֹאֲלִי, and recites the alphabetically ordered *viduy* (confession) found in the *siddur* or *machzor*. If one remembers committing a specific sin not included in the regular *viduy*, he should express it in his own words and confess tearfully with heartfelt contrition. However, one should not confess loudly to an individual sin, whether one sinned toward God or toward one's fellow (*O.C.* 607:1-2, with *M.B.*, *M.E.* 607:8). One may confess again to a sin committed a long time ago for which he has already confessed on a previous Yom Kippur (*O.C.* 607:4).

87. When confessing, one must stand, but his posture should express humility and contrition: slightly bent at the waist, head down, and shoulders hunched (M.B. 607:10). It is customary to strike the left side or middle of the chest lightly while mentioning each sin of the confession.

88. When confessing, one must stand upright, without leaning on anything. One is permitted to hold or be in contact with some support; one is considered to be leaning only if he would fall should his support be removed. If he confessed while leaning, there is question whether the confession should be repeated (O.C. 607:3, M.B. §10). *Birkei Yosef*, however, cites the view of earlier authorities that an elderly or sick person may lean on something. It may be assumed that these authorities hold that *viduy* recited while leaning is valid. (Surely one can rely on these authorities at least for the *viduy* recited during the *chazzan's* repetition — see R' Tzvi Pesach Frank, *Mikraei Kodesh*, p. 165.) [One may infer from the authorities that a confession said while sitting is invalid and should be repeated while standing, if at all possible.] One should remain standing until after וְעַל חֲטָאִים ... אַרְבַּע מִיתוֹת בֵּית דִּין (M.B. §10).

89. While an individual is reciting the *viduy*, he may respond to *Kaddish* and *Kedushah*. If he has not yet said the verse, וְיִהְיוּ לְרָצוֹן ... וְגָאֲלִי, he should do so before responding (M.E. 607:6). However, he may interrupt his *viduy* only for the responses that are permitted during the *Shema* (see Halachah section of the ArtScroll *Siddur*, §42).

◆§ Seudah HaMafsekes — The Meal Before the Fast

90. The last meal before the fast is eaten after *Minchah*. One should eat easily digestible foods, e.g., poultry rather than meat. One should avoid foods that would make him thirsty, as well as alcoholic beverages, for these would interfere with his concentration during prayers. The food for this meal should not be highly spiced. Fish are customarily not eaten at this meal (M.B. 608:16; M.E. 608:1). It is customary to dip the *challah* over which one recites the *hamotzi* blessing in honey (M.E. 608:1).

91. After the meal, psalm 126 [שִׁיר הַמַּעֲלוֹת בְּשׁוּב ה׳] is recited. *Bircas HaMazon* contains many intense prayer passages imploring for the reconstruction of Jerusalem and the Holy Temple, the Messiah, good life, prosperity, and prayers for other crucial things. One should take advantage of this opportunity to focus his concentration to petition the King of Justice for these things before the awesome Day of Judgment (M.E. 608:2).

92. At the end of the meal, before beginning *Bircas HaMazon*, it is preferable to make a mental or oral declaration that one does not yet accept the fast, so that he may eat or drink afterward, if he so chooses. Without such a declaration, some authorities hold that there is an assumption that one accepts the fast upon completion of the meal. However, if one failed to make this declaration, he may still eat, provided he has not accepted the fast, either orally or mentally (O.C. 608:3, 553:1, M.B. §12).

93. Once one assumes the fast upon himself, he is prohibited from doing anything forbidden on Yom Kippur, i.e., eating, drinking, washing, working, etc. Wearing shoes is an exception to this rule; one is automatically presumed not to have assumed this prohibition until it is required (M.B. 608:15, 553:2; M.E. 608:6).

◆§ Preparations for the Festival

94. It is customary for the father and the mother to bless their children before going to the synagogue. They should also pray that they be inscribed in the 'Book of Good Life' and that their hearts be receptive to the fear and love of God (see "Observance/Prayers and Ritual" for the text of these prayers). Many also visit their prominent relatives and acquaintances to solicit a blessing from them and to ask that they remember them in their prayers (M.E. 619:2).

95. Although no meals will be eaten on Yom Kippur, nevertheless the tables should be covered with festive tablecloths in honor of the day just as they are on the Sabbath (O.C. 610:4). The tables in the synagogue should be covered as well (M.E. 609:7).

96. Candles are lit just as before the Sabbath and the blessings ... לְהַדְלִיק נֵר שֶׁל יוֹם הַכִּפּוּרִים, ... to kindle the light of Yom Kippur, and ... שֶׁהֶחֱיָנוּ, Who has kept us alive ... are recited over them. [The procedure should be the same as before the Sabbath — the blessings are recited after the candles have been lit.] If Yom Kippur occurs on the Sabbath, the concluding phrase of the first blessing is changed to ... לְהַדְלִיק נֵר שֶׁל שַׁבָּת וְשֶׁל יוֹם הַכִּפּוּרִים, ... to kindle the light of the Sabbath and of Yom Kippur. A lit candle should also be put in the bedroom where a married couple sleeps (O.C. 610:1-2 with M.B.).

ⱸ Special Yom Kippur Candles

97. In addition to the Festival lights kindled on Yom Kippur Eve, two special candles are lit on Yom Kippur Eve, both of which should be large enough to remain lit throughout the entire day. (a) One נֵר הַבָּרִיא, light of the healthy [in Yiddish דָאס גֶעזוּנְטֶע לִיכְט], is lit for each married man. Magen Avraham (610:3) explains that the reasons for this candle apply only to men. Nevertheless, a widow may light one for herself if she wishes. (2) One נֵר נְשָׁמָה, light of the soul (sometimes referred to as a yizkor or memorial lamp), is lit by each man or woman with a deceased parent. Whether one or both

parents are deceased, only one candle need be lit (Matteh Ephraim 603:8).

It is preferable that the נֵר הַבָּרִיא, light of the healthy, be larger than the נֵר נְשָׁמָה, light of the soul (ibid.).

98. Customs vary regarding the place where these lights are kindled. Some take the light of the healthy to the synagogue and leave the light of the soul at home so as to have a light which burned throughout Yom Kippur available for havdalah (see §174). Matteh Ephraim (603:8) objects to this custom and asserts that both lights should be taken to the synagogue. Chayei Adam and others, however, agree with the idea that one light be kept at home. They assert that it should be the light of the healthy. A Yiddish saying has been formulated based on this custom: גֶעזוּנד זָאל מֶען זַיין אִין דֶער הֵיים, One should be healthy at home (Eleph HaMagen 603:18). [In any case, no blessing is recited over either of these special Yom Kippur lights.]

ⱸ Wearing White

99. It is a common practice to wear a white garment on Yom Kippur to honor the holiday with a garment whose color is reminiscent of the angels. Also, since burial shrouds are white, such garments remind one of the vulnerability of human life; thus humbled, one will be moved to repentance (O.C. 610:4).

100. The Ashkenazic practice is for every married male to wear a white, tunic-like garment called a kittel. Women, although they do not don the kittel, wear white garments. Moreover, in deference to the awe befitting the Judgment Day, they should not wear their regular holiday and Sabbath jewelry (M.B. 610:16, M.E. 609:9).

101. It is commendable to don the kittel at home and wear it to the synagogue so as to be constantly reminded of the awesome nature of the holiday that is about to begin (*M.E.* 619:5).

◦§ Tallis

102. It is customary to wear the *tallis* during the evening prayers on Yom Kippur (*M.E.* 619:7; see *Rama* in *O.C.* 18:1). Since it is questionable whether one can recite the blessing over the *tallis* at night, one should take care to don it while it is yet day (ibid.). If night has already fallen, one can don the *tallis*, but should not recite the blessing (*Rama* in *O.C.* 18:1).

THE FIVE RESTRICTIONS OF YOM KIPPUR

103. A distinctive feature of Yom Kippur is its designation in the Torah as both a 'Sabbath' and a fast day. Fasting on Yom Kippur, which the Torah expresses with the term עֱנּוּ, *affliction*, is a broader concept than a mere abstention from food and drink. The Sages (see *Yoma* 76a-77b) derive from Biblical exegesis that *affliction* implies abstention from five activites: (a) eating and drinking; (b) washing one's body; (c) anointing oneself with oils; (d) wearing leather shoes; and (e) marital relations. In addition, all labors that are forbidden on the Sabbath are forbidden on Yom Kippur as well. It is not within the scope of this summary to discuss the details of the laws of labor. We will, however, summarize the laws of the 'five afflictions' since these are relevant to Yom Kippur specifically.

◦§ Eating and Drinking

104. Although the Sages state that one does not fully violate the prohibition against eating on Yom Kippur unless he consumes a certain minimum quantity of food or drink, this refers only to incurring the severe punishment of *kares* [spiritual *excision*, premature death]. It is forbidden on a Biblical level [מדאורייתא], however, to consume even the least amount of food or drink (*O.C.* 612:5 with *M.B.*).

105. It is permitted to touch food; there is no apprehension that the person may forget himself and eat the food. It is also permitted to feed young children, even if they are capable of taking their food themselves (*O.C.* 612:10; c.f. *Magen Avraham* §6, *M.E.* 612:10).

106. Whenever there is even a slight possibility that to fast would be life threatening, one should not fast. If possible, however, one who must eat should eat less than the minimum quantity specified in regard to *kares* (*O.C.* 619:7); a competent halachic authority should be consulted to advise on how much may be eaten or drunk at one time, and how long one must wait between feedings.

107. [Whenever there is even the slightest question of danger one should not take it upon himself to fast, but should rather consult a doctor and a competent halachic authority.] It is a false and foolish piety to fast when one should not do so because of reasons of health; if the person should, God forbid, die as a result, this may be tantamount to committing suicide. In regard to such conduct it is said (*Koheles* 7:16): *Do not be overly righteous.* Where necessary, the person should be fed even against his will (*M.E.* 619:15).

◦§ Washing

108. It is forbidden to wash even a minute part of the body, whether in hot or cold water, or even to dip one's finger in water. However, the prohibition refers only to washing done for pleasure, not to that which is necessary to remove dirt. Thus, one may wash the parts of his body which have become dirty with mud, blood, etc. (O.C. 613:1). However, one may wash only that part of the body which is dirty. If one's body is dirtied in many places and it is cumbersome to wash each dirty part separately, he may immerse as much of his body as is necessary and wash the dirty areas together. He should intend not to derive any pleasure from this washing (M.B. §1).

109. One may wash his hands three times upon arising in the morning as usual [נְטִילַת יָדַיִם], provided that he washes only the minimum required area — the fingers, but not the palm of the hand. He should intend not to derive any pleasure (O.C. 613:2).

110. It is forbidden to rinse one's mouth upon arising in the morning even if one is accustomed to do so every day and is uncomfortable without doing it (O.C. 613:4; see M.B. 567:11).

111. Kohanim may wash their entire hands before ascending to recite the Bircas Kohanim (O.C. 613:3, M.B. §7; M.E. 613:8). In communities where it is customary for the Levites to wash their own hands prior to washing the Kohanim's hands, they may do so (M.B. ibid.).

112. If one has performed his bodily functions and is returning to his prayers, he may also wash his fingers (as above). Thus, during the Yom Kippur day, when one is continually at prayer, he may wash his fingers after going to the bathroom (O.C. 613:2; M.B. §4). If it is his custom to wash three times, he may wash his fingers three times (M.E. 613:5).

113. However, it is questionable whether one may wash his hands at night, after Maariv, after merely urinating. In order to avoid this problem, one should make sure to touch a part of his body, that is generally covered, thus incurring an unquestionable obligation to wash his hands before reciting the bless-

ing of אֲשֶׁר יָצַר (see O.C. 613:3, M.B. §4,6, M.E. 613:4).

114. If one merely entered a bathroom, he may not wash his hands even if this is his practice throughout the year. Rather, one should wipe his hands on a clean cloth or board, in lieu of washing. However, if he is upset at praying with unwashed hands and as a result is distracted, he may wash them (M.E. 613:7; see Eleph LaMatteh §7). [One may assume that the device of touching a generally covered part of the body is applicable here too.]

115. If one has touched a covered part of the body, and he wishes to pray or recite a blessing, he should wash all the fingers of that hand. But if he has touched dirt or mud, he may wash only the soiled area (M.B. 613:6).

116. Although it is customary to wash one's face and rinse the mouth every morning before praying, it is forbidden to do so on Yom Kippur. However, if one has mucus on his eyes, he may moisten his fingers and rub them over his eyes (M.B. 613:9).

◄§ Anointing

117. One may not anoint [i.e., smear upon the body a viscous or liquid substance to be absorbed in the skin, such as moisturizer or skin cream] even a small part of the body. This prohibition is more stringent than that against washing; one may not anoint himself even if his purpose is to remove dirt or sweat. Anointing is a greater pleasure than washing [so that it is considered to be done for pleasure] (O.C. 614:1, M.B. §1, Magen Avraham §1, Eleph HaMagen §1; c.f. Turei Zahav 613:1). [This may apply to certain cosmetics as well.]

118. Anointing for medicinal purposes is not prohibited, even if the condition is not life threatening. Nevertheless this may be forbidden because of the ban on healing or taking medicines on the Sabbath or Yom Tov for minor ailments (O.C. 614:1 with M.B. §2); a halachic authority should be consulted.

ﻉ Wearing Shoes

119. It is forbidden to wear leather shoes on Yom Kippur. This ban applies to all types of footgear, even those which are only partially leather. It makes no difference whether the leather is in the uppers or the soles; even if only covered or lined with leather (O.C. 614:2).

120. Shoes made of materials other than leather are permitted (ibid). There are, however, some *Poskim* who rule that shoes should not be worn, regardless of the material they are made of (see M.B. §5).

121. There are extenuating circumstances in which one may be permitted to wear leather shoes, but it is doubtful if these leniencies are applicable today when shoes made of synthetic materials are so readily available; at any rate, one should consult a halachic authority.

ﻉ Marital Relations

122. Marital relations are forbidden on Yom Kippur. Furthermore, all of the stringencies which are practiced by a husband and wife when she is a *niddah* (e.g., not to hand objects from one to the other, etc., as detailed in *Yoreh Deah* §195) should also be observed on the entire day of Yom Kippur (M.B. 615:1).

ﻉ Children

123. The involvement of children in *mitzvos* is defined by two Torah concepts: (a) חִינוּךְ, *chinuch*, the obligation to accustom and train children to perform the precepts of the Torah so

that they will be ready to perform them properly upon attaining their majority; and (b) the constraint placed upon adults not to feed prohibited food to a child or otherwise be directly involved in the violation of Torah laws by children [e.g., carrying a male child *Kohen* into a room in which there is a human corpse] (see *Yevamos* 114a and O.C. 343).

124. There are a number of differences between these two concepts in regard to the scope of one's responsibilities. The concept of *chinuch* applies only to the father or, according to some, also to the mother; the prohibition to directly cause a child's transgression, however, is applicable to every Jew. *Chinuch* is relevant only to children old enough to understand the significance of the constraints being placed upon them and to those who are trainable; the prohibition to bring about a transgression through a child applies even to babies (see O.C. 343 with M.B. §1-8; see further, *Rama* ad loc. and M.B. 343:7).

125. Small children before the age of *chinuch* (see further) need not be subjected to any of the afflictions except for the ban on wearing leather shoes. [The *Gemara* (*Yoma* 78b) explains that food, drink, washing, and anointing are essential to a child's growth.] Hence it was permitted in times past for an adult to feed, give drink to, wash (with cold water), and anoint small children on Yom Kippur. In our days it is not so essential to wash and anoint children; therefore adults may not wash, anoint, or dress even small children in leather shoes (O.C. 616:1 with M.B.).

126. The concept of *chinuch* applies to the *mitzvah* of fasting and afflicting oneself on Yom Kippur as it does to other *mitzvos*. However, the manner in which *chinuch* is accomplished differs in regard to this *mitzvah*. Here the criterion is not only whether the child understands the *mitzvah*, but also whether he can bear the rigor of fasting and 'afflicting' without undue difficulty and harm to his health. Therefore, even after a child reaches the age of *chinuch* he need not as yet fulfill the *mitzvah* of fasting completely; it is sufficient that he be trained to do this partially, as will be explained below.

127. The age of *chinuch* varies from child to child. Generally children are divided into two classes in this regard. Children who are robust reach the age of *chinuch* on their ninth birthday, while those whose constitution is frail reach it on their tenth birthday. The same rule is applied to female children in spite of the fact that they reach their majority one year before their male counterparts (O.C. 616:2).

128. Even when a child reaches the age of *chinuch* he is not yet obligated to fast completely. Rather he is trained to fast 'by hours', e.g., he is trained to eat some hours later than he is accustomed to. The amount of time the child is obliged to fast depends upon the strength of the individual child (ibid.).

129. The obligation to train a child once he reaches the age of *chinuch* devolves only upon the father (and perhaps the mother). Others are not obligated to train the child and need not interfere with a child who does not train to fast. However, since such fasting will

not be detrimental to an older child's health, one may not actively feed the child, just as one may not feed a child other forbidden materials, as explained earlier (M.B. 616:5; cf. *Shaar HaTziyun* there).

130. According to many *Poskim*, there is yet another level in the age of *chinuch* when the child is obligated to complete the fast. In their view, once a child — whether male or female — reaches its eleventh birthday, it must complete the fast, while others hold that a child need never complete the fast. R' Yoseph Caro — the author of the *Shulchan Aruch* — accepts the stringent opinion, while *Rama* rules that one can rely on the lenient view in regard to a child whose health is frail. However, later *Poskim* testify that it is not customary for children in their twelfth year to complete the fast. They justify this custom on the basis that in our days 'a weakness has descended upon the world' so that every eleven-year-old should be deemed to be of frail health. Others extend this principle even to twelve-year-old boys (twelve-year-old girls are considered adults according to Torah law, and as such have their own Scriptural obligation to fast). Still others argue that the lenient view be accepted entirely (O.C. 616: with M.B. §9 and *Beur Halachah*). [There are various customs in this matter; in the absence of a well-defined custom one should consult a halachic authority.]

KOL NIDREI AND MAARIV

ᴥᔈ Viduy before Maariv — Tefillah Zakkah

131. Although *viduy* is said in the Minchah prayer, some authorities (*Ramban, Ran*, et al.) state that one should recite it again because it is possible that a sin was committed during the meal. The Sages did not obligate the public to recite the *viduy* again, but it is commendable that every individual do so on his

own. He should say the short *Viduy*, אָשַׁמְנוּ ... תִּעְתָּעְנוּ (M.E. 619:8). *Chayei Adam* gives the text of a prayer that he found in 'old' sources — *Tefillah Zakkah* (see ArtScroll *Machzor*, Nusach Ashkenaz p. 38, Nusach Sefard p. 46) — which has found its way into most *machzorim* and has gained wide acceptance. In addition to being a moving prayer and confession, *Tefillah Zakkah* has an important feature: a formula in which one forgives those whom may have wronged him during the year. If one does not say the *tefillah*, he should at least substitute a similar declaration.

✎§ Kol Nidrei

132. The *chazzan* should prolong the recitation of *Kol Nidrei* until it is certainly night, so as to begin *Maariv* at the proper time (O.C. 619:1). If *Kol Nidrei* is over before nightfall, chapters of *Tehillim* should be recited until *Maariv* (M.B. §6). [A full discussion of Kol Nidrei and the customs surrounding it appears in "Backgrounds and Insights."]

133. After the *chazzan* has concluded the recitation of *Kol Nidrei* and the verses which follow it, he pronounces the blessing שֶׁהֶחֱיָנוּ, *Shehechiyanu*, out loud. The congregants should not rely on the *chazzan's* blessing to fulfill their obligation to say this blessing, but should each say it quietly together with him; they should make sure to finish their recitation before the *chazzan's* in order to be able to respond *amen* to it. Nevertheless, the *chazzan* should intend his blessing to include those who, for whatever reason, do not recite it themselves. Women who have already recited *Shehechiyanu* when kindling the Yom Tov lights should not recite it again now (M.E. 619:12).

KABBALAS SHABBOS

134. There are various customs regarding the *Kabbalas Shabbos* service when Yom Kippur falls on the Sabbath. In some communities the service commences with מִזְמוֹר שִׁיר לְיוֹם הַשַּׁבָּת [psalm 92] (M.E. 619:15) [while in others the service is said in the same way as on Yom Tov].

✎§ Shema

135. When the *chazzan* reaches the *Shema*, the entire congregation recites the first verse שְׁמַע יִשְׂרָאֵל ה׳ אֱלֹהֵינוּ ה׳ אֶחָד, aloud together with him, as on every day (M.E. 619:15; see (O.C. 61:4, 26).

136. The congregation then waits for the *chazzan* to begin the second verse בָּרוּךְ שֵׁם כְּבוֹד מַלְכוּתוֹ לְעוֹלָם וָעֶד and recites it aloud together with him. This procedure is repeated during the morning recitation of the *Shema* (O.C. 619:2). *Tur* (O.C. 619) explains this divergence from the usual custom to say this verse quietly. The *Midrash* (*Devarim Rabbah* 2:36) relates that when Moses went up to Heaven to receive the Torah, he overheard the ministering angels saying the verse בָּרוּךְ...וָעֶד. in their praise to

G-d. Upon coming down to the Israelite camp he taught the Jews to say this verse. Because of the angelic source of this utterance, it is said quietly throughout the year. R' Yose illustrated this with a parable: Someone took a precious piece of jewelry from the king's palace and gave it to his wife, cautioning her not to display her new finery in public. The *Midrash* concludes that on Yom Kippur, when we are pure as angels, we can recite this praise of God aloud just as the angels do.

✎§ The Amidah (Shemoneh Esrei)

137. All of the changes and insertions made in the *Shemoneh Esrei* during the Ten Days of Repentance are also made in the *Amidah* of Yom Kippur, wherever applicable. The laws stated concerning these changes during the Ten Days of Repentance are also true in regard to Yom Kippur (see above §26-32), except in the case set forth below (§139).

138. In the prayers of Yom Kippur, a lengthy interpolation of special prayers, beginning וּבְכֵן תֵּן פַּחְדְּךָ [in *Nusach Ashkenaz*; וּבְכֵן יִתְקַדֵּשׁ in *Nusach*

Sefard] is inserted in the third blessing of the *Shemoneh Esrei.* However, if someone omitted the insertion but ended the blessing correctly with הַמֶּלֶךְ הַקָּדוֹשׁ, he need not repeat the *Amidah.*

139. If one inserted the prescribed prayers but is in doubt whether he ended the blessing correctly, he may assume (contrary to §30 above) that he recited the correct formula. In this case, logic dictates that since he was reciting the special holiday formula he must have concluded it with the holiday ending (*M.B.* 582:4).

140. If one omitted the special prayers but correctly recited הַמֶּלֶךְ הַקָּדוֹשׁ, and has already begun the next blessing [i.e., אַתָּה בְחַרְתָּנוּ] before realizing his omission, it is clearly forbidden to interrupt and insert the omitted passage. However, if he has not yet begun the next blessing, there is a difference of opinion among the authorities as to what procedure should be followed. *Derech HaChaim* rules that once הַמֶּלֶךְ הַקָּדוֹשׁ has been said, one must continue the *Amidah.* However, R' *Tzvi Pesach Frank* (*Mikraei Kodesh* p. 212) demonstrates that according to *Eishel Avraham,* one may, if he wishes, recite the omitted paragraphs before beginning אַתָּה בְחַרְתָּנוּ.

141. In the fourth blessing of *Shemoneh Esrei* [... אַתָּה בְחַרְתָּנוּ], the *Yom Tov* is mentioned, as on all Festivals. There are two versions for Yom Kippur: אֶת יוֹם הַכִּפֻּרִים הַזֶּה, *this Day of Atonement;* and אֶת יוֹם צוֹם הַכִּפֻּרִים הַזֶּה, *this Fast Day of Atonement.* Each congregation should follow its own custom (*M.E.* 619:16).

◆§ The Amidah on the Sabbath

142. If Yom Kippur falls on the Sabbath several additions are made to the liturgy of the *Shemoneh Esrei.* Some of them are essential and, if omitted,

the *Amidah* must be repeated, while others are not.

143. One group of additions, which is essential in nature, consists of the inclusion of the Sabbath wherever the *Yom Tov* Yom Kippur is mentioned (except in יַעֲלֶה וְיָבֹא where our custom omits the mention of the Sabbath). Thus we say ... וַתִּתֶּן לָנוּ ... אֶת יוֹם הַשַּׁבָּת הַזֶּה and בָּרוּךְ אַתָּה ה' מְקַדֵּשׁ וְאֶת יוֹם הַכִּפוּרִים הַזֶּה הַשַּׁבָּת וְיִשְׂרָאֵל וְיוֹם הַכִּפוּרִים. If *both* of these additions were omitted — so that the Sabbath was not mentioned at all — the blessing must be repeated. Accordingly, if one has not yet finished the *Amidah,* he must return to the beginning of the blessing אַתָּה בְחַרְתָּנוּ and continue from there. If he has already concluded the *Amidah,* he must repeat it from the beginning. The conclusion of the *Amidah* in this regard is defined as the recitation of the verse יִהְיוּ לְרָצוֹן ... וְגֹאֲלִי just before עוֹשֶׂה [הַ]שָּׁלוֹם.

144. However, if one mentioned the Sabbath at the beginning of the blessing [i.e., in וַתִּתֶּן לָנוּ], but failed to do so in the concluding formula [i.e., בָּרוּךְ אַתָּה ה'], it is questionable whether the blessing has to be repeated (see *M.B.* 487:7, *Beur Halachah* there). *Mishnah Berurah* does not give a clear ruling on this question (although he implies his preference for certain of the views). In the absence of a ruling from a competent halachic authority, one should not repeat the *Amidah* in this case, since the general rule is that סָפֵק בְּרָכוֹת לְהָקֵל, *when there is doubt whether a blessing should be repeated, we rule leniently,* in order to avoid the possibility of reciting a blessing that is not required.

145. Conversely, if one mentioned Yom Kippur in וַתִּתֶּן לָנוּ but concluded the blessing with a mention only of the Sabbath, there is controversy over whether the blessing must be repeated. According to *Magen Avraham* (*O.C.* 487:2), in this case one should not repeat the blessing. However, many authorities differ (*Pri Chadash, Beur Halachah*, et al.; see *Hagahos R' Akiva Eiger*).

146. If the omission occurred in the concluding formula, one can correct it by immediately saying only the words הַשַּׁבָּת וְיִשְׂרָאֵל וְיוֹם הַכִּפֻּרִים. This correction is valid only if it was begun before enough time to say the words שָׁלוֹם עָלֶיךָ רַבִּי has elapsed from when the erroneously phrased conclusion was recited.

147. If, however, the blessing has not yet been concluded, there are instances in which the error can be corrected and the entire problem avoided. If one omitted mentioning the Sabbath in וַתִּתֶּן לָנוּ, he simply goes back to וַתִּתֶּן לָנוּ and continues from there. If he has said the three words בָּרוּךְ אַתָּה ה' of the concluding formula, he should add the words לַמְּדֵנִי חֻקֶּיךָ. [By doing so he has recited the verse בָּרוּךְ אַתָּה ה' לַמְּדֵנִי חֻקֶּיךָ, *Blessed are You, HASHEM, teach me Your statutes* (Psalms 119:12); thus no wrong or needless blessing has been recited, while at the same time, he has avoided concluding this fourth blessing of the *Amidah*.] Then he can go back to וַתִּתֶּן לָנוּ and repeat the entire blessing properly, thereby correcting his omission. However, if he has recited more than three words of the blessing [i.e., בָּרוּךְ אַתָּה ה' מֶלֶךְ . . .], he can no longer avoid concluding the blessing; he must finish the blessing and is subject to the questionable situation described above.

148. In the concluding paragraph of this blessing, the words אֱלֹהֵינוּ וֵאלֹהֵי אֲבוֹתֵינוּ רְצֵה בִמְנוּחָתֵינוּ, *Our God and God of our fathers, may You be pleased with our rest*, are omitted according to some authorities. Since it is a fast day, they maintain that we should not describe it as a day of contented rest (*M.E. 619:16*).

149. If Yom Kippur falls on the Sabbath, מָגֵן אָבוֹת and וַיְכֻלּוּ are recited immediately after the *Amidah* as

they are on an ordinary Sabbath. However, since it is Yom Kippur, the blessing must include the substitution of the words הַמֶּלֶךְ הַקָּדוֹשׁ in place of the usual הָאֵל הַקָּדוֹשׁ. If the *chazzan* recited the usual version instead, and has not yet concluded the blessing, he must return to that part of the blessing, correct his error and continue from there. However, if he has already concluded the blessing, he should not repeat it (*M.E. 582*; see *O.C. 582:3* with *M.B. §10*).

150. In times past it was universal custom to say *selichos* during every prayer of Yom Kippur (see *Rosh, Yoma 8:20*). Nowadays the custom in most congregations is to say *selichos* only at *Maariv* after the conclusion of the *Amidah* and during the *chazzan's* repetition of the *Amidah* of Ne'ilah.

151. The recitation of the Thirteen Attributes of Mercy is a vital element of the *selichos*. The Thirteen Attributes of Mercy should be said only with a *minyan*. Therefore, every individual should take care to be up to the congregation during this recital, or to interrupt whatever he is saying (if permissible) in order to recite them. However, if one has not yet concluded his recitation of the personal *Amidah*, he does not interrupt to join in saying the Thirteen Attributes of Mercy. Even if one is reciting the *viduy* at the end of his *Amidah* he does not interrupt to say the Thirteen Attributes of Mercy (see §89).

152. Ideally one should stand while saying *selichos*. If this is difficult, he should at least stand up for the recitation of the prayers אֵל מֶלֶךְ יוֹשֵׁב and אֵל אֶרֶךְ אַפַּיִם which introduce the recitation of the Thirteen Attributes [and surely for the recitation of the Thirteen Attributes themselves] (*M.E. 581:18*).

153. The *chazzan* repeats the *viduy* (confession) during every prayer of Yom Kippur. This is for the most part done during the *chazzan's* repetition of the *Amidah* (during the middle *berachah*); for *Maariv* it is done after *selichos*. The congregants should rise and repeat the *viduy* together with the *chazzan* (*O.C.* 607:3). [See above, §86-89, for more details about the laws of *viduy*.]

154. Many people remain in the synagogue after the service, reciting psalms and prayers, thereby emulating the procedure followed in the Temple (*O.C.* 619:6; see *Yoma* 1:6-7). However *Levush* (cited by *Magen Avraham* §11) asserts that it is better to go home and sleep, so that one should not be drowsy during the daytime prayers.

155. It is also commendable to study *Mishnah Yoma* (*M.E.* 619:24), and the laws of the sacrifices on Yom Kippur in *Rambam, Hilchos Avodas Yom KaKippurim* (see *Minhagei Chasam Sofer*).

156. It is proper for a person to recite at least one hundred blessings during the course of each day. On Yom Kippur, however, this presents difficulties, since all the blessings associated with food are missing. Some people, therefore, have aromatic herbs or spices with them in the synagogue, in order to recite the blessing בּוֹרֵא מִינֵי בְשָׂמִים over them from time to time. Thus, they are able to complete the total of one hundred blessings which should be recited every day (*M.E.* 619:26).

SHACHARIS OF YOM KIPPUR

ᵛ§ Shema

157. One should take care to be ready to join with the congregation in reciting aloud the verses שְׁמַע יִשְׂרָאֵל and בָּרוּךְ שֵׁם. If he is still reciting *Pesukei D'Zimrah*, he may interrupt to recite these verses together with the congregation. If he is reciting the Blessings of the *Shema*, he should merely pretend to be responding with the congregation (by covering his eyes with his right hand) while reciting aloud the passage he is up to. When he does reach the *Shema* he should say the verse בָּרוּךְ שֵׁם aloud, as he does for the verse שְׁמַע (*M.E.* 619:40).

ᵛ§ The Chazzan's Repetition of the Amidah

158. Just before the *chazzan* completes the first blessing of his repetition, he chants the preamble (רְשׁוּת, *reshus*) composed for him. Because of its moving contents, many congregants may also wish to say this prayer. They may do so, provided they say it in an undertone and skip the passages that refer specifically to the *chazzan* (*M.E.* 619:42).

159. When the *chazzan* reaches the *viduy*, every individual should recite it as well (*O.C.* 607:3). Care should be taken not to rush mindlessly through even the repetition of the *viduy*, for an unthinking, rushed, confession is no better, if not worse, than no confession at all (*M.E.* 619:44).

160. *Mussaf* should be begun before half of the seventh hour of the day has elapsed, i.e., approximately a half-hour after the astronomical noon. If it is realized during *Shacharis* that time will be short, some *piyutim* of *Shacharis*, and even *Avinu Malkeinu*, should be omitted in order to start *Mussaf* on time (*O.C.* 620; *M.B.* §1).

ᵛ§ The Torah Readings

161. When Yom Kippur occurs on a weekday, six people (not counting *maftir*) are called to the Torah; and on the Sabbath, seven. No additional *aliyos* should be made, even on a Yom Kippur that occurs on the Sabbath (*M.E.* 619:53).

162. It is customary for the *gabbai* to recite a מִי שֶׁבֵּרַךְ (a special blessing said for the person called to the Torah and whomever he wishes to bless). Nevertheless, care should be taken not to overburden the congregation by taking too much time doing this (*M.E.* 619:53).

163. There are two customs regarding the conclusion of the bless- ings following the *haftarah.* Some recite: בָּרוּךְ אַתָּה ה' מְקַדֵּשׁ [הַשַּׁבָּת] וְיִשְׂרָאֵל וְיוֹם הַכִּפֻּרִים. Others recite: בָּרוּךְ אַתָּה ה' מֶלֶךְ מוֹחֵל וְסוֹלֵחַ ... מֶלֶךְ עַל כָּל הָאָרֶץ ... מְקַדֵּשׁ... Each community should conduct itself according to its custom (*M.E.* 619:54). *R' Yaakov Emden* in his *siddur* expresses his preference for the latter custom (cf. *Magen Avraham* to *O.C.* 621 with *Dagul Merevavah*).

MUSSAF OF YOM KIPPUR

164. When the *chazzan* reaches the words וַאֲנַחְנוּ כּוֹרְעִים וּמִשְׁתַּחֲוִים וּמוֹדִים in *Aleinu* of his *Mussaf* (ArtScroll *Machzor, Nusach Ashkenaz* p. 550, *Nusach Sefard* p. 580), it is customary for him and the congregation to kneel (and bow their heads) all the way to the floor (*O.C.* 621:4; *M.B.* 16; cf. *M.E.* 621:4, 592:1 with *Ketzeh HaMatteh*).

165. In his repetition of the *Amidah* the *chazzan* says the *Avodah*, i.e., a poetic rendition of the Temple service on Yom Kippur. The *chazzan* leads the congregation, who should recite the *Avodah* along with him. It is important that one familiarize himself before Yom Kippur with the *piyut* recited by the congregation, so that he will understand the details of the service described in the *piyut* (*M.E.* 621:10). [This recital is all we have today to replace the atonement service performed in the Temple on behalf of the entire nation. It is the tradition of the Sages that in the absence of the Temple, recital of the Temple offering service may serve in its stead (*Yoma* 86b, *Menachos* 110a).]

166. The individual should try to keep up with the congregation and the *chazzan,* so that he will reach the passages describing the kneeling prostration practiced in the Temple with them. At these points, as well as during *Aleinu,* the entire congregation kneels and prostrates itself in simulation of the Temple service (*O.C.* 621:4). If an individual lags behind the congregation, he should nevertheless prostrate himself together with the congregation (*M.E.* 621:11).

⇐§ The Prostrations

167. There is a Scriptural ban on prostrating oneself on a stone floor anywhere except in the Holy Temple (see *Lev.* 26:1). The Scriptural ban is confined to full prostrations performed on a stone floor. Full prostrations are defined as stretching out the limbs — hands and feet — upon the floor with the head touching the ground. The Scriptural ban is confined to stone floors; wooden and brick floors are excluded. However the Sages prohibited kneeling on a stone floor and full prostrations on any floor; kneeling on a floor of a material other than stone is however permitted (see *M.B.* 131:40). In order to avoid the problem of prohibited prostrations on Yom Kippur, it is custom- ary to spread something upon the floor before performing the prostrations (*Rama, O.C.* 131:8). If one has nothing to spread out he may lean slightly to a side [thereby removing the act from the category of a full prostration] (ibid.), or interpose the *talis* between the floor and his face (*M.E.* 621:14).

168. According to most authorities, the *chazzan* should not pros- trate himself if it is impossible for him to do so while remaining in his place, since he may not move in the middle of his *Amidah* (*O.C.* 621:4). Nowadays, it has become the custom to place an additional lectern in front of the one regularly used by the chazzan. When the chazzan is about to prostrate himself, the additional lectern is removed, giving the chazzan space to prostrate himself without moving his feet. However, in some communities it is customary for the chazzan to move from his place for the prostrations, in accordance with the lenient ruling given by some Poskim (M.B. 621:16; M.E. 621:15).

169. When the descriptions of the three confessions (viduyim) recited by the Kohen Gadol [High Priest] in his service are reached in the Avodah, each individual strikes himself on the chest while saying the words constituting the viduy. For example, during the recital of the Kohen Gadol's personal viduy, each individual imagines how he would repent and confess were he the Kohen Gadol. So, in regard with the prostrations, one imagines that he is now in the Holy Temple

hearing the Kohen Gadol chant 'the glorious, awesome Name' and prostrates himself accordingly (M.E. 621:16).

170. The full Kaddish following the chazzan's repetition of the Amidah marks the end of the Mussaf service. אֵין כֵּאלֹהֵינוּ is not said on Yom Kippur (O.C. 622:1). Some authorities (Magen Avraham, Turei Zahav) feel that each individual should recite the incense service (M.B. 622:5). However, those who preface Minchah with Korbanos need not recite פִּטּוּם הַקְּטוֹרֶת, for the Korbanos section already includes the incense service (Eleph LaMatteh §16).

171. The prayers of אַשְׁרֵי and וּבָא לְצִיּוֹן are omitted at Minchah, and are deferred to Ne'ilah. The verse וַאֲנִי תְפִלָּתִי, which is usually said before reading the Torah on the Sabbath, is omitted; rather, the service begins with the opening of the Ark and וַיְהִי בִּנְסֹעַ (O.C. 622:1). צִדְקָתְךָ is also omitted (ibid. §3).

NE'ILAH

172. Ne'ilah is the culmination of the Yom Kippur prayers. It is recited just as the Heavenly gates which had been opened wide for acceptance of prayer are about to close. Although one is now tired from the fast, he should gather his strength and concentrate with great intensity and fervor upon this prayer (M.E. 623:2).

173. Ideally, Ne'ilah should be commenced a short while before sundown and be concluded close to nightfall (O.C. 623:2, M.B. §2). It should not begin before plag haminchah, i.e., approximately an hour and a quarter before sundown (M.E. 623:2).

174. The chazzan's repetition includes a passage beginning הַיּוֹם יִפְנֶה, the day will fade away... If it is already night, the passage should be reworded to read in the past tense, הַיּוֹם פָּנָה, הַשֶּׁמֶשׁ בָּא וּפָנָה, the day has faded

away, the sun has set and is gone ... However, if it is still twilight and not yet definitely night, the wording does not have to be changed (M.E. 623:7).

175. When Yom Kippur occurs on the Sabbath, the Sabbath is mentioned in the Ne'ilah prayer, as in all the previous prayers. If it was not mentioned, the prayer must be repeated just as the other prayers (see §134-139). However, the Sabbath is not mentioned in the prayer אַתָּה הִבְדַּלְתָּ, which the individual recites in the conclusion of the Amidah. In the chazzan's repetition, this prayer is said in the fourth (middle) blessing of the Amidah, and the Sabbath is mentioned there (O.C. 623:3).

176. At the end of the prayer, Avinu Malkeinu is said, even on the Sabbath (M.B. 623:10, M.E. 623:7).

177. At the conclusion of Ne'ilah, a single tekiah is sounded on the

623:6). There are varying customs as to the exact place of sounding the *shofar* in the prayer sequence; whether before *Kaddish*, after it (*M.E.* 623:7), or in the middle of *Kaddish*, before תִּתְקַבֵּל.

178. The *tekiah* may not be sounded when it is still surely day, but it may be blown in the twilight period, even on the Sabbath. There are varying views on the exact definition of the term 'twilight,' בֵּין הַשְּׁמָשׁוֹת. Each congregation should follow its tradition and the ruling of its recognized halachic authority.

THE CONCLUSION OF YOM KIPPUR

⋅≶ Maariv

179. If *Ne'ilah* was concluded early, the congregation must wait for nightfall before commencing *Maariv*. The *chazzan* should not prolong *Maariv* unnecessarily, because there are many people for whom the fasting is difficult. Neither should he rush through *Maariv*. Those who finish earlier should take care not to jostle or distract those congregants who are still reciting *Shemoneh Esrei* (*M.E.* 624:1).

180. *Maariv* begins with וְהוּא רַחוּם and proceeds in the usual manner until *Shemoneh Esrei*.

181. The passage אַתָּה חוֹנַנְתָּנוּ is included in the fourth blessing (אַתָּה חוֹנֵן). If one forgot to say it and has already said בָּרוּךְ אַתָּה ה׳, he should continue the prayer; he should not include the אַתָּה חוֹנַנְתָּנוּ passage in the blessing of שְׁמַע קוֹלֵנוּ (*M.B.* 296:6).

182. When Yom Kippur occurs on the Sabbath, וַיְהִי נֹעַם and וְאַתָּה קָדֹשׁ are omitted. However, וְיִתֶּן לְךָ is recited as usual.

⋅≶ Kiddush Levanah

183. If it is a clear night, *Kiddush Levanah* (which is not recited during the Ten Days of Repentance) is recited immediately after *Maariv*, so as to begin the year with a *mitzvah* (*M.E.* 624:4).

184. After the conclusion of the prayer, one should greet others with a blessing for a good year (*M.E.* 624:5). In some communities it is customary to use the greeting, *Gut Yom Tov*, for the night is yet a semi-*Yom Tov* (*Rama*, *O.C.* 624:5; *Ketzeh HaMatteh* 624:9).

⋅≶ Havdalah

185. All restrictions pertaining to Yom Kippur are ended once night has fallen (and one has recited אַתָּה חוֹנַנְתָּנוּ in *Shemoneh Esrei*, or has spoken the words בָּרוּךְ הַמַּבְדִּיל בֵּין קוֹדֶשׁ לְחוֹל). However, one is forbidden to eat or drink before *Havdalah* (*M.B.* 624:3; *M.E.* 624:2).

186. Some authorities rule that even when Yom Kippur falls on the Sabbath, the blessing over aromatic herbs is not included in *Havdalah* (*O.C.* 624:3). However, many later authorities dispute this ruling and state that the blessing should be said; this is the prevalent custom nowadays (*M.B.* 624, *M.E.* 624:5).

187. Unlike other festivals, the blessing בּוֹרֵא מְאוֹרֵי הָאֵשׁ is said even when Yom Kippur falls on a weekday. However there is a restriction on how the fire may be obtained, which does not apply on *Motzaei Shabbos*: namely, the source of the flame must be a fire that has been burning from *before* Yom Kippur (*O.C.* 624:4). Ideally, the blessing should be recited directly over a fire that had burned on Yom Kippur, but should this prove to be impossible, it may be recited over a flame kindled from such a flame (see *Rama* in *O.C.* 624:5, *M.B.* there §12). If such a flame is unobtainable, the blessing should not be recited at all. One should not rely on the view (cited in *O.C.* 624:4) that one can recite the blessing over a flame which has been lit from a newly lit flame, or from a gentile's fire which was lit on Yom Kippur (*Beur Halachah* there).

188. The reason for this differentiation between the flame of *Motzaei Shabbos* and that of *Motzaei Yom Kippur* derives from the fundamental difference in the reasons for using a flame in the *Havdalah* of these two nights. On *Motzaei Shabbos* we thank God for teaching Adam how to create fire; since this occurred on the first *Motzaei Shabbos* after Creation, we commemorate this event with a blessing in *Havdalah*. Since that fire was newly made, the *Havdalah* flame, too, may be new. But on *Motzaei Yom Kippur* the blessing accentuates the difference between Yom Kippur, when it is forbidden to use fire for kindling, and other Festivals, when we are permitted to use fire for cooking. Since the blessing demonstrates that only now has the fire been rendered permissible for use, it must be recited only over a flame that has burned on Yom Kippur and has now become permissible (*M.B.* 624:7).

189. In view of the above, when Yom Kippur occurs on the Sabbath, one may recite the blessing over any flame, if a flame that burned on Yom Kippur is not available. However, even when *Motzaei* Yom Kippur falls on *Motzaei Shabbos* it is customary to use an old fire. If on *Motzaei Shabbos* such a flame is not available, it is preferable to kindle a new flame and then to use that one to make a *second* flame. The *Havdalah* should then be recited over the second flame (*M.B.* 624:7; cf. *M.B.* 624:8 with *Ketzeh HaMatteh* §12).

190. There are differences of opinion whether one may recite the blessing over the candles which have been lit in the synagogue since they were intended not for use, but to lend honor to the day. (The same applies to the flame of the Yom Kippur *yahrzeit* lamps.) If this is the only eligible fire available, one should

kindle another candle from it and recite the blessing over both flames together. In order to avoid such problems, it is advisable on Erev Yom Kippur to light an additional candle in the house for use on *Motzaei Yom Kippur* (*M.B.* 624:13).

191. As on *Motzaei Shabbos*, it is preferable that women should not recite *Havdalah* themselves on *Motzaei Yom Kippur*, but should hear it from a man. The reason for this is that some authorities hold that *Havdalah* is a time-related *mitzvah*, from which women are exempt. They may do work after reciting אַתָּה חוֹנַנְתָּנוּ in *Shemoneh Esrei* or the formula בָּרוּךְ הַמַּבְדִּיל בֵּין קוֹדֶשׁ לְחוֹל; but may not eat or drink until after *Havdalah* (*M.E.* 624:7). Should this be impractical, they may recite *Havdalah* themselves (*O.C.* 296:8; *M.B.* §35, 36).

◆§ After The Fast

192. Motzaei Yom Kippur is a semi-Yom Tov, and one should eat a festive meal (*Rama, O.C.* 624:5). The Midrash says that on this night a Heavenly voice *[bas kol]* proclaims: 'Go and eat your bread with joy!' (*M.B.* 625:15).

193. One should begin to build the *succah*, if possible, on *Motzaei Yom Kippur*, in order to go from one *mitzvah* to another (ibid.).

194. One should pray *Shacharis* early on the morrow of Yom Kippur (*Ba'er Heitev* 625:6 citing *Sefer HaMinhagim*).

195. The first Temple was dedicated in the days between Yom Kippur and Succos (see *I Kings* 8:2, 66, *Moed Kattan* 9a). Therefore, during this period *Tachanun, Tzidkas'cha* (in the *Minchah* of the Sabbath) [and *Av HaRachamim* (before *Mussaf*)] are not recited. Nor are *Pirkei Avos* or *Shir HaMaalos* recited on the Sabbath afternoon (*Rama* in *O.C.* 624:5 with *M.B.* §18).

◄§ Observance /
Prayers and Ritual

Blessing of the Children

Kol Nidrei

Avinu Malkeinu

Yizkor

– Rabbi Avie Gold

⊰{ ברכת הבנים }⊱

There is a widespread custom for parents to bless their children — young and old — before leaving for the synagogue on the eve of Yom Kippur.

<table>
<tr><td align="center">FOR A GIRL:</td><td align="center">FOR A BOY:</td></tr>
<tr><td align="center">יְשִׂמֵךְ אֱלֹהִים
כְּשָׂרָה רִבְקָה
רָחֵל וְלֵאָה.</td><td align="center">יְשִׂמְךָ אֱלֹהִים
כְּאֶפְרֵיִם
וְכִמְנַשֶּׁה.¹</td></tr>
</table>

יְבָרֶכְךָ יהוה וְיִשְׁמְרֶךָ.

יָאֵר יהוה פָּנָיו אֵלֶיךָ וִיחֻנֶּךָּ.

יִשָּׂא יהוה פָּנָיו אֵלֶיךָ, וְיָשֵׂם לְךָ שָׁלוֹם.²

⊰{ בִּרְכַּת הַבָּנִים / BLESSING OF THE CHILDREN }⊱

It is customary for parents to bless their children, young and old, before leaving for the synagogue, after the final Erev Yom Kippur meal. The flow of Divine beneficence and blessing which comes with the onset of this sacred day makes this a particularly auspicious time for such blessings. Both hands should be laid upon the head of the child to signify that the blessing is conveyed with complete generosity of spirit. Each parent may add personal blessings to the customary text, as he sees fit (*Bais Yaakov*).

⊰§ יְשִׂמְךָ אֱלֹהִים כְּאֶפְרֵיִם וְכִמְנַשֶּׁה — *May God make you like Ephraim and Menashe.* This blessing is taken from Jacob's blessing to the two sons of Joseph. He prefaced his blessing with the words, בְּךָ יְבָרֵךְ יִשְׂרָאֵל לֵאמֹר, *by you* (i.e., with the blessing given your children) *shall Israel invoke blessing, saying, "May God make you . . ."* Thus Jacob himself pronounced the text of the blessing that Jewish parents would give their children throughout history.

Ephraim and Menashe were singled out as the models for blessing because they were unique. Although they were Jacob's grandchildren, he elevated them to the status of his sons, granting each his own portion of *Eretz Yisrael* and the same rights as the other tribes. Therefore, in effect, the Blessing of the Children implies that each child so blessed should be granted heavenly assistance to rise to greatness.

A central feature of Jacob's blessing is that he gave priority to the younger son, Ephraim, over his older brother (see *Genesis* 48:13-20). Joseph was upset that his father slighted Menashe, but the two sons reacted differently. Menashe was not jealous of his brother's superiority, and Ephraim did not display arrogance as a result of his preferred status. Seeing this, Jacob declared that this display of unselfish brotherhood should become the model for the entire nation. When Jews seek to bless their children, they can find nothing better to wish upon them than such sterling perfection of character (*Agra d'Pirka*).

Yalkut Yehudah finds another reason for the choice of these two as Israel's blessing. They were the first Jews born and raised in exile. What is more, they were raised in Pharaoh's court at a time when there was no Jewish religious life in Egypt except for the intimacy of their own family. That they grew up to be sources of pride to the Patriarch makes them eminently worthy to be the showpieces of Israel.

❧ BLESSING OF THE CHILDREN ❧

There is a widespread custom for parents to bless their children — young and old — before leaving for the synagogue on the eve of Yom Kippur.

FOR A BOY:	FOR A GIRL:
May God make you like Ephraim and Menashe.[1]	May God make you like Sarah, Rebeccah, Rachel and Leah.

May HASHEM bless you and safeguard you.

May HASHEM illuminate His countenance for you and be gracious to you.

May HASHEM turn His countenance to you and establish peace for you.[2]

---

(1) *Genesis* 48:20. (2) *Numbers* 6:24-26.

It has been suggested that in naming his sons Ephraim and Menashe, Joseph alluded to the three Patriarchs, Abraham, Isaac, and Jacob.

According to *Daas Zekeinim*, the name Ephraim is a plural form of אֵפֶר, *ashes*. Of Abraham, it is written, וְאָנֹכִי עָפָר וָאֵפֶר, *I am dust and ashes* (*Genesis* 18:27); and Isaac is considered as if his ashes were upon the altar (at the *Akeidah*).

And in explaining why he called his firstborn Menashe, Joseph invoked his father, Jacob, כִּי נַשַּׁנִי אֱלֹהִים . . . וְאֵת כָּל בֵּית אָבִי, *For God made me forget . . . all my father's household* (ibid. 41:51).

Thus, when we bless our sons that they should be like Ephraim and Menashe, we also express our wish that they be like the three Patriarchs.

This reasoning also explains why Jacob placed Ephraim's name before Menashe's. Since the name Menashe alludes to his own, it would be presumptuous of Jacob to place that name before Ephraim, which alludes to his forebears Abraham and Isaac (*Metzareif Dahava*).

יְשִׂמְךָ אֱלֹהִים כְּשָׂרָה רִבְקָה רָחֵל וְלֵאָה ◆§ — *May God make you life Sarah, Rebeccah, Rachel and Leah.* Unlike that of sons, this blessing is not a Scriptural quote. However, it is logical to wish Jewish girls that they be like the Matriarchs who grew up in alien surroundings and surmounted infertility and other difficulties to become the mothers of the nation.

יְבָרֶכְךָ ה' — *May HASHEM bless you.* These verses are the Priestly Blessing (*Numbers* 6:24-26; see pages 648-653). In the verse following these blessings, God states that when the *Kohanim* (priests) bless the nation, He will confer His *own* blessing upon the Children of Israel. This makes clear that *Kohanim* have no independent power of blessing; rather, they are the instruments through which God allows His blessing to rest upon Israel (*R' Hirsch*). Similarly, parents are the agents whose love and devotion to their children is the conduit for God's infinite blessing.

The three verses of the Priestly Blessing are variously explained by the Midrashim and commentaries. Generally, the first verse is understood as an allusion to material prosperity; the second to spiritual inspiration and Torah knowledge; and the third to God's compassion above and beyond what one deserves.

וְיָשֵׂם לְךָ שָׁלוֹם — *And establish peace for you.* One may have prosperity, health, food and drink, but, if there is no peace, it

FOR A BOY:

וִיהִי רָצוֹן

מִלְּפָנֶי אָבִינוּ שֶׁבַּשָׁמַיִם,
שֶׁיִּתֵּן בְּלִבְּךָ אַהֲבָתוֹ
וְיִרְאָתוֹ. וְתִהְיֶה יִרְאַת
יהוה עַל פָּנֶיךָ כָּל יָמֶיךָ,
שֶׁלֹּא תֶחֱטָא. וִיהִי
חֶשְׁקְךָ בַּתּוֹרָה וּבַמִּצְוֹת.
עֵינֶיךָ לְנֹכַח יַבִּיטוּ;[1] פִּיךָ
יְדַבֵּר חָכְמוֹת;[2] וְלִבְּךָ
יֶהְגֶּה אֵימוֹת;[3] יָדֶיךָ
יַעַסְקוּ בְמִצְוֹת; רַגְלֶיךָ
יָרוּצוּ לַעֲשׂוֹת רְצוֹן
אָבִיךָ שֶׁבַּשָׁמַיִם. יִתֵּן לְךָ
בָּנִים וּבָנוֹת, צַדִּיקִים
וְצִדְקָנִיּוֹת, עוֹסְקִים
בַּתּוֹרָה וּבְמִצְוֹת כָּל
יְמֵיהֶם. וִיהִי מְקוֹרְךָ
בָּרוּךְ.[4] וְיַזְמִין לְךָ
פַּרְנָסָתְךָ בְּהֶתֵּר בְּנַחַת
וּבְרֶוַח, מִתַּחַת יָדוֹ
הָרְחָבָה, וְלֹא עַל יְדֵי
מַתְּנַת בָּשָׂר וָדָם;
פַּרְנָסָה שֶׁתִּהְיֶה פָנוּי
לַעֲבוֹדַת יהוה. וְתִכָּתֵב
וְתֵחָתֵם לְחַיִּים טוֹבִים
וַאֲרוּכִים, בְּתוֹךְ כָּל
צַדִּיקֵי יִשְׂרָאֵל. אָמֵן.

FOR A GIRL:

וִיהִי רָצוֹן

מִלְּפָנֶי אָבִינוּ שֶׁבַּשָׁמַיִם,
שֶׁיִּתֵּן בְּלִבֵּךְ אַהֲבָתוֹ
וְיִרְאָתוֹ. וְתִהְיֶה יִרְאַת
יהוה עַל פָּנַיִךְ כָּל יָמַיִךְ,
שֶׁלֹּא תֶחֱטָאִי. וִיהִי
חֶשְׁקֵךְ בַּתּוֹרָה וּבַמִּצְוֹת.
עֵינַיִךְ לְנֹכַח יַבִּיטוּ;[1] פִּיךְ
יְדַבֵּר חָכְמוֹת;[2] וְלִבֵּךְ
יֶהְגֶּה אֵימוֹת;[3] יָדַיִךְ
יַעַסְקוּ בְמִצְוֹת; רַגְלַיִךְ
יָרוּצוּ לַעֲשׂוֹת רְצוֹן
אָבִיךְ שֶׁבַּשָׁמַיִם. יִתֵּן לָךְ
בָּנִים וּבָנוֹת, צַדִּיקִים
וְצִדְקָנִיּוֹת, עוֹסְקִים
בַּתּוֹרָה וּבְמִצְוֹת כָּל
יְמֵיהֶם. וִיהִי מְקוֹרֵךְ
בָּרוּךְ.[4] וְיַזְמִין לָךְ
פַּרְנָסָתֵךְ בְּהֶתֵּר בְּנַחַת
וּבְרֶוַח, מִתַּחַת יָדוֹ
הָרְחָבָה, וְלֹא עַל יְדֵי
מַתְּנַת בָּשָׂר וָדָם;
פַּרְנָסָה שֶׁתִּהְיִי פְנוּיָה
לַעֲבוֹדַת יהוה. וְתִכָּתְבִי
וְתֵחָתְמִי לְחַיִּים טוֹבִים
וַאֲרוּכִים, בְּתוֹךְ כָּל
צַדִּיקֵי יִשְׂרָאֵל. אָמֵן.

וִיהִי רָצוֹן *May it be the will of our Father in heaven, that He instill in your heart His love and reverence. May the fear of HASHEM be upon your face all your days, in order that you not sin. May your craving be for the Torah and the commandments. May your eyes gaze toward truth;*[3] *may your mouth speak wisdom;*[4] *may your heart meditate with awe;*[5] *may your hands engage in the commandments; may your feet run to do the will of your Father in heaven. May He grant you righteous sons and daughters who engage in the Torah and the commandments all their days. May the source of your posterity be blessed.*[6] *May He arrange your livelihood for you in a permissible way, with contentment and with relief, from beneath His generous hand, and not through the gifts of flesh and blood; a livelihood that will free you to serve HASHEM. And may you be inscribed and sealed for a good, long life, among all the righteous of Israel. Amen.*

---

(1) *Proverbs* 4:25. (2) Cf. *Psalms* 49:4. (3) Cf. *Isaiah* 33:18. (4) Cf. *Proverbs* 5:18.

is all worthless. Therefore the blessings are sealed with the gift of peace (*Sifra*). As the Sages taught in the very last Mishnah (*Uktzin* 3:12): "The Holy One, Blessed is He, could find no container capable of holding blessing except peace, as it says; HASHEM *will give might to His people,* HASHEM *will bless his people with peace"* (*Psalms* 29:11).

Thus we find that שָׁלוֹם, *peace,* is the last word in the Priestly Blessing; the last word in *Bircas HaMazon* (Grace after Meals); the last word in the essential part of the *Amidah;* the last word in the Mishnah; and the theme of the last verse of *Kaddish.*

וִיהִי רָצוֹן — *May it be the will.* One should bless his children that he merit to raise them to Torah, marriage, and good deeds; that they be truly God fearing with no ulterior motives but with complete sincerity; that they live long lives dedicated to the service of God and to His Torah in utter truth; that they have children and grandchildren who will engage sincerely in Torah and the commandments; and that they merit both tables [i.e., spiritual and material wealth and comfort] according to God's abundant compassion and unlimited kindness (*Besamim Rosh*).

ᴇ§ Kol Nidrei — Prelude to Yom Kippur

The emotion-laden chanting of *Kol Nidrei* in its moving, centuries-old melody begins the Yom Kippur service at a feverish pitch. Although *Kol Nidrei's* author is unknown, its text dates back at least to the ninth century, and is found in the *Seder Rav Amram Gaon* of that period. It is recited in all Ashkenazic and the great majority of Sephardic communities. Although *Kol Nidrei* is not part of *Maariv* — rather, it is a separate service whose purpose will be discussed below — the entire evening service is commonly referred to as that of 'Kol Nidrei Night.' Perhaps the most surprising thing of all is why the most solemn day of the year begins with a prayer that is not even a prayer. *Kol Nidrei* makes no mention of repentance and seems to be no more than an attempt to free oneself from past or future vows (see below). Two explanations are offered, one rational and one kabbalistic.

(1) *Kol Nidrei* emphasizes for us the extreme gravity that the Torah attaches not only to formal vows and oaths, but to the general concept that one must keep his word. The Talmud teaches that vows should be avoided (*Nedarim* 22a) and that violation of vows can lead to the death of loved ones (*Shabbos* 32b). Consequently, when we preface the Yom Kippur prayers not with pleas for forgiveness, but with a declaration regarding vows, we are reminding ourselves of the importance of scrupulously honoring our commitments. Thus we begin Yom Kippur with the recognition that a Jew's word is sacred. If he cannot carry out a vow, he must seek nullification through the halachically prescribed means, but under no circumstances may he simply ignore it. It is indicative of the gravity Judaism attaches to vows and promises that the Jew prefaces his Yom Kippur prayers for forgiveness and repentance with *Kol Nidrei*; we cannot make peace with God until we absolve ourselves from the grievous sin of violating our word. It should be stressed, however, that most vows cannot be invalidated by *Kol Nidrei*, as will be explained below.

(2) Kabbalistically, the message of *Kol Nidrei* is addressed primarily as a plea to God. Since the beginning of its national existence, Israel's sins have provoked God to take oaths that He would punish, exile, or even do away with the nation. In the Torah we find Moses interceding with God on more than one occasion on behalf of a sinful Israel. The Talmud relates that Rabba bar Bar Chana heard a heavenly voice saying, "Woe is Me that I have sworn [to exile My people], but now that I have sworn, who can annul it for Me?" (*Bava Basra* 74a). Thus, *Kol Nidrei* implies to God that just as we seek to annul vows we should not have taken, so may He annul His oaths to remove His Presence from His people and His City. This theme is echoed in קָם רַבִּי שִׁמְעוֹן, *R' Shimon stood up*, the kabbalistic selection that some congregations recite before *Kol Nidrei*.

ᴇ§ Nullification of Vows: Past or Present?

When *Kol Nidrei* was composed, its purpose was to nullify vows and oaths that had been made and violated during the *previous* year. While the *Halachah* requires that such oaths be specified, and can be nullified only if the court is satisfied that they were undertaken under some misapprehension, *Kol Nidrei* refers to vows that have been forgotten and for which the standard remedy is impossible. Thus, *Kol Nidrei* is similar to the nullification of vows that is customarily done on Erev Rosh Hashanah. The verse וְנִסְלַח, *May it be forgiven*, that is recited immediately after *Kol Nidrei* is intended as a plea for forgiveness for violations that may have taken place before the nullification. According to this view, *Kol Nidrei* must be phrased in the past tense, since it refers to previous vows, and the text should read מִיּוֹם כִּפּוּרִים שֶׁעָבַר עַד יוֹם כִּפּוּרִים זֶה, *from the past Yom Kippur until this Yom Kippur*.

Rabbeinu Tam forcefully objected on halachic grounds to this formulation. In his opposition, he followed the view of his father, R' Meir ben Shmuel, and the *geonim* R' Natronai and R' Hai. They argued that *Kol Nidrei* did not conform with the halachic procedure of nullification, and thus could not be a valid method of canceling vows. If so, what was the purpose of *Kol Nidrei*? *Rabbeinu Tam*, therefore, advanced a new rationale. *Kol Nidrei* is *not* a nullification of vows made in the past, but a declaration regarding those of the *future*. In this view, *Kol Nidrei* is based on the Talmudic teaching that one may nullify in advance any vows he may make in the future (*Nedarim* 23b). It is as if someone were to declare publicly that his forthcoming pronouncement should have no legal force. According to *Rabbeinu Tam*, the verse וְנִסְלַח, *May it be forgiven*, that is recited after *Kol Nidrei*, is not a plea for forgiveness — since no sin has yet been committed. Rather, the verse is an expression of hope that the *Kol Nidrei* declaration will help one avoid the grievous sin of unfulfilled vows. Furthermore, according to *Rabbeinu Tam*, *Kol Nidrei* refers to the future and the text must reflect this fact. Therefore, his text reads מִיּוֹם כִּפּוּרִים זֶה עַד יוֹם כִּפּוּרִים הַבָּא עָלֵינוּ לְטוֹבָה, *from this Yom Kippur until the next Yom Kippur, may it come upon us for good*.

Most authorities and congregations have adopted *Rabbeinu Tam's* interpretation and reading. However, the original version has many defenders among the commentators (see *Rosh, Yoma* 8:28; and *Tur Orach Chaim* 619). *R' Yaakov Emden* and *Chayei Adam* rule that it is preferable to accommodate both views. Accordingly, our text includes a bracketed insert that refers to the previous year's vows.

Kol Nidrei must be recited before evening because of the opinion that it is a nullification of existing vows. As such, it is a formal act of *beis din*, and all such legal pronouncements must be made during the day. In many congregations the *Kol Nidrei* service is prolonged so that *Maariv* can begin immediately as it is concluded. In other congregations there is a pause after *Kol Nidrei* — during which individuals recite Psalms, study Tractate *Yoma*, or other appropriate subjects — and *Maariv* is begun after dark.

⋖§ Nullification Valid Only for Specific Vows

There is a dangerous and erroneous misconception among some people that the *Kol Nidrei* nullification of vows — whether past or future, depending on the above opinions — gives people the right to break their word or to make insincere promises that will have no legal force. This is not the case. The *Kol Nidrei* declaration can invalidate only vows that one undertakes on his own volition. It has *no* effect on vows or oaths imposed by someone else, a court, or a gentile. Also, the invalidation of future vows takes effect only if someone makes the vow without having in mind his previous *Kol Nidrei* declaration. But if he makes the vow with *Kol Nidrei* in mind — thus being openly insincere in his vow — the vow is in full force.

⋖§ Torah Scrolls During Kol Nidrei

Tur (ibid.) cites a custom that the *chazzan* holds a Torah Scroll while reciting *Kol Nidrei*. *Arizal* expounds upon the importance of this custom and teaches that it is very meritorious for one or more Scrolls to be carried around the synagogue so that everyone can kiss them. *R' Yaakov Emden* writes that all the Scrolls should be removed from the Ark before *Kol Nidrei* and that those holding them should kiss and caress them, while confessing their sins. This display of love for the Torah influences people to repent and is a source of merit for them. The honor of holding the first Scroll is a very great privilege and is auctioned off in some congregations, where it is known as the *Kol Nidrei Torah. Yesod V'Shoresh HaAvodah* teaches that it is a source of merit to hold any of the Scrolls, especially the first one, during *Kol Nidrei.* The Scrolls are returned to the Ark immediately after *Kol Nidrei.*

⋅◈ Permission to Transgressors:
עַל דַּעַת הַמָּקוֹם/With the Approval of the Omnipresent

As part of its responsibility to foster compliance with Torah Law, a congregation has the right to ban transgressors from prayer in the synagogue or other interaction with the community. On the other hand, the Sages teach: A public fast in which Jewish sinners do not take part is no fast. This is derived from the fact that חֶלְבְּנָה, *galbanum,* which has a foul aroma, was included among the spices of the Temple incense (*Kereisos* 6b). *Rabbeinu Bachya* (*Exodus* 30:34) explains:

This is meant to show us that we should not ignore the sinners of Israel and exclude them from our fasts and prayers, for whenever transgressors repent, atone for their sins, and join with the righteous, the Name of God is sanctified. Otherwise, the righteous would be accountable for the sinners, because all Jews are responsible for one another.

Therefore even in the event that transgressors may have been banned for the rest of the year, they should be admitted to the congregation for the Yom Kippur services.

This dispensation is proclaimed formally just before *Kol Nidrei* through a formula introduced by R' Meir of Rothenburg. The rabbi or *chazzan* recites, עַל דַּעַת הַמָּקוֹם, *With the approval of the Omnipresent . . .*

⋅◈ The Three People at the Amud

The *chazzan* or rabbi is flanked by two leaders of the congregation, for the following reasons:

The declaration admitting transgressors is of a formal, legal nature, and therefore requires a 'court' of three.

Mechilta 17:10 states that just as Moses was flanked by Aaron and Chur when he prayed for Israel during the Amalekite attack, so too three people should represent the congregation on public fasts.

Others hold that *Kol Nidrei* itself requires a *beis din* of three, because it is a nullification of vows.

⋅◈ The Three-Time Recitation of Kol Nidrei

Kol Nidrei is recited three times by the *chazzan* and, quietly but in unison with the *chazzan,* by the congregation. Furthermore, each time the *chazzan* recites it, he does so more loudly than the previous time. Various reasons are offered for these customs:

(1) It is common for important prayers and declarations to be recited three times for emphasis (see *Menachos* 65a). Thus, both the declaration inviting transgressors to pray with the congregation and *Kol Nidrei* itself are recited three times. Since *Kol*

Nidrei is a declaration nullifying future vows (according to the generally accepted view of *Rabbeinu Tam* cited above), each congregant must recite it, for only the individual involved can make such a declaration about himself. It is customary, therefore, for everyone to recite it quietly with the *chazzan*.

(2) In this necessity for individual recitation, *Levush (Orach Chaim* 619) finds a further reason for the three-fold repetition. The second and third recitations by the *chazzan* are intended to remind members of the congregation to join in the nullification in case they have not done so. According to *Levush*, this is also why each recitation by the *chazzan* is said louder than the one before: to stress to the congregation that everyone should join in the declaration. *Maharal* writes that the increasing volume of the *chazzan's* voice is meant to intensify the congregation's mood of awe and prayer.

(3) *Machzor Vitry* writes:

The first time he should utter it softly like someone hesitating before entering the king's palace to beg for a favor from someone he is afraid to approach. The second time [as he gains confidence] he may speak a bit more loudly. The third time he may speak even more loudly, like someone who feels comfortable in the royal court and approaches his king like a friend.

◄§ Like Angels: Standing, Unity, Kittel and Tallis

Several of the widely adopted customs of the Yom Kippur services are based on the account in the ancient midrashic work, *Pirkei d'Rabbi Eliezer* (ch. 46), that compares Israel on Yom Kippur to the angels, because the people have repented and are free of sin:

When Satan sees that [Israel] is free of sin on Yom Kippur, he says before [God], 'Master of the universe, just as the ministering angels have no knee-joints [and consequently cannot sit], so Jews stand on Yom Kippur. Just as the ministering angels neither eat nor drink, so the Jews neither eat nor drink on Yom Kippur. Just as the ministering angels are united in peace, so the Jews are united in peace on Yom Kippur.'

This comparison of Israel to the angels is the source of several Yom Kippur practices: Many devout people stand during the services as much as they can. Just as the angels are at peace with one another, so Jews ask one another for forgiveness. Jews don the white *kittel* and *tallis* prior to the *Kol Nidrei* service in imitation of the angels who are dressed in white, as it were (see *Daniel* 10:5). Another outgrowth of Israel's similarity to the angels is the Yom Kippur practice of loudly reciting בָּרוּךְ שֵׁם כְּבוֹד מַלְכוּתוֹ לְעוֹלָם וָעֶד, *Blessed is the name of His glorious Kingdom for all eternity*, which is a praise associated with the angels. The *Midrash (Devarim Rabbah* 2:36) relates that when Moses ascended to heaven, he heard the angels using this verse to praise God. He learned it and taught it to Israel. [See commentary on pages 69-70.]

Other reasons for wearing the white *kittel* and *tallis* are to give honor to the solemn day and — because the dead are buried wearing *kittel* and *tallis* — to remind us that death and judgment are inevitable. This is a powerful stimulant to repentance *(Rama, Orach Chaim* 610:4). Women, too, have adapted the custom of wearing something white for the above reason *(Mishnah Berurah*, ibid.).

Another reason for wearing the *tallis* in the evening is because the Thirteen Attributes of Mercy [י"ג מדות], which are part of *Maariv*, should be recited while one is wearing a *tallis (Magen Avraham* 18:2).

Two or more Torah Scrolls are removed from the Ark. In most congregations, the Scrolls are carried around the synagogue so that each person may kiss the Torah. All but two Scrolls are returned to the Ark. The *chazzan* is flanked by the rabbi and another prominent member of the congregation, each holding a Torah.

The following verse is recited aloud responsively several times:

אוֹר זָרֻעַ לַצַּדִּיק, וּלְיִשְׁרֵי לֵב שִׂמְחָה.¹

In some congregations, the following passage from *Tikkunei Zohar* is recited at this point. Other congregations proceed directly to *Kol Nidrei*.

קָם רַבִּי שִׁמְעוֹן סָלִיק יָדוֹי לְגַבֵּי עֵלָּא, וְשַׁבַּח לְמָארֵי
עָלְמָא, וְאָמַר, רִבּוֹן עָלְמִין, עָבִיד בְּגִין
שְׁכִינְתָּא, דְּאִיהִי בְּגָלוּתָא. וְאִם אִיהִי בְּאוּמָאָה, הָא אַבָּא
וְאִמָּא, דְּאִינּוּן חָכְמָה וּבִינָה, יָכְלִין לְמֶעְבַּד הַתָּרָה. הֲדָא הוּא
דִּכְתִיב: יהוה צְבָאוֹת יָעָץ, וּמִי יָפֵר.² אִם הַתַּלְמִיד אוֹמֵי, הָרַב
יָכִיל לְמֶעְבַּד הַתָּרָה. וְאִם נָדַר אוֹ נִשְׁבַּע בֵּן, דְּאִיהוּ ו', דְּלָא
יִפְרוֹק לָהּ אֶלָּא דְּתֶהֱא בְּגָלוּתָא עַד זִמְנָא יְדִיעָא. וְנֶדֶר אוֹ
שְׁבוּעָה אִיהוּ בִּי"ה, דְּאִינּוּן חָכְמָה וּבִינָה. וְאִיהוּ אִתְחָרַט הָא
תְּלַת בְּנֵי נָשָׁא, יְכִילִין לְמִפְטַר לֵיהּ. וְאִינּוּן תְּלַת אַבָּהָן לְעֵלָּא
לְקַבְלֵיהוּ. וְאִם לָא תִתְחָרַט, אֲנָא בָּעֵינָא מִינָךְ וּמִכָּל אִינּוּן
דְּמְתִיבְתָּא, דִּלְעֵלָּא וְתַתָּא, דְּתַעֲבֵד בְּגִין רַעֲיָא מְהֵימְנָא, דְּלָא
זָז מִשְּׁכִינְתָּא בְּכָל אֲתַר, וְאִיהוּ עָאל שְׁלָם בֵּינָךְ וּבֵינָהּ זִמְנִין
סַגִּיאִין, וּמָסַר גַּרְמֵיהּ לְמִיתָה בְּגִינָהּ, וּבְגִין בְּנָהָא, הֲדָא הוּא
דִּכְתִיב: וְאִם אַיִן, מְחֵנִי נָא מִסִּפְרְךָ אֲשֶׁר כָּתָבְתָּ.³

וְאִם הוּא נֶדֶר מִסְּטְרָא דְּאַבָּא וְאִמָּא וְלָא בָּעֵי, אֲנָא סָלִיק
לְגַבֵּי הַהוּא דְּאִתְּמַר בֵּיהּ: כִּי יִפָּלֵא מִמְּךָ דָּבָר.⁴ דְּאִתְּמַר בֵּיהּ:
בְּמִפְלָא מִמְּךָ אַל תִּדְרוֹשׁ,⁵ דְּיִפְטוֹר נֶדֶר.

אוֹר זָרֻעַ לַצַּדִּיק ◆ — *Light is sown for the righteous.* Spiritual light — the reward for good deeds and the personal perfection that is their natural result — is like seeds sown in fertile soil (*Rashi; Radak*). It is because of this inspiring and optimistic message that this verse was chosen to inaugurate the Yom Kippur service.

The Talmud (*Taanis* 15a) teaches that only the *upright* are worthy of *gladness*, unlike the *righteous* who have only *light*, but not gladness. *Sfas Emes* explains that upright people are those who remain wholesome and retain their faith that whatever God does is good and holy, even though there are many events whose purpose they do not understand. As a result, nothing can shake the constant *gladness* of upright people. Righteous people, however, may not have this degree

Two or more Torah Scrolls are removed from the Ark. In most congregations, the Scrolls are carried around the synagogue so that each person may kiss the Torah. All but two Scrolls are returned to the Ark. The *chazzan* is flanked by the rabbi and another prominent member of the congregation, each holding a Torah.

The following verse is recited aloud responsively several times:

Light is sown for the righteous; and for the upright of heart, gladness.[1]

In some congregations, the following passage from *Tikkunei Zohar* is recited at this point. Other congregations proceed directly to *Kol Nidrei*.

קָם רַבִּי שִׁמְעוֹן *R' Shimon stood up, raised his hands upward, and praised the Lord of the universe saying: Master of the universe! Act for the sake of the Shechinah [Divine Presence], which is in exile. And if [the Shechinah] is under an oath [to remain in exile] then Abba and Imma, which are [also known as the sefiros of] Chachmah and Binah, can effect a dispensation. This is as it is written: HASHEM, Master of Legions, has proposed [the oath], who can nullify?[2] If the disciple has sworn, then the master can effect a dispensation. But what if Ben [son], who is also vav, has made a neder or an oath not to redeem [the Shechinah], but rather that [the Shechinah] remain in exile until a certain period? — Now a neder or oath emanates from the letters yud and hei [of the Four-Letter Name], which correspond to Chachmah and Binah. If he [i.e., Ben] regrets it, then three people can release him. They are the three Patriarchs [who are] above and parallel to [the three lower sefiros: Chessed, Gevurah and Tiferes]. But if he does not regret [the oath to keep the Shechinah in exile], then I beseech You and all of the tribunals — the upper and lower — that You act for the sake of the Faithful Shepherd [Moses] who never departed from the Shechinah anywhere, and made peace between her [the Shechinah] and You many times, and risked death for her [the Shechinah] and her children. This is as it is written: And if not, erase me from Your book that You have written.[3]*

However, if there is a neder from the side of Abba and Imma [Chachmah and Binah] so that [the neder] cannot be [annulled by the sefiros below it], then I will come up to that [sefirah] — regarding which it is said: If a thing be hidden from you;[4] and regarding which it is said: Onto what is hidden from you do not investigate[5] [i.e., Keser, the highest sefirah] — to effect a dispensation of the neder.

(1) *Psalms* 97:11. (2) *Isaiah* 14:27. (3) *Exodus* 32:32.
(4) *Deuteronomy* 17:8. (5) See Tractate *Chagigah* 13a.

---

of equanimity. Nevertheless, though the righteous may sometimes be unhappy, they benefit from the growing spiritual light of all the good they do.

◦§ קָם רַבִּי שִׁמְעוֹן — *R' Shimon stood up.* This refers to R' Shimon bar Yochai, one of the greatest of the *Tannaim* [i.e., the rabbis of the Mishnah] and the author of

וְאַף עַל גַּב דִּשְׁכִינְתָּא אִיהִי בְּגָלוּתָא לְגַבֵּי בַּעֲלָהּ כְּנִדָּה,
דְּאִיהוּ יַפְרִישׁ בֵּין דָּם לְדָם,[1] וְאִתְפְּתַח מְקוֹרָא דִּילָהּ לְדַכְּאָה
לָהּ בְּמַיִם דְּאוֹרַיְתָא; מַיִם חַיִּים דְּלָא פָסְקִין. וְאַפְרֵישׁ מִינָהּ דַּם
נִדָּה דְּאִיהִי לֵילִית, דְּלָא אִתְקְרִיבַת בַּהֲדָהּ, דְּאִיהוּ חוּבָא
דִּנְשָׁמָתָא. דְּסָאִיבַת לָהּ וְלֵית לָהּ רְשׁוּ לְסַלְּקָא נִשְׁמָתָא לְגַבֵּי
בַּעֲלָהּ, לְהַהוּא אֲתָר דְּאִתְיְהִיבַת מִתַּמָּן. וְאִתְדָּנַת בֵּין דִּין
לְדִין,[1] בֵּין דִּינֵי נַפְשׁוֹת לְדִינֵי מָמוֹנוֹת, דְּאִית מַאן דְּפָרַע
בְּמָמוֹנֵיהּ, וְאִית מַאן דְּפָרַע בְּנַפְשֵׁיהּ.

וּבֵין נֶגַע לָנֶגַע,[1] כְּמָה דְאוּקְמוּהוּ: אֵיכָה יָשְׁבָה בָדָד,[2]
דְּאִיהִי חֲשִׁיבָא שְׁכִינְתָּא בְּגָלוּתָא כִּמְצוֹרָע, דְּאִתְּמַר בֵּהּ: בָּדָד
יֵשֵׁב מִחוּץ לַמַּחֲנֶה,[3] מִחוּץ וַדַּאי דָא גָלוּתָא, דְּאִיהִי לְבַר
מֵאַרְעָא דְיִשְׂרָאֵל, דְּאִיהִי מוֹתְבָא דְּאָת (ה'). וְאִי מְקוֹרָא לָא
יָכִיל לְמִפְתַּח, עַד דְּיִפְתַּח לֵיהּ הַהוּא דְּסָגִיר לֵיהּ, אֲנָא
מְפַיֵּסְנָא לֵיהּ בְּגִין (יוּ"ד ה"א וא"ו ה"א) דְּאִיהוּ יְחוּדָא
(דִּיחוּדֵיהּ תַּמָּן) וּבְגִין לְבוּשִׁין דְּאִתְלַבַּשׁ. מִיַּד אִתְפַּתְּחַת
מְקוֹרָהּ וְאִתְדַּכִּיאַת שְׁכִינְתָּא. וְרָזָא דְמִלָּה: מִקְוֵה יִשְׂרָאֵל
יהוה, מוֹשִׁיעוֹ בְּעֵת צָרָה.[4] מוֹשִׁיעוֹ וַדַּאי, הַהוּא דִּמְקוֹרָא
דְּמִקְוֶה בִּידֵיהּ. אָמֵן.

﴾ כל נדרי ﴿

The chazzan, or one of the men at his side, recites the following three times:

עַל דַּעַת הַמָּקוֹם וְעַל דַּעַת הַקָּהָל, בִּישִׁיבָה שֶׁל
מַעְלָה, וּבִישִׁיבָה שֶׁל מַטָּה, אָנוּ מַתִּירִין
לְהִתְפַּלֵּל עִם הָעֲבַרְיָנִים.

---

the Zohar. This selection from *Tikkunei Zohar* is esoteric in the extreme. Neither the translation nor a concise commentary can give more than a very general idea of its meaning. As noted in the introduction (p. 130), this selection, like *Kol Nidrei* itself, implies that God, too, can annul His oaths, as it were. Specifically, we express the subtle hope that He will annul the oath that prevents the Redemption of Israel.

﴾ כָּל נִדְרֵי / KOL NIDREI ﴿

עַל דַּעַת הַמָּקוֹם — *With the approval of the Omnipresent.* This is a formal declaration through which the elders of the congregation invite the participation even of transgressors who may have been excluded from the synagogue. On Yom Kippur, all Jews must join together to pray and repent. [See 'Permission to Transgressors,' p. 132.]

Although the Shechinah when in exile is like a niddah to her 'husband,' nevertheless, it [Keser] will differentiate 'between [undefiled] blood and [defiled] blood,'[1] and will open the wellspring to purify [the Shechinah] with the waters of the Torah — fresh waters that do not fail. It will remove from [the Shechinah] the blood of niddah that corresponds to Lilis, to which one may not come near for she is detrimental to the soul. She defiles the soul so that she has no right to come up to her husband, to that place from which she was given. And she is judged 'between one punishment and another punishment,'[1] which means between capital punishment and monetary punishment, for some are punished with monetary fines and some are punished with [loss of] life.

'And between affliction and affliction,'[1] for as we have interpreted the verse: Alas! She sits in solitude,[2] [i.e.,] She, the Shechinah, while in exile is considered a metzora regarding whom it is said: In solitude shall he sit outside of the camp,[3] surely outside refers to the dispersion outside of Eretz Yisrael, which is the dwelling of the letter hei [i.e., the sefirah of Keser]. But if the wellspring cannot be opened until he who has shut it [the sefirah of Yesod] reopens it, then I appease it for the sake of the Four-letter Name, because His unification is in it, and for the sake of the vestments in which it is garbed. Immediately [the Shechinah] wellspring opens and the Shechinah is purified. The secret of the matter is: The hope of Israel [is] HASHEM, its Savior in time of trouble.[4] Surely its Savior is He in Whose hands is the wellspring and the hope. Amen.

❧ KOL NIDREI ❧

The *chazzan,* or one of the men at his side, recites the following three times:

עַל דַּעַת *With the approval of the Omnipresent and with the approval of the congregation; in the convocation of the Court above and in the convocation of the Court below, we sanction prayer with the transgressors.*

---

(1) *Deuteronomy* 17:8. (2) *Lamentations* 1:1.
(3) *Leviticus* 13:46. (4) Cf. *Jeremiah* 17:13 and 14:8.

In some texts the phrase order of this declaration is reversed: בִּישִׁיבָה שֶׁל מַעְלָה, וּבִישְׁבָה שֶׁל מַטָּה, עַל דַּעַת הַמָּקוֹם, וְעַד דַּעַת הַקָּהָל, *In the convocation of the Court above and in the convocation of the Court below; with the approval of the Omnipresent and with the approval of the congregation, we sanction . . .*

בִּישִׁיבָה שֶׁל מַעְלָה — *In the convocation of the Court above.* This special permission is declared by the leaders of the congregation on behalf of both the Heavenly and earthly assemblies. It should be understood, however, that this invitation to transgressors does not imply that their sins are automatically forgiven. Only

The *chazzan* recites *Kol Nidrei* aloud three times, each time louder than before, and the congregation recites along with him in an undertone.
[Some congregations add the bracketed phrase.]

כָּל נִדְרֵי, וֶאֱסָרֵי, וּשְׁבוּעֵי, וַחֲרָמֵי, וְקוֹנָמֵי, וְקִנּוּסֵי, וְכִנּוּיֵי, דְּאִנְדַּרְנָא, וּדְאִשְׁתַּבַּעְנָא, וּדְאַחֲרִמְנָא, וּדְאָסַרְנָא עַל נַפְשָׁתָנָא. מִיּוֹם כִּפּוּרִים [שֶׁעָבַר עַד יוֹם כִּפּוּרִים זֶה, וּמִיּוֹם כִּפּוּרִים] זֶה עַד יוֹם כִּפּוּרִים הַבָּא עָלֵינוּ לְטוֹבָה. בְּכֻלְּהוֹן אִחֲרַטְנָא בְהוֹן. כֻּלְּהוֹן יְהוֹן שָׁרָן, שְׁבִיקִין, שְׁבִיתִין, בְּטֵלִין וּמְבֻטָּלִין, לָא שְׁרִירִין וְלָא קַיָּמִין. נִדְרָנָא לָא נִדְרֵי, וֶאֱסָרָנָא לָא אֱסָרֵי, וּשְׁבוּעָתָנָא לָא שְׁבוּעוֹת.

personal repentance can accomplish that.

✤ **כָּל נִדְרֵי** — *All vows.* As noted in the introduction, *Kol Nidrei* is a declaration that deals with the various categories of vows and oaths. Several examples are specified, as follows:

נִדְרֵי — *Vows.* A vow through which one accepts a prohibition upon himself. In the standard form of a *neder* one says: This item should be forbidden as if it were a קָרְבָּן, *Temple offering.* By saying this, the person making the vow declares that all prohibitions forbidding the use of an offering should apply to the item in question.

וֶאֱסָרֵי — *Prohibitions.* This, too, is a *neder*, whereby one imposes a prohibition upon himself simply by saying, for example, 'All apples are hereby forbidden to me.'

וּשְׁבוּעֵי — *Oaths.* By means of a *shevuah*-oath, one obligates himself either to do or to refrain from doing or enjoying some-

thing. The difference between a *neder* and a *shevuah* is that a *neder* alters the status of the object (i.e., this apple becomes forbidden to me), while a *shevuah* alters the status of the person (i.e., I am forbidden to enjoy the apple).

וַחֲרָמֵי — *Consecrations.* This is a specific form of declaration that was used to sanctify something as the property of the *Kohanim* or of the Temple.

וְקוֹנָמֵי וְקִנּוּסֵי — *Konam-vows, konas-vows.* Essentially these are substitute terms for the word *korban*, offering. Thus they are substitutes for the classic *neder* form of 'This should be forbidden to me as if it were a קָרְבָּן, offering.' According to R' Yochanan, these words are foreign language equivalents for the word 'offering.' According to Reish Lakish, they are slang terms devised by the Sages. The Sages invented these expressions because it was common for people to use the Scrip-

The chazzan recites Kol Nidrei aloud three times, each time louder than before,
and the congregation recites along with him in an undertone.
[Some congregations add the bracketed phrase.]

כָּל נִדְרֵי *All vows, prohibitions, oaths, conse-crations, konam-vows, konas-vows, or equivalent terms that we may vow, swear, consecrate, or prohibit upon ourselves — [from the past Yom Kippur until this Yom Kippur, and] from this Yom Kippur until the next Yom Kippur, may it come upon us for good — regarding them all, we regret them henceforth. They all will be permitted, abandoned, canceled, null and void, without power and without standing. Our vows shall not be valid vows; our prohibitions shall not be valid prohibitions; and our oaths shall not be valid oaths.*

tural term קָרְבָּן לַה', a *korban to* HASHEM, and the Sages wished to discourage the unnecessary use of God's Name (*Nedarim* 10a).

וְכִנּוּיֵי — *Or equivalent terms.* Although there are standard terms used to effect a *neder,* such as *korban* or *nazir,* corruptions of these terms are also acceptable, provided their intent is clear. *Konam* and *konas* are examples of such equivalents. Another example is the use of *nazik* or *naziach* instead of *nazir* (*Nedarim* 2a and *Nazir* 2a).

דְּאַנְדְּרָנָא ... — *That we may vow ...* The form and translation of this group of words is part of the controversy whether *Kol Nidrei* refers to past or future vows, as explained in the introduction. The literal translation of דְּאַנְדְּרָנָא is *we have vowed,* in the past tense. Since most communities have adopted *Rabbeinu Tam's* version that *Kol Nidrei* refers to future vows, many authorities have changed דְּאַנְדְּרָנָא to the future tense [דִּי נַדִירְנָא], but

this change has not gained common acceptance. Our translation in the *future* tense, therefore, is not literal, but follows the context of *Kol Nidrei,* as interpreted by *Rabbeinu Tam* and most commentators.

מִיּוֹם כִּפּוּרִים שֶׁעָבַר — *From the past Yom Kippur.* The *Vilna Gaon* and R' *Yaakov Emden* interpolated this phrase, so that *Kol Nidrei* would refer both to past and to future vows. According to those who make this interpolation, the word דְּאַנְדְּרָנָא, as noted above, would be translated literally: *that we have vowed.*

כָּלְהוֹן יְהוֹן שָׁרָן — *They all will be permitted.* The word *all* is not meant literally. This declaration is valid only regarding vows that one makes of his own volition. **Note:** This declaration does *not* apply to vows or oaths imposed by someone else. Nor does it apply to vows or oaths made at the behest of a non-Jew or a court (*Yoreh Deah* 211:4; *Be'er Hagolah;* see introductory remarks).

Chazzan three times, then congregation three times:

וְנִסְלַח לְכָל עֲדַת בְּנֵי יִשְׂרָאֵל וְלַגֵּר הַגָּר
בְּתוֹכָם, כִּי לְכָל הָעָם בִּשְׁגָגָה.[1]

Chazzan:

סְלַח נָא לַעֲוֹן הָעָם הַזֶּה כְּגֹדֶל חַסְדֶּךָ,
וְכַאֲשֶׁר נָשָׂאתָה לָעָם הַזֶּה מִמִּצְרַיִם
וְעַד הֵנָּה,[2] וְשָׁם נֶאֱמַר:

Congregation three times, then chazzan three times:

וַיֹּאמֶר יהוה סָלַחְתִּי כִּדְבָרֶךָ.[3]

The *chazzan* recites the following blessing aloud. All members of the congregation, except those who recited this blessing at candle lighting, recite it along with the *chazzan* in an undertone. The congregation should finish slightly before the *chazzan* so that they may respond אָמֵן to his blessing.

בָּרוּךְ אַתָּה יהוה אֱלֹהֵינוּ מֶלֶךְ הָעוֹלָם,
שֶׁהֶחֱיָנוּ וְקִיְּמָנוּ וְהִגִּיעָנוּ לַזְּמַן הַזֶּה.

(אָמֵן. –Cong.)

וְנִסְלַח§ — *May it be forgiven.* The Scriptural context of this verse refers to a case where the Sanhedrin rules erroneously that an idolatrous practice is permitted, and the entire nation sins as a result. A sin-offering is brought on behalf of the nation, upon which it is forgiven (*Numbers* 15:22-26). The verse is borrowed and used here in connection with unwitting violation of vows. We beg forgiveness for possible past violations of vows and express the hope that we may never transgress this grievous sin.

סְלַח נָא§ — *Please forgive.* The spies Moses had sent on a reconnaissance mission to the Land of Canaan returned with an evil report about the Land. When the Israelites heard the slanderous tidings, they believed what they were told and they rebelled. God then threatened to eradicate all of Israel, leaving only Moses to rebuild the great nation He had promised would spring from Abraham, Isaac and Jacob.

Moses' supplication and God's response

have become one of the basic themes of the Yom Kippur liturgy.

סְלַח נָא לַעֲוֹן הָעָם הַזֶּה כְּגֹדֶל חַסְדֶּךָ וְכַאֲשֶׁר נָשָׂאתָה לָעָם הַזֶּה מִמִּצְרַיִם וְעַד הֵנָּה. וַיֹּאמֶר ה' סָלַחְתִּי כִּדְבָרֶךָ.

"*Please forgive the iniquity of this people according to the greatness of Your kindness, and as You have forgiven this people since [the time they left] Egypt and to this point.*"

And HASHEM said, "I have forgiven according to your words."

A novel interpretation of God's response is based on the Mishnah (*Sotah* 1:7): בְּמִדָּה שֶׁאָדָם מוֹדֵד, בָּהּ מוֹדְדִין לוֹ, *According to the standard in which one behaves, so is he treated [by Heaven].* That is, in whatever manner one conducts himself, whether positively or negatively, Divine judgment deals with him in a similar manner. For example Absalom, son of King David, was an extremely handsome man who gloried in his beautiful hair (see *II Samuel* 14:25-26). This fed his vanity to the point that he decided to take the throne

Chazzan three times, then congregation three times:

וְנִסְלַח *May it be forgiven for the entire congregation of the Children of Israel and for the stranger who dwells among them, for [the sin] befell the entire nation through carelessness.*[1]

Chazzan:

סְלַח *Please forgive the iniquity of this people according to the greatness of Your kindness, and as You have forgiven this people since Egypt and to this point.*[2] *And there it was said:*

Congregation three times, then chazzan three times:

And HASHEM said, 'I have forgiven according to your words.'[3]

The *chazzan* recites the following blessing aloud. All members of the congregation, except those who recited this blessing at candle lighting, recite it along with the *chazzan* in an undertone. The congregation should finish slightly before the *chazzan* so that they may respond *Amen* to his blessing.

בָּרוּךְ *Blessed are You, HASHEM, our God, King of the universe, Who has kept us alive, sustained us, and brought us to this season.* (Cong. – Amen.)

---

(1) *Numbers* 15:26. (2) 14:19. (3) 14:20.

away from his father. After his initial success, Absalom and his army were defeated by David (ibid. chs. 15-18). As Absalom fled his debacle, his hair got tangled in a low-hanging branch. It was there that Joab, David's general, found Absalom and killed him. The beautiful hair that had led him astray became the instrument of his undoing.

In our verse, this principle applies in the following manner: God answers one's prayers in direct proportion to one's request. He forgives in a measure commensurate with the depth of concentration and intent (כַּוָנָה) with which the penitent imbues his confession, and according to the degree of his seeking to return to God. Thus says God, "סָלַחְתִּי, *I have forgiven.*" And then He adds, "כִּדְבָרֶךָ, [but only] *according to* [the depths of] *your words*" (Botzina Dinhora).

סָלַחְתִּי – *I have forgiven.* Just as God forgave Israel then, we hope that He will forgive us this Yom Kippur.

◆§ שֶׁהֶחֱיָנוּ / The Shehecheyanu Blessing

As in the case of all seasonal commandments, such as the Festival observances, the שֶׁהֶחֱיָנוּ blessing is required. In it we thank God for keeping us alive so that we can perform the commandment again. In the case of the other festivals, *Shehecheyanu* is deferred until *Kiddush*, so that it can be recited in conjunction with the feast that celebrates the joy of the day. On Yom Kippur, when there is no *Kiddush*, the blessing is recited as the day is about to begin.

The congregation [except those who have recited this blessing at the candle lighting] should recite it quietly, together with the *chazzan*, but finish it a bit before him so that all can answer *Amen*.

אָבִינוּ מַלְכֵּנוּ ﴾

Avinu Malkeinu / Our Father, Our King

The Talmud relates the following incident regarding the origin of the אָבִינוּ מַלְכֵּנוּ prayers:

[In a year of drought,] Rabbi Eliezer [ben Hyrkanos] once decreed thirteen public fast days [as ordained in the first chapter of *Taanis*], yet no rain fell. After the final fast, the congregation began to disperse. He called out to them rhetorically, "Have you prepared your graves?" Immediately the people burst into tears. And the rains fell.

Another time, Rabbi Eliezer served as *chazzan* and recited twenty-four blessings [the eighteen regular blessings of the daily *Shemoneh Esrei*[1] plus the six extra blessings ordained for fast days in times of drought], but he was not answered. Rabbi Akiva then approached the *chazzan's* lectern and recited:

אָבִינוּ מַלְכֵּנוּ אָבִינוּ אָתָּה, *Our Father, our King, You are our Father.*

אָבִינוּ מַלְכֵּנוּ אֵין לָנוּ מֶלֶךְ אֶלָּא אָתָּה, *Our Father, our King, we have no King but You.*

אָבִינוּ מַלְכֵּנוּ חָטָאנוּ לְפָנֶיךָ, *Our Father, our King, we have sinned before You.*

אָבִינוּ מַלְכֵּנוּ רַחֵם עָלֵינוּ, *Our Father, our King, have compassion upon us.*

אָבִינוּ מַלְכֵּנוּ עֲשֵׂה עִמָּנוּ לְמַעַן שְׁמֶךָ, *Our Father, our King, deal [kindly] with us for Your Name's sake.*

And he was immediately answered.

The Rabbis began discussing this incident. [They concluded that Rabbi Akiva must be greater than his mentor Rabbi Eliezer,] when a heavenly voice resounded: "[This did] not [happen] because this one [Rabbi Akiva] is greater than that one [Rabbi Eliezer]. Rather, [it happened] because this one [Rabbi Akiva] is forgiving of personal slights, while that one [Rabbi Eliezer] is not forgiving of personal slights" (*Taanis* 25b as recorded in *Ein Yaakov*).

To this account, *Machzor Vitry* appends a historical note that explains why Rabbi Akiva's five supplications have grown to over forty sentences, and in the Sefardic rite to over fifty: "When they saw that this prayer [i.e., the verses which begin אָבִינוּ מַלְכֵּנוּ] was answered, they added other verses to it whenever the occasion arose. And they ordained that these verses be recited on days of penitence."

The Ten Days of Repentance beginning with Rosh Hashanah and concluding with Yom Kippur is such a time. The Sages therefore instituted that *Avinu Malkeinu* be recited twice each day during this period — after the *Shemoneh Esrei* of *Shacharis* and after that of *Minchah*; and on Yom Kippur after *Maariv* and *Ne'ilah* as well. On the Sabbath, however, *Avinu Malkeinu* is omitted for a variety of reasons: (a) On the Sabbath, we do not pray for specific needs, the sort with which *Avinu Malkeinu* is filled; (b) *Avinu Malkeinu* was originally composed by R' Akiva for a fast day and time of communal distress, thus it is not appropriate for the Sabbath; and (c) many of the verses of *Avinu Malkeinu* correspond to the thirteen blessings of the middle section of the weekday *Shemoneh Esrei*. [See the accompanying chart.]

---

1. The nineteenth blessing — the one beginning וְלַמַּלְשִׁינִים, *And for the slanderers* — was introduced at a later date when Jewish traitors betrayed our people to the Roman authorities.

Siddur Shaar HaShamayim points out that even supplications for the fulfillment of our basic needs must be recited for the sake of God and not just for our selfish needs. Thus, for example, when one recites the eighth blessing of the *Shemoneh Esrei* — רְפָאֵנוּ, *Heal us* — he should think not merely of the physical comfort and independence that come with good health, but he should also have in mind that he can better serve God in good health than in illness. Similarly, when reciting *Avinu Malkeinu* one must be mindful that, ultimately, our requests to be cleansed from sin, freed from adversity and supplied with all our physical needs (the major themes of *Avinu Malkeinu*) are to enable us to keep God's commandments. Thus, the climax of the *Avinu Malkeinu* supplication comes in the penultimate verse, "... act for the sake of Your great, mighty and awesome Name that is proclaimed upon us" — we ask God to help us as a means of bringing glory to His Name.

שְׁמוֹנֶה עֶשְׂרֵה	אָבִינוּ מַלְכֵּנוּ
חוֹנֵן הַדָּעַת *Gracious Giver of knowledge*	חָנֵּנוּ וַעֲנֵנוּ ... *Be gracious with us and answer us ...*
הָרוֹצֶה בִּתְשׁוּבָה *He Who desires repentance*	הַחֲזִירֵנוּ בִּתְשׁוּבָה שְׁלֵמָה ... *Return us ... in perfect repentance ...*
הַמַּרְבֶּה לִסְלוֹחַ *Who forgives abundantly*	סְלַח וּמְחַל ... *Forgive and pardon ...*
גּוֹאֵל יִשְׂרָאֵל *Redeemer of Israel*	כָּתְבֵנוּ בְּסֵפֶר גְּאֻלָּה ... *Inscribe us in the book of redemption ...*
רוֹפֵא חוֹלֵי עַמּוֹ יִשְׂרָאֵל *He Who heals the sick of His people Israel*	שְׁלַח רְפוּאָה שְׁלֵמָה ... *Send complete recovery ...*
מְבָרֵךְ הַשָּׁנִים *He Who blesses the years*	חַדֵּשׁ עָלֵינוּ שָׁנָה טוֹבָה *Inaugurate upon us a good year*
תְּקַע בְּשׁוֹפָר ... *Sound the shofar ...*	הָרֵם קֶרֶן ... *Raise high the pride (lit., horn) ...*
הָשִׁיבָה ... וְהָסֵר מִמֶּנּוּ יָגוֹן ... *Restore ... remove from us sorrow ...*	בַּטֵּל מֵעָלֵינוּ כָּל גְּזֵרוֹת קָשׁוֹת *Nullify all harsh decrees upon us*
שׁוֹבֵר אֹיְבִים ... *He Who breaks enemies ...*	כַּלֵּה כָּל צַר וּמַשְׂטִין ... *Exterminate every foe and adversary ...*
עַל הַצַּדִּיקִים ... יֶהֱמוּ נָא רַחֲמֶיךָ ... *On the righteous ...* *may Your compassion be aroused ...*	מְחוֹק בְּרַחֲמֶךָ הָרַבִּים ... *Erase through Your abundant* *compassion ...*
וְלִירוּשָׁלַיִם ... וְכִסֵּא דָוִד ... *And to Jerusalem ...* *the throne of David ...*	הָרֵם קֶרֶן מְשִׁיחֶךָ *Raise high the pride of* *Your anointed*
מַצְמִיחַ קֶרֶן יְשׁוּעָה *Who causes the pride of salvation* *to flourish*	הַצְמַח לָנוּ יְשׁוּעָה בְּקָרוֹב *Make salvation sprout* *for us soon*
שְׁמַע קוֹלֵנוּ ... *Hear our voice ...*	שְׁמַע קוֹלֵנוּ ... *Hear our voice ...*

THE ARK IS OPENED.

[As the Ark is opened, some say the words: פְּתַח שַׁעֲרֵי שָׁמַיִם לִתְפִלָּתֵנוּ.]

אָבִינוּ מַלְכֵּנוּ, חָטָאנוּ לְפָנֶיךָ.

אָבִינוּ מַלְכֵּנוּ, אֵין לָנוּ מֶלֶךְ אֶלָּא אָתָּה.

אָבִינוּ מַלְכֵּנוּ, עֲשֵׂה עִמָּנוּ לְמַעַן שְׁמֶךָ.

אָבִינוּ מַלְכֵּנוּ, חַדֵּשׁ עָלֵינוּ שָׁנָה טוֹבָה.

אָבִינוּ מַלְכֵּנוּ, בַּטֵּל מֵעָלֵינוּ כָּל גְּזֵרוֹת קָשׁוֹת.

אָבִינוּ מַלְכֵּנוּ, בַּטֵּל מַחְשְׁבוֹת שׂוֹנְאֵינוּ.

אָבִינוּ מַלְכֵּנוּ, הָפֵר עֲצַת אוֹיְבֵינוּ.

אָבִינוּ מַלְכֵּנוּ — *Our Father, our King.* By addressing God as "our Father" and "our King," we acknowledge our shortcomings and plead for mercy from two perspectives. God is our Father Who loves us and provides for us — how could we be ungrateful to Him? And He is our King Who has absolute power over us and to Whom we owe total allegiance — how dare we flout His authority? Nevertheless, He always remains merciful, like a Father; and, like a King, He remains concerned for the well-being of His subjects. Therefore, we take the courage to approach Him from both aspects in our present time of helplessness and need. If we deserve His mercy, let Him be tender. If not, at least let Him judge us as necessary cogs in His empire.

Both aspects of God's relationship to us — as Father and as King — are found in Scripture. Sometimes, He is a Father: וְעַתָּה ה' אָבִינוּ אָתָּה, *And now, Hashem, You are our Father* (Isaiah 64:7), and כֹּה אָמַר ה' בְּנִי בְכֹרִי יִשְׂרָאֵל, *Thus said Hashem, "Israel is My son, My firstborn"* (Exodus 4:22). At other times God is the King and Israel His servants — ה' מַלְכֵּנוּ הוּא יוֹשִׁיעֵנוּ, *Hashem is our King, He will save us* (Isaiah 33:22), and כִּי לִי בְנֵי יִשְׂרָאֵל עֲבָדִים ... אֲנִי ה' אֱלֹהֵיכֶם, *For unto Me are the Children of Israel servants ... I am HASHEM, your God* (Leviticus 25:55).

Alternatively, we are commanded to serve Hashem in two ways: with love — וְאָהַבְתָּ אֵת ה' אֱלֹהֶיךָ, *you shall love HASHEM, your God* (Deuteronomy 6:5); and with awe — עִבְדוּ אֶת ה' בְּיִרְאָה, *Serve HASHEM with awe* (Psalms 2:11). Children serve their parents out of a feeling of love; a desire to make them comfortable and proud. Servants, on the other hand, serve their king out of awe of their master's majesty. By addressing Hashem as "our Father, our King," we declare that we wish to fulfill our dual obligation of serving Him out of love and out of awe.

חָטָאנוּ לְפָנֶיךָ — *We have sinned before You.* When they appear in Scriptures, the expressions of confession, חָטָאתִי, *I have sinned*, and חָטָאנוּ, *we have sinned*, are followed by לְךָ, **to** *you*, never לְפָנֶיךָ, **before** *you*. The usage of לְפָנֶיךָ here may be understood according to the dictum of the *Chovas HaLevavos* (shaar 3), "Do not rebel against your Master, for He sees you." God is omnipresent and all seeing, thus we are always *before* Him. And while we are remorseful for having sinned, we are even more so for having sinned in His presence (*Siach Yitzchak*).

אֵין לָנוּ מֶלֶךְ אֶלָּא אָתָּה — *We have no King but You.* No longer is there idol worship among us as there was in ancient times. Now, you are our only King (*Eitz Yosef*).

THE ARK IS OPENED.

[As the Ark is opened, some say the words:
'Open the gates of heaven to our prayer.']

אָבִינוּ מַלְכֵּנוּ *Our Father, our King, we have sinned before You.*

Our Father, our King, we have no King but You.

Our Father, our King, deal [kindly] with us for Your Name's sake.

Our Father, our King, inaugurate upon us a good year.

Our Father, our King, nullify all harsh decrees upon us.

Our Father, our King, nullify the thoughts of those who hate us.

Our Father, our King, thwart the plan of our enemies.

Commentators explain that a slave with allegiance to two masters is not a true slave of either, because his loyalty is divided. We ask for God's mercy because he is our *only* King.

עֲשֵׂה עִמָּנוּ לְמַעַן שְׁמֶךְ — *Deal [kindly] with us for Your Name's sake.* This verse is based on *Jeremiah* (14:7): *If our sins have spoken out against us, HASHEM, deal [kindly] for Your Name's sake.* When the world sees God's concern for His errant people, His glory becomes elevated.

R' Samson Raphael Hirsch links the opening three verses: Our sins of the past, which have persisted into the present and which we have still not been successful in eliminating, are the underlying cause for the present exile in which we find ourselves. Nevertheless, despite our misdeeds and despite the resultant exile — both physical and spiritual — *we have no King but You.* Therefore, we pray that You *deal kindly with us for Your Name's sake,* which itself implies Your never-ending loving-kindness (מִדַּת הָרַחֲמִים).

חַדֵּשׁ עָלֵינוּ שָׁנָה טוֹבָה — *Inaugurate upon us a good year.* This phrase introduces all of our hopes for the new year. The remaining verses of *Avinu Malkeinu* enumerate in detail the many components of "goodness."

גְּזֵרוֹת קָשׁוֹת — *Harsh decrees.* In the simple sense, we ask God to save us from the harsh decrees of our enemies (*Eitz Yosef*). A further meaning is that sometimes God's decrees are too hard for us to bear, even though they are intended for our own good. From such decrees, we ask God to spare us (*Dover Shalom*).

בַּטֵּל מַחְשְׁבוֹת שׂוֹנְאֵינוּ . . . הָפֵר עֲצַת אוֹיְבֵינוּ — *Nullify the thoughts of those who hate us ... thwart the plan of our enemies.* Although these two supplications seem to say the same thing, *Siach Yitzchak* explains how they differ. In comparing the terminology of these two verses, he notes three key differences: (a) The root בטל, *to nullify,* refers to the total elimination of an object or cancellation of an idea, so that its existence is nullified — whether in the past, the present or the future. הפר, *to thwart,* on the other hand, means that its past or present remains unchanged, but it is prevented from going forward. (b) מַחְשָׁבוֹת are mere *thoughts,* in this case, of hatred; while עֵצוֹת are *plans* that will lead to future action. (c) A שׂוֹנֵא is *one who hates* in his heart, while an אוֹיֵב, *enemy,* is one who incites others to attack the object of his hatred. (Below we will meet the צָר, *foe,* who carries the plans to fruition and actually inflicts harm.) Thus, the two verses are quite different, as follows:

אָבִינוּ מַלְכֵּנוּ, כַּלֵּה כָּל צַר וּמַשְׂטִין מֵעָלֵינוּ.

אָבִינוּ מַלְכֵּנוּ, סְתוֹם פִּיּוֹת מַשְׂטִינֵנוּ וּמְקַטְרִיגֵנוּ.

אָבִינוּ מַלְכֵּנוּ, כַּלֵּה דֶּבֶר וְחֶרֶב וְרָעָב וּשְׁבִי

וּמַשְׁחִית וְעָוֹן וּשְׁמַד מִבְּנֵי בְרִיתֶךָ.

אָבִינוּ מַלְכֵּנוּ, מְנַע מַגֵּפָה מִנַּחֲלָתֶךָ.

אָבִינוּ מַלְכֵּנוּ, סְלַח וּמְחַל לְכָל עֲוֹנוֹתֵינוּ.

אָבִינוּ מַלְכֵּנוּ, מְחֵה וְהַעֲבֵר פְּשָׁעֵינוּ וְחַטֹּאתֵינוּ

מִנֶּגֶד עֵינֶיךָ.

First we ask that the *thoughts* of those who hate us be nullified lest they lead to evil *plans*. Yet sometimes God, in His wisdom, does not wish to nullify these thoughts, but allows them to blossom into plans designed to harm us. So our next prayer is that He "thwart the plan of our enemies."

כַּלֵּה כָּל צַר וּמַשְׂטִין מֵעָלֵינוּ ... סְתוֹם פִּיּוֹת מַשְׂטִינֵנוּ וּמְקַטְרִיגֵנוּ — *Exterminate every foe and adversary from upon us ... seal the mouths of our adversaries and our accusers.* Once again the verses seem contradictory. First we ask God to *exterminate every adversary*, then we ask Him merely to *seal [their] mouths!*

R' Ben Zion Aryeh Leib Tzizling of Shkod (cited in *Siach Yitzchak*) explains that the former verse addresses itself to our human foes and adversaries — those who hurl false accusations at us and agitate before the temporal powers to destroy us. [Thus, this verse forms a unit with the three preceding ones, which speak of *harsh decrees ... the thoughts of those who hate us ... the plan of our enemies*, and now the fourth verse speaks of the accusations of our foes.]

The latter verse, however, refers to our heavenly adversaries and accusers — those angels of destruction created by our own iniquities. As the Mishnah (*Avos* 4:13) teaches: "He who commits one transgression gains himself one accusing angel." We do not pray for the extermination of these adversaries for that would not necessarily

be in our best interest. As the Talmud (*Yoma* 86a) states: "Repentance is great, for because of it sins are accounted as merits." Therefore, we ask only that the mouths of our heavenly accusers be sealed, thus averting the punishments enumerated in the next two verses, and attaining for us the pardon and atonement of the succeeding supplications. All this will hopefully culminate in our returning *to You in perfect repentance* — and if we succeed in doing so, our sins will be converted to merits and the accusing angels will become our protagonists.

מַשְׂטִינֵנוּ וּמְקַטְרִיגֵנוּ — *Our adversaries and our accusers.* Both terms allude to the destructive angels created through our iniquities (see *Avos* 4:13 cited above). A מַשְׂטִין [or שָׂטָן], *adversary,* is one formed when we fail to perform a מִצְוַת עֲשֵׂה, *positive commandment.* A מְקַטְרֵג [sometimes called a קַטֵּגוֹר], *accuser,* comes into being when we actively transgress a מִצְוַת לֹא תַעֲשֶׂה, *negative commandment* (*Siach Yitzchak*).

חֶרֶב ... וּשְׁבִי — *Sword ... captivity.* [In accordance with R' Ben Zion Aryeh Leib Tzizling's interpretation (see above, s.v. כַּלֵּה כָּל צַר ..., *Exterminate every foe ...*), this prayer does not call for salvation from mortal enemies who seek to kill or take us captive; otherwise it would have appeared among the earlier supplications regarding our earthly enemies. Listed as they are among the heavenly retributions, they

Our Father, our King, exterminate every foe
and adversary from upon us.
Our Father, our King, seal the mouths of our adversaries
and accusers.
Our Father, our King, exterminate pestilence, sword,
famine, captivity, destruction, iniquity and eradica-
tion from the members of Your covenant.
Our Father, our King, withhold the plague
from Your heritage.
Our Father, our King, forgive and pardon
all our iniquities.
Our Father, our King, wipe away and remove our
willful sins and errors from before Your eyes.

more likely refer to periods of general hostility among nations. At these times, as history repeatedly teaches us, the Jews are most vulnerable. Therefore, we pray that even if "pestilence, sword, famine, etc." are released upon the world, may we, "the members of Your covenant," be spared.]

מְנַע מַגֵּפָה מִנַּחֲלָתֶךָ — *Withhold the plague from Your heritage.* According to the opinion of *Siddur Shaar HaShamayim*, cited above, that our requests are to enable us to enhance God's glory on earth by our fulfillment of His *mitzvos*, this prayer is based on the verse: *In the grave who will praise You? (Psalms* 6:6). Although their souls endure, the dead can no longer praise Hashem nor spread knowledge of Him in the world.

Although the words pestilence and plague are synonymous in English, there is a difference between דֶּבֶר and מַגֵּפָה, here translated "pestilence" and "plague" respectively. A visitation of דֶּבֶר afflicts all living beings, man and animal alike, whereas plague affects human beings only (*Divrei Shlomo*).

סְלַח וּמְחַל — *Forgive and pardon.* In Hebrew, סְלִיחָה, *forgiveness*, is milder than מְחִילָה, *pardon.* God forgives in the sense that He defers punishment, as He did after the sin of the Golden Calf. At that time, He agreed not to punish the Jews, in

response to Moses' prayers; however, the sin was not completely wiped away. On the other hand, מְחִילָה, *pardon*, means that repentance has been so complete that all effects of the sin are removed.

סְלַח . . . מְחֵה . . . מְחוֹק — *Forgive . . . wipe away . . . erase.* The three verses respectively beginning סְלַח וּמְחַל, *forgive and pardon*, מְחֵה וְהַעֲבֵר, *wipe away and remove*, and מְחוֹק, *erase*, appear to be repetitious. *Dover Shalom* explains that each verse pleads with God to expunge a different effect of sinfulness. Firstly, the act of sinning causes a flaw in one's soul, a condition that can be corrected only by forgiveness and pardon. Secondly, sin represents disobedience to God and His commandments. To atone for this we ask that God wipe away and erase our sins from His sight. Finally, each person owes an unrepayable debt to God Who has given him life, health, and prosperity — yet the sinner has repaid Him with evil. Thus the prayer that God erase כָּל שִׁטְרֵי חוֹבוֹתֵינוּ, *all records of our guilt*, which may also be rendered *all contracts of our indebtedness.*

מְחֵה וְהַעֲבֵר פְּשָׁעֵינוּ וְחַטֹּאתֵינוּ מִנֶּגֶד עֵינֶיךָ — *Wipe away and remove our willful sins and our errors from before Your eyes.* This verse is taken from the Yom Kippur *Amidah*, which continues: *As it is said, "I,*

אָבִינוּ מַלְכֵּנוּ, מְחוֹק בְּרַחֲמֶיךָ הָרַבִּים
כָּל שִׁטְרֵי חוֹבוֹתֵינוּ.

Each of the next nine verses is recited by the *chazzan*,
then repeated by the congregation.

אָבִינוּ מַלְכֵּנוּ, הַחֲזִירֵנוּ בִּתְשׁוּבָה שְׁלֵמָה לְפָנֶיךָ.
אָבִינוּ מַלְכֵּנוּ, שְׁלַח רְפוּאָה שְׁלֵמָה לְחוֹלֵי עַמֶּךָ.
אָבִינוּ מַלְכֵּנוּ, קְרַע רוֹעַ גְּזַר דִּינֵנוּ.
אָבִינוּ מַלְכֵּנוּ, זָכְרֵנוּ בְּזִכָּרוֹן טוֹב לְפָנֶיךָ.

only I, am He Who wipes away your willful sins for My own sake, and I shall not recall your errors'' (Isaiah 43:25). According to the Talmud (*Yoma* 36b), פֶּשַׁע, here translated *willful sin*, refers to מֶרֶד, *rebelliousness*, i.e., sin committed with the intent to defy the yoke of Heaven while חֵטְא, *error*, describes שׁוֹגֵג, *inadvertent transgression*. Therefore, the Talmud concludes, in the *Kohen Gadol's* Yom Kippur confession, he recited חָטָאתִי, *I have erred*, before פָּשַׁעְתִּי, *I have sinned willfully*. For, as *Rashi* explains, logic dictates that one ask forgiveness for the lesser sins before he asks forgiveness for the graver sins.

If so, the order of our verse is difficult. Why do we ask Hashem to wipe away our inadvertent lapses *after* having asked Him to pardon our willful, rebellious sins?

In response to this problem, some authorities reverse the order of the words, placing חַטֹאתֵינוּ, *our errors*, before פְּשָׁעֵינוּ, *our willful sins* (see e.g., *Mishnah Berurah* 684:3). This may be why many early sources omit the word וְחַטֹאתֵינוּ from both *Avinu Malkeinu* and the *Amidah*.

Nevertheless, some commentaries justify the text of our *siddurim*. The Talmud (*Yoma* 86a) teaches that תְּשׁוּבָה מִיִּרְאָה, *repentance based on fear [of Hashem]*, can serve to ameliorate premeditated sins (זְדוֹנוֹת) so that they be accounted as inadvertent errors (שְׁגָגוֹת); while תְּשׁוּבָה מֵאַהֲבָה, *repentance based on love [for Hashem]*, causes premeditated sins to be accounted as merits (זְכֻיּוֹת). Thus, we first

mention פְּשָׁעֵינוּ, implying that we beseech Hashem to treat our rebelliousness as mere error. Only then do we add וְחַטֹאתֵינוּ, asking that our whole-hearted repentance, which is due to our love for Hashem, cause our errors to be reckoned as merits.

מְחוֹק . . . כָּל שִׁטְרֵי חוֹבוֹתֵינוּ — *Erase . . . all records of our guilt*. Why do we ask only that 'the records' of our guilt be erased, and not our guilt itself? According to the *Rav* of Kovno, R' Yitzchak Elchanan, there are certain instances in which one may incur Divine punishment for deeds he never committed — namely, when one has the power to persuade others not to sin, yet remains silent. Thus, while in the previous verse we spoke of our own misdeeds, here we refer to the sins we did not commit, but which are nevertheless "on our records" (cited in *Siach Yitzchak*).

[Alternatively, this verse may be based on the aforementioned Talmudic dictum (*Yoma* 86a) that repentance of the highest degree turns one's guilt into merit. If so, we ask that only the records of our guilt be erased, but that the guilt itself be transformed to merit.]

An ingenious interpretation of this verse is offered by R' Shlomo Yanovsky in his *siddur* commentary *Divrei Shlomo*:

Why do we ask that all records of our guilt be erased? Shouldn't we ask that they be totally destroyed? The answer to these questions may be found in a verse in *Jeremiah* (17:1): *The sin of Judah is inscribed with an iron stylus . . . on the*

Our Father, our King, erase through Your abundant compassion all records of our guilt.

Each of the next nine verses is recited by the chazzan,
then repeated by the congregation.

*Our Father, our King, return us to You
in perfect repentance.*

*Our Father, our King, send complete recovery
to the sick of Your people.*

*Our Father, our King, tear up the evil of the decree
of our verdict.*

*Our Father, our King, recall us with
a favorable memory before You.*

tablet of their heart. Obviously, since "the records of our guilt" are inscribed on our own hearts, we cannot ask that the records be destroyed, only erased.

בִּתְשׁוּבָה שְׁלֵמָה — *In perfect repentance.* Sometimes a person repents his sins, only to relapse into his old ways soon after. Thus we pray for Divine assistance that our *teshuvah* be of enduring quality (*Keser Nehora*).

רְפוּאָה שְׁלֵמָה — *Complete recovery.* Rambam (*Hilchos Dayos* 2:1) teaches: People who are physically ill often confuse tastes — bitter foods taste sweet to them, while sweets seem bitter. Some sick people develop appetites for harmful objects, while losing their desire for nourishing foods. Similarly, those who are afflicted with spiritual diseases seek evil life styles, rejecting the proper manner of conduct. Just as the physically sick must seek out competent physicians to cure their ills, so must the spiritually ill seek out mentors who are capable of directing them back to the proper way.

This, then, is the meaning of the phrase רְפוּאָה שְׁלֵמָה, *complete recovery,* spiritual healing as well as physical healing (*Eitz Yosef*).

קְרַע רוֹעַ גְּזַר דִּינֵנוּ — *Tear up the evil of the decree of our verdict.* The translation follows *Turei Zahav* (*Taz* 621:6) who states that the words רוֹעַ גְּזַר should be pro-

nounced in one breath. Because, says *Taz*, if a pause is introduced between the words רוֹעַ, *evil,* and גְּזַר, *decree,* the word גְּזַר would not be a noun but an imperative verb. The verse would then mean קְרַע רוֹעַ, *tear up evil,* גְּזַר דִּינֵנוּ, *decree our verdict,* an obvious misinterpretation of our prayer.

We do not say simply *tear our verdict,* because even if the decree cannot be completely torn up, its effect can be softened. For example, a small amount of rainfall can be made beneficial if it falls at the right times. Or if a person must be deprived of a certain amount of money, he can lose it by giving it to charity. In that way, even though he will no longer have the lost money he will be rewarded for his good deed (*Eitz Yosef*).

זָכְרֵנוּ בְּזִכָּרוֹן טוֹב לְפָנֶיךָ — *Recall us with a favorable* [lit., *good*] *memory before You.* Sometimes we, with our finite understanding, think that a particular thing may be good for us, but God, in His infinite wisdom, knows what is truly good. Therefore, we pray for what is טוֹב לְפָנֶיךָ, *good before You,* i.e., totally and ultimately good (*Dover Shalom*).

Some *siddurim* vowelize בְּזִכְרוֹן, *with a good remembrance.* This is based on the Talmudic passage (*Rosh Hashanah* 16a): God said, "... On Rosh Hashanah recite before Me [verses that speak of My] Sovereignty, זִכְרוֹנוֹת, Remembrance [of all events] and Shofar blasts: Sovereignty —

אָבִינוּ מַלְכֵּנוּ, כָּתְבֵנוּ בְּסֵפֶר חַיִּים טוֹבִים.
אָבִינוּ מַלְכֵּנוּ, כָּתְבֵנוּ בְּסֵפֶר גְּאֻלָּה וִישׁוּעָה.
אָבִינוּ מַלְכֵּנוּ, כָּתְבֵנוּ בְּסֵפֶר פַּרְנָסָה וְכַלְכָּלָה.°

°While the *chazzan* recites this line, some recite this Kabbalistic prayer for sustenance. The Divine Names that appear in brackets should be scanned with the eyes and concentrated upon, but should not be spoken.

יְהִי רָצוֹן מִלְּפָנֶיךָ, יהוה אֱלֹהֵינוּ וֵאלֹהֵי אֲבוֹתֵינוּ, הָאֵל הַגָּדוֹל
הַגִּבּוֹר וְהַנּוֹרָא, עֲשֵׂה לְמַעֲנֶךָ וּלְמַעַן שֵׁם הַגָּדוֹל
וְהַקָּדוֹשׁ [**דִּיקַרְנוּסָא**] הַיּוֹצֵא מִפָּסוּק: וַהֲרִיקֹתִי לָכֶם בְּרָכָה עַד בְּלִי
דָי.[1] וּמִפָּסוּק: נָסָה עָלֵינוּ אוֹר פָּנֶיךָ יהוה.[2] שֶׁתַּזְמִין לָנוּ וְתִתֵּן לָנוּ
וּלְכָל הַסְּמוּכִים בְּשֻׁלְחָנֵנוּ, הַיּוֹם וּבְכָל יוֹם, פַּרְנָסָתֵנוּ וּמְזוֹנוֹתֵינוּ
בְּמִלּוּי וּבְרֶיוַח, בְּכָבוֹד וְלֹא בְאִיסוּר, לֹא בְעָמָל וְלֹא בְטוֹרַח
וּבִיגִיעָה רַבָּה, רַק בְּנַחַת וּבְשַׁלְוָה וּבְהַשְׁקֵט, כְּדֵי שֶׁנּוּכַל לַעֲבוֹד
עֲבוֹדָתְךָ הַטְּהוֹרָה וְהַקְּדוֹשָׁה בְּלִי טִרְדַת פַּרְנָסָה. וְשֶׁלֹּא יִהְיֶה בָה
שׁוּם בּוּשָׁה וּכְלִימָה, וְשֶׁלֹּא תַצְרִיכֵנוּ לִידֵי מַתְּנַת בָּשָׂר וָדָם, כִּי אִם
לְיָדְךָ הַפְּתוּחָה וְהַקְּדוֹשָׁה. וְתַצְלִיחֵנוּ וְהַרְוִיחֵנוּ וּבָרְכֵנוּ בְּכָל מַעֲשֵׂה
יָדֵינוּ וַעֲסָקֵינוּ. וְתֵן לָנוּ מֵאוֹצַר מַתְּנַת יָדֶךָ. וְשֶׁיִּהְיֶה בֵיתִי מָלֵא
בִּרְכַּת יהוה [**יַהְוָה**] בִּזְכוּת שִׁמְךָ הַגָּדוֹל [**דִּיקַרְנוּסָא**].

so that you make Me King over you; Remembrance — so that your remembrance should ascend before Me, with the result that it will be לְטוֹבָה, *for [your] good . . .*" (*Iyun Tefillah*).

בְּסֵפֶר חַיִּים טוֹבִים — *In the book of good life.* R' Kruspedai said in the name of R' Yochanan: Three books are opened [before the Heavenly Tribunal] on Rosh Hashanah — one for the unquestionably wicked; one for the unquestionably righteous; and one for those in between [these extremes]. The unquestionably righteous are immediately inscribed and sealed for life; the unquestionably wicked are immediately inscribed and sealed for death. [But the judgment of] those in between is held in abeyance from Rosh Hashanah until Yom Kippur. If they are found worthy, they are inscribed for life; if they are not found worthy, they are inscribed for death (*Rosh Hashanah* 6b).

The book of life refers not primarily to physical life; in its fuller sense it means the book of righteous people. They are called

'living,' because theirs is the worthwhile life. On the other hand, the book of death means the list of those who are considered to be dead even though they eat and breathe, i.e., the wicked. Thus, we pray that our deeds and repentance make us worthy of inclusion in the book of the living (*Rashi*).

We don't pray merely to be inscribed in the book of life, but in the book of good life. Just being included among the righteous does not necessarily mean our lives will be pleasant, for God's wisdom may decree that some wicked people should luxuriate while some righteous people should suffer. Therefore, we pray also for a *good* life, a life of blessing, peace, and prosperity (*R' Moshe Chaim Luzzatto*).

גְּאֻלָּה וִישׁוּעָה — *Redemption and salvation.* The Prophet states: גֹּאֲלֵנוּ, *Our Redeemer* — HASHEM, *Master of Legions, is His name* (*Isaiah* 47:4). And the Psalmist writes: *For God is my King from days of old,* פֹּעֵל יְשׁוּעוֹת, *working salvations in the midst of the earth* (*Psalms* 74:12).

Our Father, our King, inscribe us in the book of good life.

Our Father, our King, inscribe us in the book of redemption and salvation.

Our Father, our King, inscribe us in the book of sustenance and support.°

°While the *chazzan* recites this line, some recite this Kabbalistic prayer for sustenance. The Divine Names that appear in brackets should be scanned with the eyes and concentrated upon, but should not be spoken.

יְהִי רָצוֹן *May it be Your will, HASHEM our God and the God of our forefathers, the great, mighty and awesome God, that You act for Your sake and for the sake of the great and sacred Name* [דִּיקַרְנוּסָא] — *that emanates from the verse: And I shall pour out blessing for you without limit;[1] and from this verse: Let the light of Your face shine upon us, HASHEM[2] — that You prepare for us, and give to us and to all who depend upon our table, today and every day, our sustenance and our food, with fullness and relief, with honor and not in a forbidden manner, without exertion and without bother and great effort, but pleasantly with tranquillity and calm, in order that we be able to perform Your pure and holy service without the preoccupation of sustenance. May there be neither inner shame nor humiliation, and may we not require the gifts of human hands, but only of Your open and holy hand. May You grant us success and ease, and bless us in all our handiwork and involvement. And give us from the treasure of Your handiwork. And may my house be filled with the blessing of HASHEM* [וַיְהֹוָה] *in the merit of Your great Name* [דִּיקַרְנוּסָא].

(1) *Malachi* 3:10. (2) *Psalms* 4:7.

Homiletically, God is considered to be a close relative to the Jews, as it is written, *For the Children of Israel,* עַם קְרֹבוֹ, *the people that are His relative* (*Psalms* 148:14). And, regarding the commandment to redeem the property of an impoverished Jew who was forced to sell his ancestral estate, the Torah places the responsibility upon *His redeemer shall come,* הַקָּרֹב אֵלָיו, *one who is related to him* (*Leviticus* 25:25). Thus, we are relatives to God and, as such, He must redeem us (*Divrei Shlomo*).

Alternatively, this verse refers to redemption and salvation from the impure shells that surround the soul, preventing it from attaining greater levels of holiness (*R' Yaakov Emden*).

פַּרְנָסָה וְכַלְכָּלָה — *Sustenance and support.* These two words are often paired or used interchangeably, but there is a difference between them: פַּרְנָסָה is related to פֶּרֶס, *a broken piece,* i.e., the bare minimum, and implies a subsistence level with nothing to spare. כַּלְכָּלָה, on the other hand, stems from the root כָּל, *everything;* the doubling of its letters indicates an intense form. Thus, it means complete and total support, an outpouring of unending beneficence (*Iyun Tefillah*).

◄§ Divine Names

It is common for prayers composed according to the mysteries of Kabbalistic wisdom to contain sacred and mystical Divine Names which are composed of the initials of words or of names of angels. The masters of Kabbalah teach that while the supplicant should look at the Names and concentrate on them, under no circumstances should they be pronounced.

אָבִינוּ מַלְכֵּנוּ, כָּתְבֵנוּ בְּסֵפֶר זְכֻיּוֹת.

אָבִינוּ מַלְכֵּנוּ, כָּתְבֵנוּ בְּסֵפֶר סְלִיחָה וּמְחִילָה.

End of responsive reading. All continue:

אָבִינוּ מַלְכֵּנוּ, הַצְמַח לָנוּ יְשׁוּעָה בְּקָרוֹב.

אָבִינוּ מַלְכֵּנוּ, הָרֵם קֶרֶן יִשְׂרָאֵל עַמֶּךָ.

אָבִינוּ מַלְכֵּנוּ, הָרֵם קֶרֶן מְשִׁיחֶךָ.

אָבִינוּ מַלְכֵּנוּ, מַלֵּא יָדֵינוּ מִבִּרְכוֹתֶיךָ.

אָבִינוּ מַלְכֵּנוּ, מַלֵּא אֲסָמֵינוּ שָׂבָע.

אָבִינוּ מַלְכֵּנוּ, שְׁמַע קוֹלֵנוּ, חוּס וְרַחֵם עָלֵינוּ.

אָבִינוּ מַלְכֵּנוּ, קַבֵּל בְּרַחֲמִים וּבְרָצוֹן אֶת תְּפִלָּתֵנוּ.

זְכֻיּוֹת — *Merits*. Grammarians are at odds regarding the vowelization of this word in both its singular and plural forms. Some place the word in the same family as גָּלוּת/גָּלֻיּוֹת, *exile/exiles*, reading זְכוּת for the singular and זְכֻיּוֹת for the plural. Others vowelize the word in the same way as חֲנוּת/חֲנֻיּוֹת, *store/stores*, reading זְכוּת for the singular and זְכֻיּוֹת for the plural. Two other versions are זָכֻיּוֹת and זְכֻיוֹת. [In any case, the use of the word זְכוּתִים in the vernacular has no grammatical basis and is akin to the use of טַלִיתִים as the plural of טַלִּית in place of its proper plural טַלִּיּוֹת.]

The word זְכוּת, *merit*, implies a favorable tilt of the scales of justice, while its counterpart חוֹב, *guilt*, indicates an unfavorable tilt (*Iyun Tefillah*).

How can we ask God to inscribe us in the book of merits? If we actually have merits, He will certainly inscribe us there, whether we request it or not. But if we are undeserving, how do we dare ask Hashem to 'falsify the records,' as it were? We can answer these questions by once again citing the Talmudic teaching (*Yoma* 86a) that repentance based on fear of Hashem serves to ameliorate premeditated sins and account them as inadvertent errors, while repentance based on love for God can turn sins into merits. Thus, we beseech Hashem to accept our whole-hearted repentance and inscribe even our sins in the book of merits (*Siddur Menachem Yitzchak*).

סְלִיחָה וּמְחִילָה — *Forgiveness and pardon*. For the difference between these two terms, see above s.v. סְלַח וּמְחַל, *Forgive and pardon*.

Eitz Yosef homiletically relates the five books just mentioned to the Five Books of Moses:

חַיִּים טוֹבִים, *good life*, alludes to בְּרֵאשִׁית, *Genesis*, which describes how God breathed life into His creatures;

גְּאֻלָּה וִישׁוּעָה, *redemption and salvation*, refers to שְׁמוֹת, *Exodus*, in which the Jews were redeemed and saved from Egyptian slavery;

פַּרְנָסָה וְכַלְכָּלָה, *sustenance and support*, coincides with בַּמִּדְבָּר, *Numbers*, which tells of the incidents of the מָן, *manna*, the שְׂלָיו, *quails*, and the בְּאֵר, *well*, through which God sustained and supported the nation during its sojourn in the wilderness;

זְכֻיּוֹת, *merits*, corresponds to דְּבָרִים, *Deuteronomy*, the book that enumerates the outstanding traits and merits of Moses;

and, finally, סְלִיחָה וּמְחִילָה, *forgiveness and pardon*, is representative of the sin-offerings and guilt-offerings described in וַיִּקְרָא, *Leviticus*.

הַצְמַח לָנוּ יְשׁוּעָה בְּקָרוֹב — *Make salvation sprout for us soon*. At the time of the Exodus from Egypt, total salvation did not come in one fell swoop. It came in stages, like a tree that sprouts and grows gradually until it reaches maturity. First there were

Our Father, our King, inscribe us in the book of merits.

*Our Father, our King, inscribe us in the book of
forgiveness and pardon.*

End of responsive reading. All continue:

Our Father, our King, make salvation sprout for us soon.

*Our Father, our King, raise high the pride of Israel,
Your people.*

*Our Father, our King, raise high the pride
of Your anointed.*

Our Father, our King, fill our hands from Your blessings.

Our Father, our King, fill our storehouses to satiety.

*Our Father, our King, hear our voice,
pity and be compassionate to us.*

*Our Father, our King, accept — with compassion
and favor — our prayer.*

ten plagues, during which the Jewish servitude ended. Then there was the Exodus itself. This was followed by the giving of the Torah; a forty-year sojourn in the wilderness; seven years of conquering *Eretz Yisrael*; seven more years of dividing it among the tribes; more than three centuries during which the land was ruled by the זְקֵנִים, *Elders*, and שׁוֹפְטִים, *Judges*; and the forty-two years of King Saul and King David. Then, finally, the *Beis HaMikdash* was built by King Solomon. Similarly we pray that even if we are undeserving of the full glory of *Mashiach*, at least let the events leading to his coming begin to sprout and develop (*Divrei Shlomo*).

הָרֵם קֶרֶן יִשְׂרָאֵל עַמֶּךְ — *Raise high the pride of Israel, Your people.* The literal meaning of קֶרֶן is *horn*. It is usually interpreted as a metaphor for pride or strength. The Midrash (*Eichah Rabbah* on 2:3) enumerates various "horns" mentioned in Scripture. The horns of Abraham, Isaac, Joseph, Moses, the Torah, the *Kohanim*, the Levites, the Prophets, the Temple, Israel, and Messiah. All of these "horns" were conferred upon Israel, but when the nation sinned, they were removed and presented to the other nations. When Israel will have repented fully, Hashem will return these "horns" to them. Thus, we pray that we be deserving of such restoration (*Eitz Yosef*).

הָרֵם... הָרֵם — *Raise high ... raise high* ... These two verses are based on the two verses: וַיָּרֶם קֶרֶן לְעַמּוֹ, *and He will have raised the pride of His nation* (Psalms 148:14), and וְיָרֵם קֶרֶן מְשִׁיחוֹ, *may He raise the pride of His anointed* (I Samuel 2:10).

מַלֵּא יָדֵינוּ מִבִּרְכוֹתֶיךָ — *Fill our hands from Your blessings.* Even when we toil with our hands to earn our living, let us realize that in the final analysis it is not "my strength and the power of my hands that has gathered this wealth for me" (*Deuteronomy* 8:17), but the blessings of Hashem "have given you the strength to gather this wealth" (ibid. v. 18). In return for this recognition by us ...

מַלֵּא אֲסָמֵינוּ שָׂבָע — *Fill our storehouses to satiety.* As the wise King Solomon wrote: *Honor HASHEM with your possessions ... and your storehouses will be filled to satiety* (*Proverbs* 3:9-10).

שְׁמַע קוֹלֵנוּ חוּס וְרַחֵם עָלֵינוּ — *Hear our voice, pity and be compassionate to us.* First we ask that Hashem hear us out; then, that He

אָבִינוּ מַלְכֵּנוּ, פְּתַח שַׁעֲרֵי שָׁמַיִם לִתְפִלָּתֵנוּ.

אָבִינוּ מַלְכֵּנוּ, זְכוֹר כִּי עָפָר אֲנָחְנוּ.

אָבִינוּ מַלְכֵּנוּ, נָא אַל תְּשִׁיבֵנוּ רֵיקָם מִלְּפָנֶיךָ.

אָבִינוּ מַלְכֵּנוּ, תְּהֵא הַשָּׁעָה הַזֹּאת שְׁעַת רַחֲמִים

וְעֵת רָצוֹן מִלְּפָנֶיךָ.

אָבִינוּ מַלְכֵּנוּ, חֲמוֹל עָלֵינוּ וְעַל עוֹלָלֵינוּ וְטַפֵּנוּ.

be compassionate. *Eitz Yosef* explains that this order is based on an event recorded in the Talmud (*Taanis* 25b):

Once, during a drought, Shmuel HaKattan declared a fast for the next day. Before sunrise, it began to rain. Everyone accepted this as credit to the community (for even as they were merely preparing to pray for rain, the rains began to fall). Then Shmuel HaKattan told them, "The incident is not a sign of communal virtue. Rather, it is comparable to a servant who (has fallen from grace and) stands before his master begging for a bit of bread. "Give it to him," cried the master, "as long as I don't have to hear his voice!' "

Thus, we pray that Hashem hear us out and find favor in our prayers and supplication. Then His pity and compassion will have been earned.

חוּס וְרַחֵם — *Pity and be compassionate.* The term חוּס, *pity*, refers to an artisan's special regard for the product of his hands; while רַחֲמִים, *compassion*, describes the emotion aroused upon seeing someone who is pathetically helpless. O God — *pity* us because we are Your handiwork, and *be compassionate* because we are nothing without You! (*Vilna Gaon*).

קַבֵּל בְּרַחֲמִים וּבְרָצוֹן — *Accept — with compassion and favor.* We ask God to accept our prayers even though we are unaware of the full depth of their meaning. We ask *His compassion* because of our physical needs and *His favor* in view of our limited intelligence (*Eitz Yosef*).

פְּתַח שַׁעֲרֵי שָׁמַיִם לִתְפִלָּתֵנוּ — *Open the gates of heaven to our prayer.* Arizal explains

the divergent liturgies that have arisen among Jewish communities throughout the world. There are twelve gateways in heaven that correspond to the twelve tribes of Israel. These are the very gates referred to in *Ezekiel* (48:31-34), which describes the twelve gates of the Third Temple. Each gateway differs from the others and each tribe's prayer that enters heaven through its gate is different from that of every other tribe's. It is these gates that we ask Hashem to open so that our prayers may enter (*Iyun Tefillah* based on *Pri Eitz Chaim*).

זְכוֹר כִּי עָפָר אֲנָחְנוּ — *Remember that we are but dust.* This verse is based on *Psalms* 103:14 which reads: זָכוּר כִּי עָפָר אֲנָחְנוּ, *He remembers that we are dust.* [Indeed, many *siddurim* read זָכוּר for זְכוֹר.]

God told Adam (*Genesis* 3:19), כִּי עָפָר אַתָּה וְאֶל עָפָר תָּשׁוּב, "*For dust are you, and to dust shall you return.*"

Man is composed of two aspects: the body and the soul. If he focuses primarily on the celestial realm of the spirit, then the soul is supreme and man resembles an angel. But if man focuses primarily on the coarse physical realm, then he will become akin to the animals and beasts (*Radak*), the physical part of man that God fashioned from the dust of the earth.

God recognizes that our physicality — the part of us that was formed from the dust — drags us toward the animal aspect of our natures, and therefore He is lenient and merciful with us (*Ibn Yachya*).

אַל תְּשִׁיבֵנוּ רֵיקָם מִלְּפָנֶיךָ — *Do not turn us away from before You empty handed.*

*Our Father, our King, open the gates of heaven
to our prayer.*

Our Father, our King, remember that we are but dust.

*Our Father, our King, please do not turn us away from
before You empty handed.*

*Our Father, our King, may this moment be a moment of
compassion and a time of favor before You.*

*Our Father, our King, take pity upon us, and upon our
toddlers and our youngsters.*

After having supplicated, "fill our hands from Your blessings," and "fill our storehouses to satiety" why do we suddenly forgo all of that and merely plead that we not be sent away empty handed? The key word here is מִלְּפָנֶיךָ, *from before You*. True, we asked for blessings and abundance. And we even trust that those requests will be fulfilled. Nevertheless, we ask now that they come to us directly from the hand of Hashem (מִלְּפָנֶיךָ, *from before You*) and not merely through the agency of some angel or law of nature (*Shem Yaakov* cited in *Menachem Yitzchak*).

Kabbalistically, רֵיקָם, *empty*, alludes to a place devoid of holiness and the "breeding ground" of the קְלִיפּוֹת, *impure shells*, that separate the holiness inherent in all creation from its source. That place is called בּוֹר רֵק, *the empty pit*, from which the waters of holiness are absent, yet which is filled with the serpents of evil (see *Rashi* to *Genesis* 37:24). Thus, we pray that our supplications not be rejected and relegated to the empty pit (*R' Yaakov Emden*).

תְּהֵא הַשָּׁעָה הַזֹּאת שְׁעַת רַחֲמִים — *May this moment be a moment of compassion.* There was once a righteous innkeeper who treated all his guests respectfully. His doors were open to rich and poor alike. The itinerant beggar who appeared at mealtime ate the same sumptuous foods as the nobleman who lodged overnight at the inn and paid a pretty penny for his stay. Yet there was one difference between the paying guest and the pauper: After retiring for the night, the innkeeper and his family

didn't mind being awakened by an affluent wayfarer who came knocking on their door. That guest paid well for his stay and so could dictate when he would be served. Not so the beggar. When the dining room was open, he was welcome. But once it was closed for the night, he would have to wait until the next day for his meal. Thus, an indigent wanderer would pray that he reach the inn before nightfall, at an opportune time. The rich man, on the other hand, would travel at his leisure and arrive at any time.

Similarly, we in our spiritual paucity pray that our supplication reach heaven at an opportune time, while the gates of heaven are open for the prayers of the righteous. Then our prayers will be able to enter along with theirs (*Menachem Yitzchak*).

חֲמוֹל עָלֵינוּ וְעַל עוֹלָלֵינוּ וְטַפֵּנוּ — *Take pity upon us, and upon our toddlers and our youngsters.* Sometimes Hashem is merciful to us because He wants us to have the opportunity to repent the evil of our past and serve Him whole-heartedly in the future. At other times He is merciful to us because of our posterity, so that we can raise future generations to serve Him. Thus, we pray that He take pity upon the future generations, "our toddlers and our youngsters" (*Dover Shalom*).

Our translation follows *Iyun Tefillah* who defines עוֹלְלִים as those who have been weaned from their mothers and are beginning to talk and walk, and טַף as those who are already capable of running and jumping.

אָבִֽינוּ מַלְכֵּֽנוּ, עֲשֵׂה לְמַֽעַן הֲרוּגִים עַל שֵׁם קָדְשֶֽׁךָ.

אָבִֽינוּ מַלְכֵּֽנוּ, עֲשֵׂה לְמַֽעַן טְבוּחִים עַל יִחוּדֶֽךָ.

אָבִֽינוּ מַלְכֵּֽנוּ, עֲשֵׂה לְמַֽעַן בָּאֵי בָאֵשׁ וּבַמַּֽיִם
עַל קִדּוּשׁ שְׁמֶֽךָ.

אָבִֽינוּ מַלְכֵּֽנוּ, נְקוֹם לְעֵינֵֽינוּ נִקְמַת
דַּם עֲבָדֶֽיךָ הַשָּׁפוּךְ.

אָבִֽינוּ מַלְכֵּֽנוּ, עֲשֵׂה לְמַעַנְךָ אִם לֹא לְמַעֲנֵֽנוּ.

אָבִֽינוּ מַלְכֵּֽנוּ, עֲשֵׂה לְמַעַנְךָ וְהוֹשִׁיעֵֽנוּ.

אָבִֽינוּ מַלְכֵּֽנוּ, עֲשֵׂה לְמַֽעַן רַחֲמֶֽיךָ הָרַבִּים.

אָבִֽינוּ מַלְכֵּֽנוּ, עֲשֵׂה לְמַֽעַן שִׁמְךָ הַגָּדוֹל הַגִּבּוֹר
וְהַנּוֹרָא, שֶׁנִּקְרָא עָלֵֽינוּ.

אָבִֽינוּ מַלְכֵּֽנוּ, חָנֵּֽנוּ וַעֲנֵֽנוּ, כִּי אֵין בָּֽנוּ מַעֲשִׂים,
עֲשֵׂה עִמָּֽנוּ צְדָקָה וָחֶֽסֶד וְהוֹשִׁיעֵֽנוּ.

THE ARK IS CLOSED.

הֲרוּגִים ... טְבוּחִים ... בָּאֵי בָאֵשׁ וּבַמַּֽיִם — *Those who were murdered ... were slaughtered ... went into fire and water.* We pray that, even if we are undeserving, we be forgiven and protected in the merit of our forebears who were martyred for their devotion to Hashem.

Homiletically, these three verses may be interpreted in light of the verse, *And I will remember My covenant with Jacob, and also My covenant with Isaac, and also My covenant with HASHEM will I remember ... (Leviticus 26:42).*

The term הֲרוּגִים, from הרג, alludes to the threat that Esau made against Jacob — *When the days of mourning for my father arrive,* וְאַהַרְגָה, *I shall murder my brother Jacob (Genesis 27:41).* The word טְבוּחִים, *slaughtered,* brings to mind the Akeidah, the Binding of Isaac, who was on the verge of being slaughtered as an offering (ibid. ch. 22). And the expression בָּאֵי בָאֵשׁ וּבַמַּֽיִם, *who went into fire and water,* recalls Abraham, who was thrown into the fiery furnace by Nimrod (see

Rashi to Genesis 11:28), and whose path Satan tried to block by turning into a raging river when Abraham led Isaac to the Akeidah (see *Yalkut Shimoni* I:99). Thus, we pray that we be saved in the merit of Abraham, Isaac, and Jacob (*Eitz Yosef*).

דַּם עֲבָדֶֽיךָ הַשָּׁפוּךְ — *The spilled blood of Your servants.* Their blood was spilled only because they were Your servants (*Dover Shalom;* see *Psalms* 79:10).

עֲשֵׂה לְמַעַנְךָ אִם לֹא לְמַעֲנֵֽנוּ ... וְהוֹשִׁיעֵֽנוּ — *Act for Your sake if not for our sake ... and save us.* Israel cries: *Not for our sake, HASHEM, not for our sake* —not because our deeds make us deserving — *but for Your Name's sake give honor, for the sake of Your loving-kindness and Your truth (Psalms* 115:1; *Targum Yonasan*).

God responds: לְמַעֲנִי לְמַעֲנִי אֶעֱשֶׂה, *For My sake, for My sake, shall I act ... (Isaiah* 48:11).

As long as Israel is in exile, the שְׁכִינָה

Our Father, our King, act for the sake of those who were
murdered for Your Holy Name.

Our Father, our King, act for the sake of those who were
slaughtered for Your Oneness.

Our Father, our King, act for the sake of those who went
into fire and water for the sanctification
of Your Name.

Our Father, our King, avenge before our eyes the spilled
blood of Your servants.

Our Father, our King, act for Your sake
if not for our sake.

Our Father, our King, act for Your sake and save us.

Our Father, our King, act for the sake of
Your abundant compassion.

Our Father, our King, act for the sake of Your great,
mighty, and awesome Name
that is proclaimed upon us.

Our Father, our King, be gracious with us and answer
us, though we have no worthy deeds;
treat us with charity and kindness, and save us.

THE ARK IS CLOSED.

[Shechinah], the Divine Presence, is in exile with them — as the prophet declares: In all their troubles, He is troubled (Isaiah 63:9), and as God says: I am with you in trouble (Psalms 91:15). The Talmud discusses this at length:

Come and observe how beloved Israel is to the Holy One, Blessed is He, for wherever they [Israel] are exiled, the Shechinah is with them ... and when they will be redeemed, the Shechinah will be [redeemed] with them ... This teaches that the Holy One, Blessed is He, returns with them from their exiles (Taanis 16a; Megillah 29a).

Says God, "Anyone who joins in communal [i.e., synagogue] prayer is considered as having redeemed Me and My children from among the nations [of their exile]" (Berachos 8a).

רַחֲמֶיךָ הָרַבִּים — Your abundant compassion. Scripture spells out clearly that salvation is dependent upon God's abundant compassion: וּכְרַחֲמֶיךָ הָרַבִּים, And according to Your abundant compassion You gave them saviors who saved them from their oppressors (Nehemiah 9:27).

שְׁמֶךָ ... שֶׁנִּקְרָא עָלֵינוּ — Your ... Name that is proclaimed upon us. This verse is based on Jeremiah 14:9, You, HASHEM, are among us, and Your Name is proclaimed upon us, forsake us not. Since we are known as עַם ה', the nation of HASHEM, it is incumbent upon You to act on our behalf. Alternatively, Your Name, אֵל, is contained within our name יִשְׂרָאֵל (Radak).

יִזְכֹּר / Yizkor

The ancient custom of recalling the souls of the departed and contributing to charity in their memory is rooted in the fundamental Jewish belief in the eternity of the soul. When physical life ends, only the body dies, but the soul ascends to the realm of the spirit where it regularly attains higher levels of purity and holiness.

When this life is over, the soul can no longer perform good deeds; that method of attaining merit is the sole province of mortal man who must struggle with the baseness and selfishness of his animal nature. But there is a way for the disembodied soul to derive new sources of merit. History is a continuum. If we, the living, give charity or do good deeds due to the lasting influence or in memory of a departed parent or other loved one, the merit is truly that of the soul in its spiritual realm. Moreover, God in His mercy credits our deed to the departed one because he or she, too, would have done the same were it possible. Even if the departed one was too poor to have made contributions to charity, the soul benefits nonetheless, because it may be assumed that he or she would have been charitable had sufficient means been available. But mere intentions do not suffice; only accomplishment can achieve this purpose. The intention to give and the fulfillment of that intention are both necessary; consequently, the pledges to charity should be redeemed as soon as possible after Yom Kippur.

The Yom Kippur customs of pledging to charity on behalf of the departed and of praying for their souls are recorded in *Orach Chaim* 621:6. *Beis Yosef* records the custom of pledging and *Rama* adds the custom of Yizkor. *R' Yaakov Weil (Mahariv)* explains that the proper name of the day, *Yom HaKippurim*, is in the plural, because there are indeed *two* atonements — one for the living and one for the dead. Consequently, it is incumbent upon the living to seek ways to bring spiritual benefits upon their departed parents and other loved ones.

There are other reasons, too, for *Yizkor* on Yom Kippur. *Kol Bo* explains that we recall the dead as a prod to repentance, because the reminder that life is fleeting helps to make us humble and contrite. An opposite point of view is given in *Levush*, who explains that we invoke the memory of righteous parents and others so that their memory will act on our behalf before the Heavenly Court.

It is for all these reasons that *Yizkor* is one of the highlights of the Yom Kippur service. The reason is neither emotional nor sentimental — although it is undeniable that *Yizkor* touches the most sentimental chords in the human heart — but because of the spiritual benefits it confers, both above and below.

The earliest source of the *Yizkor* custom is *Midrash Tanchuma, Haazinu*, which cites the custom of recalling the departed and pledging charity on their behalf on Yom Kippur. Ashkenazic Jewry's custom of reciting *Yizkor* on Pesach, Shavuos, and Shemini Atzeres is of a later origin, possibly the time of the Crusades when bloody massacres wiped out many Jewish communities and seriously hurt many others.

It is virtually a universal custom that those whose parents are still living leave the synagogue during *Yizkor*. This is done to avoid the 'evil eye,' i.e., the resentment that might be felt by those without parents toward those whose parents are still living. *R' Elie Munk* suggests a further reason: We wish to avoid the possibility that people with living parents may mistakenly join in reciting *Yizkor*.

Those congregants whose parents are both living do not participate in the *Yizkor* service, but leave the synagogue and return when the congregation begins אַב הָרַחֲמִים at the end of *Yizkor*.

Although the following verses are not part of the traditional *Yizkor* service, some congregations have adopted the custom of reciting them responsively before *Yizkor*:

יהוה, מָה אָדָם וַתֵּדָעֵהוּ, בֶּן אֱנוֹשׁ וַתְּחַשְּׁבֵהוּ.
אָדָם לַהֶבֶל דָּמָה, יָמָיו כְּצֵל עוֹבֵר.[1]
בַּבְּקֶר יָצִיץ וְחָלָף, לָעֶרֶב יְמוֹלֵל וְיָבֵשׁ.[2]
לִמְנוֹת יָמֵינוּ כֵּן הוֹדַע, וְנָבִא לְבַב חָכְמָה.[3]
שְׁמָר תָּם וּרְאֵה יָשָׁר, כִּי אַחֲרִית לְאִישׁ שָׁלוֹם.[4]
אַךְ אֱלֹהִים יִפְדֶּה נַפְשִׁי מִיַּד שְׁאוֹל, כִּי יִקָּחֵנִי סֶלָה.[5]
כָּלָה שְׁאֵרִי וּלְבָבִי, צוּר לְבָבִי וְחֶלְקִי אֱלֹהִים לְעוֹלָם.[6]
וְיָשֹׁב הֶעָפָר עַל הָאָרֶץ כְּשֶׁהָיָה, וְהָרוּחַ תָּשׁוּב אֶל הָאֱלֹהִים אֲשֶׁר נְתָנָהּ.[7]

תהלים צא

יֹשֵׁב בְּסֵתֶר עֶלְיוֹן, בְּצֵל שַׁדַּי יִתְלוֹנָן. אֹמַר לַיהוה,
מַחְסִי וּמְצוּדָתִי, אֱלֹהַי אֶבְטַח בּוֹ. כִּי הוּא יַצִּילְךָ
מִפַּח יָקוּשׁ, מִדֶּבֶר הַוּוֹת. בְּאֶבְרָתוֹ יָסֶךְ לָךְ, וְתַחַת כְּנָפָיו
תֶּחְסֶה, צִנָּה וְסֹחֵרָה אֲמִתּוֹ. לֹא תִירָא מִפַּחַד לָיְלָה, מֵחֵץ
יָעוּף יוֹמָם. מִדֶּבֶר בָּאֹפֶל יַהֲלֹךְ, מִקֶּטֶב יָשׁוּד צָהֳרָיִם. יִפֹּל
מִצִּדְּךָ אֶלֶף, וּרְבָבָה מִימִינֶךָ, אֵלֶיךָ לֹא יִגָּשׁ. רַק בְּעֵינֶיךָ
תַבִּיט, וְשִׁלֻּמַת רְשָׁעִים תִּרְאֶה. כִּי אַתָּה יהוה מַחְסִי, עֶלְיוֹן
שַׂמְתָּ מְעוֹנֶךָ. לֹא תְאֻנֶּה אֵלֶיךָ רָעָה, וְנֶגַע לֹא יִקְרַב
בְּאָהֳלֶךָ. כִּי מַלְאָכָיו יְצַוֶּה לָּךְ, לִשְׁמָרְךָ בְּכָל דְּרָכֶיךָ. עַל
כַּפַּיִם יִשָּׂאוּנְךָ, פֶּן תִּגֹּף בָּאֶבֶן רַגְלֶךָ. עַל שַׁחַל וָפֶתֶן תִּדְרֹךְ,
תִּרְמֹס כְּפִיר וְתַנִּין. כִּי בִי חָשַׁק וַאֲפַלְּטֵהוּ, אֲשַׂגְּבֵהוּ, כִּי
יָדַע שְׁמִי. יִקְרָאֵנִי וְאֶעֱנֵהוּ, עִמּוֹ אָנֹכִי בְצָרָה, אֲחַלְּצֵהוּ
וַאֲכַבְּדֵהוּ. אֹרֶךְ יָמִים אַשְׂבִּיעֵהוּ, וְאַרְאֵהוּ בִּישׁוּעָתִי. אֹרֶךְ
יָמִים אַשְׂבִּיעֵהוּ, וְאַרְאֵהוּ בִּישׁוּעָתִי.

---

(1) *Psalms* 144:3-4. (2) 90:6. (3) 90:12. (4) 37:37.
(5) 49:16. (6) 73:26. (7) *Ecclesiastes* 12:7.

⊰ YIZKOR ⊱

Those congregants whose parents are both living do not participate in the Yizkor service, but leave the synagogue and return when the congregation begins Father of Compassion *at the end of Yizkor.*

Although the following verses are not part of the traditional Yizkor service, some congregations have adopted the custom of reciting them responsively before Yizkor:

יהוה *HASHEM, what is man that You recognize him? The son of a frail human that You reckon with him?*

Man is like a breath, his days are like a passing shadow.[1]

In the morning it blossoms and is rejuvenated, by evening it is cut down and brittle.[2]

According to the count of our days, so may You teach us; then we shall acquire a heart of wisdom.[3]

Safeguard the perfect and watch the upright, for the destiny of that man is peace.[4]

But God will redeem my soul from the grip of the Lower World, for He will take me, Selah![5]

My flesh and my heart yearn — Rock of my heart, and my portion is God, forever.[6]

Thus the dust returns to the ground as it was, and the spirit returns to God who gave it.[7]

Psalm 91

ישֵׁב *Whoever sits in the refuge of the Most High, he shall dwell in the shadow of the Almighty. I will say of HASHEM, "He is my refuge and my fortress, my God, I will trust in Him." That He will deliver you from the ensnaring trap and from devastating pestilence. With His pinion He will cover you, and beneath His wings you will be protected; shield and armor is His truth. You shall not be afraid of the terror of night, nor of the arrow that flies by day; nor the pestilence that walks in gloom, nor the destroyer who lays waste at noon. Let a thousand encamp at your side and a myriad at your right hand, but to you they shall not approach. You will merely peer with your eyes and you will see the retribution of the wicked. Because [you said], "You, HASHEM, are my refuge"; you have made the Most High your dwelling place. No evil will befall you, nor will any plague come near your tent. He will charge His angels for you, to protect you in all your ways. On their palms they will carry you, lest you strike your foot against a stone. Upon the lion and the viper you will tread; you will trample the young lion and the serpent. For he has yearned for Me and I will deliver him; I will elevate him because he knows My Name. He will call upon Me and I will answer him, I am with him in distress, I will release him and I will honor him. I will satisfy him with long life and show him My salvation. I will satisfy him with long life and show him My salvation.*

Whenever the name of the deceased is mentioned in the *Yizkor* service, it is given in the following form: the Hebrew name of the deceased followed by the word בֶּן, *son of* — or, בַּת, *daughter of* — and then the deceased's father's Hebrew name.

FOR ONE'S FATHER

יִזְכּׂר אֱלֹהִים נִשְׁמַת אָבִי מוֹרִי (name of the deceased) שֶׁהָלַךְ לְעוֹלָמוֹ, בַּעֲבוּר שֶׁבְּלִי נֶדֶר אֶתֵּן צְדָקָה בַּעֲדוֹ. בִּשְׂכַר זֶה תְּהֵא נַפְשׁוֹ צְרוּרָה בִּצְרוֹר הַחַיִּים[1] עִם נִשְׁמוֹת אַבְרָהָם יִצְחָק וְיַעֲקֹב, שָׂרָה רִבְקָה רָחֵל וְלֵאָה, וְעִם שְׁאָר צַדִּיקִים וְצִדְקָנִיּוֹת שֶׁבְּגַן עֵדֶן. וְנֹאמַר: אָמֵן.

FOR ONE'S MOTHER

יִזְכּׂר אֱלֹהִים נִשְׁמַת אִמִּי מוֹרָתִי (name of the deceased) שֶׁהָלְכָה לְעוֹלָמָהּ, בַּעֲבוּר שֶׁבְּלִי נֶדֶר אֶתֵּן צְדָקָה בַּעֲדָהּ. בִּשְׂכַר זֶה תְּהֵא נַפְשָׁהּ צְרוּרָה בִּצְרוֹר הַחַיִּים[1] עִם נִשְׁמוֹת אַבְרָהָם יִצְחָק וְיַעֲקֹב, שָׂרָה רִבְקָה רָחֵל וְלֵאָה, וְעִם שְׁאָר צַדִּיקִים וְצִדְקָנִיּוֹת שֶׁבְּגַן עֵדֶן. וְנֹאמַר: אָמֵן.

יִזְכּׂר אֱלֹהִים — *May God remember.* In calling upon God to 'remember' the soul of the departed, we do not suggest that the possibility of forgetting exists before the All-Knowing One. Rather, we pray that in return for our devotion and generosity, God should take cognizance of the new source of merit for the soul whose memory is now influencing our conduct.

אָבִי מוֹרִי — *My father, my teacher.* This expression (and the parallel אִמִּי מוֹרָתִי, *my mother, my teacher*) is commonly used as a deferential reference to one's parent, lest someone seem to place himself on the same plane as his parents. It appears also in the הָרַחֲמָן verses that form the latter part of *Bircas HaMazon* (Grace after Meals). *Eitz Yosef* and *Likutei Mahariach* question the propriety of their use in that prayer. For according to *Sefer Chassidim* (800), one should not append any titles to

the name of a person about whom he is praying; such titles are meaningless before God. Thus we find that King Solomon, in his lengthy prayer at the dedication of the *Beis HaMikdash* (I Kings ch. 8), mentions דָּוִד אָבִי, *David, my father*, no less than seven times, never once with any additional title such as הַמֶּלֶךְ, *the king.* Similarly, the prophet Elisha invoked "HASHEM, the God of Elijah" (II Kings 2:14) without adding "my teacher," "my master," or "the prophet."

Likutei Mahariach (in his commentary to *Bircas HaMazon*) suggests that *Sefer Chassidim's* injunction applies only where God's Name is mentioned in the prayer, as in the instances of Solomon and Elisha cited above. In the section of *Bircas HaMazon* in question, however, God's Name does not appear; He is addressed only as הָרַחֲמָן, *the Compassionate One.* Therefore, we are permitted to use deferential titles for our parents, even when

Whenever the name of the deceased is mentioned in the *Yizkor* service, it is given in the following form: the Hebrew name of the deceased followed by the word בֶּן, *son of* — or, בַּת, *daughter of* — and then the deceased's father's Hebrew name.

FOR ONE'S FATHER

יִזְכֹּר‎ *May God remember the soul of my father, my teacher,* (name of the deceased) *who has gone on to his world, because, without making a vow, I shall give to charity on his behalf. As reward for this, may his soul be bound in the Bond of Life,[1] together with the souls of Abraham, Isaac, and Jacob; Sarah, Rebecca, Rachel, and Leah; and together with the other righteous men and women in the Garden of Eden. Now let us respond: Amen.*

FOR ONE'S MOTHER

יִזְכֹּר‎ *May God remember the soul of my mother, my teacher,* (name of the deceased) *who has gone on to her world, because, without making a vow, I shall give to charity on her behalf. As reward for this, may her soul be bound in the Bond of Life,[1] together with the souls of Abraham, Isaac, and Jacob; Sarah, Rebecca, Rachel, and Leah; and together with the other righteous men and women in the Garden of Eden. Now let us respond: Amen.*

(1) Cf. *I Samuel* 25:29.

---

they are the subject of our supplication.

An alternative resolution is proposed in *Shirusa Ditzlosa*: Since *Bircas HaMazon* is often recited in the presence of one's parents, it would be unseemly to omit deferential titles when asking God to bless them. In order not to cause confusion by varying the language of the blessing, the same wording is kept, even in their absence.

Neither of these solutions is applicable to *Yizkor*, for (a) the Divine Name אֱלֹהִים does appear in this prayer, and (b) *Yizkor* is never recited in the presence of the parent for whom it is said. Surprisingly, we have not found any *siddur* or commentary that deals with this question in regard to *Yizkor*.

בַּעֲבוּר שֶׁבְּלִי נֶדֶר — *Because, without*

making a vow. It should be noted that many *siddurim* use the phrase בַּעֲבוּר שֶׁאֲנִי נוֹדֵר צְדָקָה, *because I vow to give charity.* However since a נֶדֶר, *vow,* is a very serious matter in Jewish law, and one must be scrupulous in fulfilling his vows, in order to avoid the possibility that one may make a pledge to charity and then forget to redeem it, we follow the practice of many *machzorim* in not using that formula in the *Yizkor* text. Instead, we use the form שֶׁבְּלִי נֶדֶר אֶתֵּן, *without making a vow I shall give.*

בִּצְרוֹר הַחַיִּים — *In the Bond of Life.* This phrase is an abbreviated form of the blessing with which Abigail, wife of Naval, blessed King David: "וְהָיְתָה נֶפֶשׁ אֲדֹנִי צְרוּרָה בִּצְרוֹר הַחַיִּים אֶת ה' אֱלֹהֶיךָ, *May the soul of my lord [David] be bound in*

אֱלֹהִים נִשְׁמַת **יִזְכֹּר**

husband	son	brother	uncle	grandfather
בַּעְלִי	בְּנִי	אָחִי	דּוֹדִי	זְקֵנִי

שֶׁהָלַךְ לְעוֹלָמוֹ, בַּעֲבוּר שֶׁבְּלִי נֶדֶר (name of the deceased)
אֶתֵּן צְדָקָה בַּעֲדוֹ. בִּשְׂכַר זֶה תְּהֵא נַפְשׁוֹ צְרוּרָה
בִּצְרוֹר הַחַיִּים[1] עִם נִשְׁמוֹת אַבְרָהָם יִצְחָק וְיַעֲקֹב,
שָׂרָה רִבְקָה רָחֵל וְלֵאָה, וְעִם שְׁאָר צַדִּיקִים
וְצִדְקָנִיּוֹת שֶׁבְּגַן עֵדֶן. וְנֹאמַר: אָמֵן.

FOR A FEMALE RELATIVE

אֱלֹהִים נִשְׁמַת **יִזְכֹּר**

wife	daughter	sister	aunt	grandmother
אִשְׁתִּי	בִּתִּי	אֲחוֹתִי	דּוֹדָתִי	זְקֵנְתִּי

שֶׁהָלְכָה לְעוֹלָמָהּ, בַּעֲבוּר שֶׁבְּלִי נֶדֶר (name of the deceased)
אֶתֵּן צְדָקָה בַּעֲדָהּ. בִּשְׂכַר זֶה תְּהֵא נַפְשָׁהּ צְרוּרָה
בִּצְרוֹר הַחַיִּים[1] עִם נִשְׁמוֹת אַבְרָהָם יִצְחָק וְיַעֲקֹב,
שָׂרָה רִבְקָה רָחֵל וְלֵאָה, וְעִם שְׁאָר צַדִּיקִים
וְצִדְקָנִיּוֹת שֶׁבְּגַן עֵדֶן. וְנֹאמַר: אָמֵן.

FOR ONE'S EXTENDED FAMILY

יִזְכֹּר אֱלֹהִים נִשְׁמוֹת זְקֵנַי וּזְקֵנוֹתַי, דּוֹדַי
וְדוֹדוֹתַי, אַחַי וְאַחְיוֹתַי, הֵן מִצַּד אָבִי, הֵן
מִצַּד אִמִּי, שֶׁהָלְכוּ לְעוֹלָמָם, בַּעֲבוּר שֶׁבְּלִי נֶדֶר אֶתֵּן
צְדָקָה בַּעֲדָם. בִּשְׂכַר זֶה תִּהְיֶינָה נַפְשׁוֹתֵיהֶם צְרוּרוֹת
בִּצְרוֹר הַחַיִּים[1] עִם נִשְׁמוֹת אַבְרָהָם יִצְחָק וְיַעֲקֹב,
שָׂרָה רִבְקָה רָחֵל וְלֵאָה, וְעִם שְׁאָר צַדִּיקִים
וְצִדְקָנִיּוֹת שֶׁבְּגַן עֵדֶן. וְנֹאמַר: אָמֵן.

the Bond of Life with HASHEM, your God" (I Samuel 25:29).

The Bond of Life refers to the ultimate which is unlimited by the constraints of time and space and the weakness of flesh. The greater the merit achieved by a soul during its time on earth — or as a result of our good deeds in its mem-

יִזְכֹּר *May God remember the soul of my grandfather/
grandmother / uncle / aunt / brother / sister / son/
daughter / husband / wife* (name of the deceased) *who has
gone on to his/her world, because, without making a
vow, I shall give to charity on his/her behalf. As reward
for this, may his/her soul be bound in the Bond of Life,[1]
together with the souls of Abraham, Isaac, and Jacob;
Sarah, Rebecca, Rachel, and Leah; and together with the
other righteous men and women in the Garden of Eden.
Now let us respond: Amen.*

FOR ONE'S EXTENDED FAMILY

יִזְכֹּר *May God remember the souls of my grandfa-
thers and grandmothers, uncles and aunts,
brothers and sisters, both on my father's side and on my
mother's side, who have gone on to their world, because,
without making a vow, I shall give to charity on their
behalf. As reward for this, may their souls be bound in
the Bond of Life,[1] together with the souls of Abraham,
Isaac, and Jacob; Sarah, Rebecca, Rachel, and Leah; and
together with the other righteous men and women in the
Garden of Eden. Now let us respond: Amen.*

(1) Cf. *I Samuel* 25:29.

ory — the more it is bound together with the souls of the Patriarchs and Matriarchs.

Kabbalistically, the Bond of Life alludes to גַּן עֵדֶן, *the* [heavenly] *Garden of Eden*, in which rest the souls of the righteous, enjoying the radiance of the *Shechinah* [Divine Presence].

Alternatively, the phrase refers to the esoteric concept of transmigration of the soul. Each soul implanted in a body is charged with perfecting itself through *mitzvos* and Torah study so that it may enjoy everlasting reward in *Gan Eden*. The unfortunate soul that does not fulfill its mission must return to earth in a different body and make a new attempt to perfect itself. This transmigration repeats itself until the soul finally succeeds in

accomplishing its assigned tasks. Then it becomes bound in "the Bond of Life with HASHEM."

In *Yizkor* we express our hopes that the souls of our departed relatives have reached this level of accomplishment and are settled in their exalted places in *Gan Eden* (*Anaf Yosef* citing *Avkas Rochel* and *Nishmas Chaim*).

בְּגַן עֵדֶן — *In the Garden of Eden.* Originally, this name referred only to גַּן עֵדֶן שֶׁל מַטָּה, *the earthly Garden of Eden*, where Adam and Eve lived until their sin caused them to be driven out. Because this name implies spiritual perfection and bliss, the name is used also to refer to the spiritual paradise, גַּן עֵדֶן שֶׁל מַעְלָה, *the heavenly Garden of Eden.*

יִזְכֹּר אֱלֹהִים נִשְׁמוֹת (כָּל קְרוֹבַי וּקְרוֹבוֹתַי, הֵן מִצַּד אָבִי, הֵן מִצַּד אִמִּי) הַקְּדוֹשִׁים וְהַטְּהוֹרִים שֶׁהוּמְתוּ וְשֶׁנֶּהֶרְגוּ וְשֶׁנִּשְׁחֲטוּ וְשֶׁנִּשְׂרְפוּ וְשֶׁנִּטְבְּעוּ וְשֶׁנֶּחְנְקוּ עַל קִדּוּשׁ הַשֵּׁם, בַּעֲבוּר שֶׁבְּלִי נֶדֶר אֶתֵּן צְדָקָה בְּעַד הַזְכָּרַת נִשְׁמוֹתֵיהֶם. בִּשְׂכַר זֶה תִּהְיֶינָה נַפְשׁוֹתֵיהֶם צְרוּרוֹת בִּצְרוֹר הַחַיִּים[1] עִם נִשְׁמוֹת אַבְרָהָם יִצְחָק וְיַעֲקֹב, שָׂרָה רִבְקָה רָחֵל וְלֵאָה, וְעִם שְׁאָר צַדִּיקִים וְצִדְקָנִיּוֹת שֶׁבְּגַן עֵדֶן. וְנֹאמַר: אָמֵן.

FOR MEMBERS OF THE ISRAEL DEFENSE FORCE

[The following text is taken from the *Minchas Yerushalayim Siddur.*]

יִזְכֹּר אֱלֹהִים אֶת נִשְׁמוֹת חַיָּלֵי צְבָא הַהֲגַנָּה לְיִשְׂרָאֵל שֶׁמָּסְרוּ נַפְשָׁם עַל קְדֻשַּׁת הַשֵּׁם, הָעָם וְהָאָרֶץ, וְנָפְלוּ מוֹת גִּבּוֹרִים בְּמִלְחֶמֶת הַשִּׁחְרוּר, וּבְמַעַרְכוֹת סִינַי בְּתַפְקִידֵי הַהֲגַנָּה וּבִטָּחוֹן. מְנֻשָּׁרִים קַלּוּ, וּמֵאֲרָיוֹת גָּבֵרוּ, בְּהֵחָלְצָם לְעֶזְרַת הָעָם, וְהִרְווּ בְּדָמָם הַטָּהוֹר אֶת רִגְבֵי אַדְמַת קָדְשֵׁנוּ וּמִדְבְּרוֹת סִינָי. זֵכֶר עֲקֵדָתָם וּמַעֲשֵׂי גְבוּרָתָם לֹא יָסוּפוּ מֵאִתָּנוּ לְעוֹלָמִים. תִּהְיֶינָה נִשְׁמוֹתֵיהֶם צְרוּרוֹת בִּצְרוֹר הַחַיִּים[1] עִם נִשְׁמוֹת אַבְרָהָם יִצְחָק וְיַעֲקֹב, וְעִם נִשְׁמוֹת שְׁאָר גִּבּוֹרֵי יִשְׂרָאֵל וּקְדוֹשָׁיו שֶׁבְּגַן עֵדֶן. אָמֵן.

יִזְכּוֹר *May God remember the souls of (all my relatives, both on my father's side and on my mother's side,) the holy and pure ones who were killed, murdered, slaughtered, burned, drowned and strangled for the sanctification of the Name, because, without making a vow, I shall give to charity on their behalf. As reward for this, may their souls be bound in the Bond of Life,[1] together with the souls of Abraham, Isaac, and Jacob; Sarah, Rebecca, Rachel, and Leah; and together with the other righteous men and women in the Garden of Eden. Now let us respond: Amen.*

FOR MEMBERS OF THE ISRAEL DEFENSE FORCE

[The following text is taken from the *Minchas Yerushalayim Siddur.*]

יִזְכּוֹר *May God remember the souls of the fighters of the Israel Defense Force who gave their lives for the sanctification of the Name, the People and the Land; who died a heroic death in the War of Independence and the battlefields of Sinai in missions of defense and safety. They were quicker than eagles and stronger than lions as they volunteered to assist the people and with their pure blood soaked the clods of our holy earth and the deserts of Sinai. The memory of their self-sacrifice and heroic deeds will never perish from us. May their souls be bound in the Bond of Life[1] with the souls of Abraham, Isaac and Jacob, and with the souls of the other Jewish heroes and martyrs who are in the Garden of Eden. Amen.*

---

(1) Cf. *I Samuel* 25:29.

אֵל מָלֵא רַחֲמִים

After reciting *Yizkor* it is customary to recite the following prayers. It is permitted to mention many names in this prayer, but it is preferable to recite separate prayers for men and women.

FOR A MAN

אֵל מָלֵא רַחֲמִים, שׁוֹכֵן בַּמְּרוֹמִים, הַמְצֵא מְנוּחָה נְכוֹנָה עַל כַּנְפֵי הַשְּׁכִינָה, בְּמַעֲלוֹת קְדוֹשִׁים וּטְהוֹרִים כְּזֹהַר הָרָקִיעַ מַזְהִירִים,¹ אֶת נִשְׁמַת (name of the deceased) שֶׁהָלַךְ לְעוֹלָמוֹ, בַּעֲבוּר שֶׁבְּלִי נֶדֶר אֶתֵּן צְדָקָה בְּעַד הַזְכָּרַת נִשְׁמָתוֹ, בְּגַן עֵדֶן תְּהֵא מְנוּחָתוֹ, לָכֵן בַּעַל הָרַחֲמִים

אֵל מָלֵא רַחֲמִים ◆
Keil Malei Rachamim

הַמְצֵא מְנוּחָה נְכוֹנָה — *Grant proper rest.* The fact that a soul is in Paradise does not guarantee it complete contentment. Its level there depends on its prior achievements here on earth; consequently, there are as many degrees there as there are degrees of righteousness on earth. Through our prayers and deeds, we hope to earn God's compassion upon the departed soul.

עַל כַּנְפֵי הַשְּׁכִינָה — *On the wings of the Divine Presence.* Some prayers use the expression תַּחַת כַּנְפֵי הַשְּׁכִינָה, **under** *the wings of the Shechinah* [Divine Presence]; other prayers say עַל כַּנְפֵי הַשְּׁכִינָה, **on** *the wings of the Shechinah.* When Heavenly protection from danger is meant, we say תַּחַת, *under* the wings, using the analogy of a bird spreading its protective wings over its young. This is obviously not the intent of this prayer, which speaks of spiritual elevation. Here the analogy is reversed and God's Presence is compared to a soaring eagle that puts its young upon its wings and carries them aloft.

Kabbalistically, **under** and **on** the wings of the *Shechinah* refer to two exalted positions assigned to the souls of the righteous, in accordance with the following principles:

Each nation, other than Israel, is represented by a guardian angel who pleads its cause before the Heavenly Tribunal. Every non-Jewish soul comes under the aegis of its nation's angel. Israel, however, is not under the domination of any angel. Rather, in the words of the prophet, it is *borne from the belly, carried from the womb* (Isaiah 46:3) on the wings of the *Shechinah.* Thus, after it departs this world, a righteous Jewish soul is restored to its position **on** the wings of the *Shechinah.* The soul of a righteous גֵּר, *proselyte,* which until its conversion to Judaism was **under** an angel's protection, moves from there to a position **under** the protective wings of the *Shechinah* — as Scripture testifies regarding the righteous convert Ruth, "*May you reward be full from* HASHEM, *the God of Israel,* **under** *whose wings you have come to seek refuge*" (Ruth 2:12). "Thus," in the words of *Shaloh* (*Maseches Shavuos*), "those *chazzanim* who recite the memorial prayers for worthy people and say, 'Grant proper rest **under** the wings ...' would do better to remain silent. For [by assigning them wrong positions] they lower [rather than elevate] these worthy souls."

◈ Keil Malei Rachamim

After reciting *Yizkor* it is customary to recite the following prayers. It is permitted to mention many names in this prayer, but it is preferable to recite separate prayers for men and women.

FOR A MAN

אֵל *O God, full of mercy, Who dwells on high, grant proper rest on the wings of the Divine Presence — in the lofty levels of the holy and the pure ones, who shine like the glow of the firmament[1] — for the soul of* (name of the deceased) *who went on to his world, because, without making a vow, I will contribute to charity in remembrance of his soul. May his resting place be in the Garden of Eden — therefore may the Master of mercy*

(1) Cf. *Daniel* 12:3.

קְדוֹשִׁים וּטְהוֹרִים — *The holy and the pure ones*, a reference to the angels. Alternatively, this alludes to the souls of the righteous in *Gan Eden*.

כְּזֹהַר הָרָקִיעַ מַזְהִירִים — *Who shine like the glow of the firmament*. This phrase is borrowed from Scriptures (*Daniel* 12:3) which describes the souls of the righteous who will merit תְּחִיַּת הַמֵּתִים, *the resurrection of the dead*: "The wise יַזְהִרוּ כְּזֹהַר הָרָקִיעַ, *will shine like the glow of the firmament, and those who bring the masses to righteousness [will shine] like the stars forever."*

The Talmud (*Bava Basra* 8b) explains that "the wise" refers to those appointed to collect and distribute charity, while "those who bring the masses to righteousness" alludes to the Torah teachers of young children. According to *Tosafos*, since the glow of the stars appears brighter than the glow of the firmament, the implication here is that teachers are considered to be on a higher plane than charity officials. But, asks *Tosafos*, this contradicts the Talmudic dictum (*Pesachim* 49b) that teaches that one should always seek to marry the daughter of a Torah scholar; if he cannot find such a bride, he should marry a charity official's daughter; if he cannot find even this, then

he should seek the daughter of one who teaches Torah to young children. This latter statement obviously places charity officials on a more lofty level than teachers.

To resolve this contradiction, *Tosafos* cites the Midrash (*Pirkei d'Rabbi Eliezer* 4) which states that the רָקִיעַ, *firmament*, mentioned in *Daniel* is not to be understood in the usual sense of "heaven" or "sky." Rather, it refers to the רָקִיעַ above the heads of *Chayos* seen by Ezekiel in his vision of the Heavenly Chariot. There, רָקִיעַ refers to a heavenly platform held aloft by the angelic *Chayos* and upon which rests the Divine Throne. Ezekiel (1:22) describes that רָקִיעַ as כְּעֵין הַקֶּרַח הַנּוֹרָא, *resembling the awesome ice*, i.e., it is awe inspiring in its brilliance and whiteness (*Radak*). It is to this hidden-from-human-eyes רָקִיעַ, says *Tosafos*, that charity officials are compared. Hence, both Talmudic passages assign a more exalted position to charity officials than to teachers.

As noted above, one of the purposes for the institution of *Yizkor* is the donation of charity in memory of, and as a source of merit for, the souls of our departed relatives. If so, these souls are the cause of our contributions and, as such, they may be considered charity collectors. It is

יַסְתִּירֵהוּ בְּסֵתֶר כְּנָפָיו לְעוֹלָמִים, וְיִצְרוֹר בִּצְרוֹר
הַחַיִּים אֶת נִשְׁמָתוֹ,[1] יהוה הוּא נַחֲלָתוֹ, וְיָנְוּחַ
בְּשָׁלוֹם עַל מִשְׁכָּבוֹ.[2] וְנֹאמַר: אָמֵן.

FOR A WOMAN

אֵל מָלֵא רַחֲמִים, שׁוֹכֵן בַּמְּרוֹמִים, הַמְצֵא
מְנוּחָה נְכוֹנָה עַל כַּנְפֵי הַשְּׁכִינָה, בְּמַעֲלוֹת
קְדוֹשִׁים וּטְהוֹרִים כְּזֹהַר הָרָקִיעַ מַזְהִירִים,[3] אֶת
נִשְׁמַת (name of the deceased) שֶׁהָלְכָה לְעוֹלָמָהּ, בַּעֲבוּר
שֶׁבְּלִי נֶדֶר אֶתֵּן צְדָקָה בְּעַד הַזְכָּרַת נִשְׁמָתָהּ, בְּגַן
עֵדֶן תְּהֵא מְנוּחָתָהּ, לָכֵן בַּעַל הָרַחֲמִים יַסְתִּירֶהָ
בְּסֵתֶר כְּנָפָיו לְעוֹלָמִים, וְיִצְרוֹר בִּצְרוֹר הַחַיִּים אֶת
נִשְׁמָתָהּ,[1] יהוה הוּא נַחֲלָתָהּ, וְתָנְוּחַ בְּשָׁלוֹם עַל
מִשְׁכָּבָהּ.[2] וְנֹאמַר: אָמֵן.

FOR A GROUP OF MEN

אֵל מָלֵא רַחֲמִים, שׁוֹכֵן בַּמְּרוֹמִים, הַמְצֵא
מְנוּחָה נְכוֹנָה עַל כַּנְפֵי הַשְּׁכִינָה, בְּמַעֲלוֹת
קְדוֹשִׁים וּטְהוֹרִים כְּזֹהַר הָרָקִיעַ מַזְהִירִים,[3] אֶת
נִשְׁמוֹת (names of the deceased) שֶׁהָלְכוּ לְעוֹלָמָם, בַּעֲבוּר
שֶׁבְּלִי נֶדֶר אֶתֵּן צְדָקָה בְּעַד הַזְכָּרַת נִשְׁמוֹתֵיהֶם,
בְּגַן עֵדֶן תְּהֵא מְנוּחָתָם, לָכֵן בַּעַל הָרַחֲמִים
יַסְתִּירֵם בְּסֵתֶר כְּנָפָיו לְעוֹלָמִים, וְיִצְרוֹר בִּצְרוֹר

---

therefore fitting that we pray for their souls to be included with the souls of the charity officials which "shine like the glow of the firmament" upon which rests the Divine Throne.

בְּסֵתֶר כְּנָפָיו — *In the shelter of His wings.* Sometimes a bird's wings provide shelter from above, as when a mother bird spreads her wings over her nest to protect her brood from the elements and from predators. At other times, the wings provide shelter from below, such as when an eagle soars with its young perched on its wings, thereby protecting them from the hunter's arrows (see *Rashi to Exodus* 19:4). Similarly, God protects "in the shelter of his wings" both those souls that rest עַל כַּנְפֵי הַשְּׁכִינָה, **on** *the wings of the Shechinah,* and those that are תַּחַת כַּנְפֵי

shelter him in the shelter of His wings for eternity; and may He bind his soul in the Bond of Life.[1] HASHEM is his heritage, and may he repose in peace on his resting place.[2] Now let us respond: Amen.

FOR A WOMAN

אֵל O God, full of mercy, Who dwells on high, grant proper rest on the wings of the Divine Presence — in the lofty levels of the holy and the pure ones, who shine like the glow of the firmament[3] — for the soul of (name of the deceased) who has gone on to her world, because, without making a vow, I will contribute to charity in remembrance of her soul. May her resting place be in the Garden of Eden — therefore may the Master of mercy shelter her in the shelter of His wings for eternity; and may He bind her soul in the Bond of Life.[1] HASHEM is her heritage, and may she repose in peace on her resting place.[2] Now let us respond: Amen.

FOR A GROUP

אֵל O God, full of mercy, Who dwells on high, grant proper rest on the wings of the Divine Presence — in the lofty levels of the holy and the pure ones, who shine like the glow of the firmament[3] — for the souls of (names of the deceased) who have gone on to their world, because, without making a vow, I will contribute to charity in remembrance of their souls. May their resting place be in the Garden of Eden — therefore may the Master of mercy shelter them in the shelter of His wings for eternity; and may He bind their souls in the Bond

---

(1) Cf. *I Samuel* 25:29. (2) Cf *Isaiah* 57:1-2. (3) Cf. *Daniel* 12:3.

הַשְּׁכִינָה, **under** the wings of the Shechinah (see above).

ה' הוּא נַחֲלָתוֹ — *HASHEM is his heritage.* This clause appears twice in *Deuteronomy*: the first time (10:9) in reference to the Tribe of Levi; the second (18:2), to the *Kohanim*. In each case, *Targum Onkelos* paraphrases, "the presents given them by HASHEM are their heritage." Or, in the

words of *Rashi*, "they take their wages directly from the King's house." (Compare the similar passages in *Joshua* 13:14 and 33 which bear out this interpretation.)

Thus, we pray that the souls of our departed relatives receive their eternal rewards "directly from the King's house," and not through mere intermediaries.

וְיָנוּחַ בְּשָׁלוֹם עַל מִשְׁכָּבוֹ — *And may he*

הַחַיִּים אֶת נִשְׁמוֹתֵיהֶם,[1] יהוה הוּא נַחֲלָתָם, וְיָנְוּחוּ בְּשָׁלוֹם עַל מִשְׁכְּבוֹתֵיהֶם.[2] וְנֹאמַר: אָמֵן.

FOR A GROUP OF WOMEN

אֵל מָלֵא רַחֲמִים, שׁוֹכֵן בַּמְּרוֹמִים, הַמְצֵא מְנוּחָה נְכוֹנָה עַל כַּנְפֵי הַשְּׁכִינָה, בְּמַעֲלוֹת קְדוֹשִׁים וּטְהוֹרִים כְּזְהַר הָרָקִיעַ מַזְהִירִים,[3] אֶת נִשְׁמוֹת (names of the deceased) שֶׁהָלְכוּ לְעוֹלָמָן, בַּעֲבוּר שֶׁבְּלִי נֶדֶר אֶתֵּן צְדָקָה בְּעַד הַזְכָּרַת נִשְׁמוֹתֵיהֶן, בְּגַן עֵדֶן תְּהֵא מְנוּחָתָן, לָכֵן בַּעַל הָרַחֲמִים יַסְתִּירֵן בְּסֵתֶר כְּנָפָיו לְעוֹלָמִים, וְיִצְרוֹר בִּצְרוֹר הַחַיִּים אֶת נִשְׁמוֹתֵיהֶן,[1] יהוה הוּא נַחֲלָתָן, וְתָנְוּחוּ בְּשָׁלוֹם עַל מִשְׁכְּבוֹתֵיהֶן.[2] וְנֹאמַר: אָמֵן.

FOR MARTYRS

אֵל מָלֵא רַחֲמִים, שׁוֹכֵן בַּמְּרוֹמִים, הַמְצֵא מְנוּחָה נְכוֹנָה עַל כַּנְפֵי הַשְּׁכִינָה, בְּמַעֲלוֹת קְדוֹשִׁים וּטְהוֹרִים כְּזְהַר הָרָקִיעַ מַזְהִירִים,[3] אֶת נִשְׁמוֹת (כָּל קְרוֹבַי וּקְרוֹבוֹתַי, הֵן מִצַּד אָבִי, הֵן מִצַּד אִמִּי) הַקְּדוֹשִׁים וְהַטְּהוֹרִים שֶׁהוּמְתוּ וְשֶׁנֶּהֶרְגוּ וְשֶׁנִּשְׁחֲטוּ וְשֶׁנִּשְׂרְפוּ וְשֶׁנִּטְבְּעוּ וְשֶׁנֶּחְנְקוּ עַל קִדּוּשׁ הַשֵּׁם, (עַל יְדֵי הַצוֹרְרִים הַגֶּרְמָנִים, יִמַּח שְׁמָם וְזִכְרָם) בַּעֲבוּר שֶׁבְּלִי נֶדֶר אֶתֵּן צְדָקָה בְּעַד הַזְכָּרַת נִשְׁמוֹתֵיהֶם, בְּגַן עֵדֶן תְּהֵא מְנוּחָתָם, לָכֵן בַּעַל הָרַחֲמִים יַסְתִּירֵם בְּסֵתֶר כְּנָפָיו לְעוֹלָמִים, וְיִצְרוֹר בִּצְרוֹר הַחַיִּים אֶת נִשְׁמוֹתֵיהֶם,[1] יהוה הוּא נַחֲלָתָם, וְיָנְוּחוּ בְּשָׁלוֹם עַל מִשְׁכְּבוֹתֵיהֶם.[2] וְנֹאמַר: אָמֵן.

repose in peace on his resting place. This phrase is borrowed from the Prophets.

"The righteous person is lost [i.e., has died] but no man takes it to heart; men of of Life.[1] HASHEM is their heritage, and may they repose in peace on their resting places.[2] Now let us respond: Amen.

FOR MARTYRS

אֵל O God, full of mercy, Who dwells on high, grant proper rest on the wings of the Divine Presence — in the lofty levels of the holy and the pure ones, who shine like the glow of the firmament[3] — for the souls of (all my relatives, both on my father's side and on my mother's side,) the holy and pure ones who were killed, murdered, slaughtered, burned, drowned and strangled for the sanctification of the Name, (through the hands of the German oppressors, may their name and memory be obliterated) because, without making a vow, I will contribute to charity in remembrance of their souls. May their resting place be in the Garden of Eden — therefore may the Master of mercy shelter them in the shelter of His wings for eternity; and may He bind their souls in the Bond of Life.[1] HASHEM is their heritage, and may they repose in peace on their resting places.[2] Now let us respond: Amen.

---

(1) Cf. *I Samuel* 25:29. (2) Cf *Isaiah* 57:1-2. (3) Cf. *Daniel* 12:3.

kindness are gathered in [another euphemism for death], yet none understand that the righteous one has been gathered in because of the bad [times that will befall his generation]; יָבוֹא שָׁלוֹם, may he [the righteous one] come [to his ancestors] peacefully [i.e., without having witnessed these bad times], יָנוּחוּ עַל מִשְׁכְּבוֹתָם, may they repose on their resting places — each of these who have gone [on the] straightforward [path]" (Isaiah 57:1-2). Thus, the inclusion of this phrase should jolt us into taking to heart and understanding the lesson to be learned from the death of the righteous; as King Solomon writes, "May the living take it into his heart" (Ecclesiastes 7:2).

The Rebbe of Alesk (cited in *Taamei HaMinhagim* 1076) explains the expression, "and may he repose in peace on his resting place." It is customary to visit the gravesite of one's parents and grandparents. There one pours out his heart and asks his deceased forebears to intercede with the Heavenly Court on behalf of their descendants. The tales of woe and anguish related there cause unrest for the souls of the departed. However, when the visitors at the grave report happy events and praise God for blessing them in their endeavors, the souls are able to rest peacefully. Thus, by asking that they "repose in peace" we are, in reality, also praying for our own needs. For when our lives are peaceful, their rest is too.

At the conclusion of the *Yizkor* service, it is customary for the *gabbai*
to recite a prayer on behalf of the rabbi of the congregation.

מִי שֶׁבֵּרַךְ אֲבוֹתֵינוּ אַבְרָהָם יִצְחָק וְיַעֲקֹב,
מֹשֶׁה וְאַהֲרֹן, דָּוִד וּשְׁלֹמֹה, הוּא
יְבָרֵךְ אֶת רַבִּי (name) בֶּן (father's name) שֶׁיִּתֵּן לִצְדָקָה
בַּעֲד הַנְּשָׁמוֹת שֶׁהִזְכִּיר הַיּוֹם, לִכְבוֹד הַמָּקוֹם,
לִכְבוֹד הַתּוֹרָה, בִּשְׂכַר זֶה, הַקָּדוֹשׁ בָּרוּךְ הוּא
יִשְׁמְרֵהוּ וְיַצִּילֵהוּ מִכָּל צָרָה וְצוּקָה, וּמִכָּל נֶגַע
וּמַחֲלָה, וְיִכְתְּבֵהוּ וְיַחְתְּמֵהוּ לְחַיִּים טוֹבִים בְּזֶה יוֹם
הַדִּין, וְיִשְׁלַח בְּרָכָה וְהַצְלָחָה בְּכָל מַעֲשֵׂה יָדָיו, עִם
כָּל יִשְׂרָאֵל אֶחָיו. וְנֹאמַר: אָמֵן. (אָמֵן. –Cong.)

Congregation and *chazzan*:

אַב הָרַחֲמִים, שׁוֹכֵן מְרוֹמִים, בְּרַחֲמָיו
הָעֲצוּמִים הוּא יִפְקוֹד
בְּרַחֲמִים, הַחֲסִידִים וְהַיְשָׁרִים וְהַתְּמִימִים, קְהִלּוֹת
הַקֹּדֶשׁ שֶׁמָּסְרוּ נַפְשָׁם עַל קְדֻשַּׁת הַשֵּׁם, הַנֶּאֱהָבִים
וְהַנְּעִימִים בְּחַיֵּיהֶם, וּבְמוֹתָם לֹא נִפְרָדוּ.
מִנְּשָׁרִים קַלּוּ, וּמֵאֲרָיוֹת גָּבֵרוּ,[1] לַעֲשׂוֹת רְצוֹן קוֹנָם

אַב הָרַחֲמִים ﬔ/**Father of compassion.**
This is a memorial prayer, as the text
makes clear, for the martyrs who died to
sanctify God's Name. It was originally
written, although we do not know by
whom, in memory of those martyred
during the First Crusade.

הַנֶּאֱהָבִים וְהַנְּעִימִים ... מֵאֲרָיוֹת גָּבֵרוּ — *Who
were beloved and pleasant ... stronger
than lions.* These words are taken from
King David's eulogy of King Saul and his
son Jonathan when he heard that they
had been killed on the battlefield. In that
context, the commentaries offer a variety
of interpretations: — Saul and Jonathan
were beloved to each other during their
lifetimes, and did not separate from each
other even in death (*Radak*).

— Saul and Jonathan were beloved to God
during their lifetimes, and did not separate
from Him even though it meant giving up
their lives in a battle to save His people.
Indeed, they fought to the bitter end, and
did not try to flee to safety when the
chance arose (*Targum Yonasan* as understood by *Radak*).

— Saul and Jonathan were beloved by the
people, and, even after their death, that
love did not wane (*Metzudos*).

All of these interpretations are appropriate regarding the martyrs memorialized
in this prayer.

מִנְּשָׁרִים קַלּוּ מֵאֲרָיוֹת גָּבֵרוּ לַעֲשׂוֹת רְצוֹן קוֹנָם —
*They were quicker than eagles, stronger
than lions to do their Creator's will.* We
evoke the memory of our martyred ances-

At the conclusion of the *Yizkor* service, it is customary for the *gabbai* to recite a prayer on behalf of the rabbi of the congregation.

מִי שֶׁבֵּרַךְ *He Who blessed our forefathers Abraham, Isaac and Jacob, Moses and Aaron, David and Solomon — may He bless Rabbi (name) son of (father's name) because he shall contribute to charity on behalf of the souls remembered today, in honor of the Omnipresent, in honor of the Torah, in honor of the Day of Judgment. As reward for this, may the Holy One, Blessed is He, protect him and rescue him from every trouble and distress, from every plague and illness; and May He inscribe him and seal him for good life on this Day of Judgment, and may He send blessing and success in his every endeavor, together with all Israel, his brethren. Now let us respond: Amen. (Cong.— Amen.)*

Congregation and *chazzan:*

אַב הָרַחֲמִים *Father of compassion, Who dwells on high, in His powerful compassion may He recall with compassion the devout, the upright, and the perfect ones; the holy congregations who gave their lives for the sanctification of the Name. They were beloved and pleasant in their lifetimes and in their death were not parted; they were quicker than eagles, stronger than lions[1] to do their Creator's will*

(1) *II Samuel* 1:23.

tors, hoping to be inspired by the lesson of their death and their life. The oppressors tried everything in their power to drag these martyrs down from their spiritual and moral heights into the miserable dirt of sensuality and baseness. But our ancestors soared like eagles, and remained high above in their own lofty world. With the strength and courage of lions, they defied the rest of the world for the sake of the truth which they had received and lived and passed on to future generations. Scattered, defenseless, abused with scorn, they had the courage to remain a constant living protest against the ideals touted by

the rest of humanity. For these martyrs had a Master and they knew His will, and they dedicated themselves to it in all earnestness. They had the courage to bear the fury of a population gone mad and to remain steadfastly loyal to Hashem and His Torah despite all the violent threats and enticements to stray. They were butchered, burned at the stake with their families and children, and out of their lives as well as their deaths came a *Kiddush Hashem* of the highest order. They died — and still they triumphed (see *R' Hirsch, Collected Writings,* vol. 1, *Iyar III*).

וְחֵפֶץ צוּרָם. יִזְכְּרֵם אֱלֹהֵינוּ לְטוֹבָה, עִם שְׁאָר
צַדִּיקֵי עוֹלָם, וְיִנְקוֹם לְעֵינֵינוּ נִקְמַת דַּם עֲבָדָיו
הַשָּׁפוּךְ, כַּכָּתוּב בְּתוֹרַת מֹשֶׁה אִישׁ הָאֱלֹהִים:[1]
הַרְנִינוּ גוֹיִם עַמּוֹ כִּי דַם עֲבָדָיו יִקּוֹם, וְנָקָם יָשִׁיב
לְצָרָיו, וְכִפֶּר אַדְמָתוֹ עַמּוֹ.[2] וְעַל יְדֵי עֲבָדֶיךָ
הַנְּבִיאִים כָּתוּב לֵאמֹר: וְנִקֵּיתִי דָמָם לֹא נִקֵּיתִי,
וַיהוה שֹׁכֵן בְּצִיּוֹן.[3] וּבְכִתְבֵי הַקֹּדֶשׁ נֶאֱמַר: לָמָּה
יֹאמְרוּ הַגּוֹיִם, אַיֵּה אֱלֹהֵיהֶם, יִוָּדַע בַּגּוֹיִם לְעֵינֵינוּ,
נִקְמַת דַּם עֲבָדֶיךָ הַשָּׁפוּךְ.[4] וְאוֹמֵר: כִּי דֹרֵשׁ דָּמִים
אוֹתָם זָכָר, לֹא שָׁכַח צַעֲקַת עֲנָוִים.[5] וְאוֹמֵר: יָדִין
בַּגּוֹיִם מָלֵא גְוִיּוֹת, מָחַץ רֹאשׁ עַל אֶרֶץ רַבָּה.
מִנַּחַל בַּדֶּרֶךְ יִשְׁתֶּה, עַל כֵּן יָרִים רֹאשׁ.[6]

וְיִנְקוֹם — *May He ... exact retribution.*
We do not pray that we be strong enough
to avenge our martyrs; Jews are not
motivated by a lust to repay violence and
murder with violence and murder. Rather,
we pray that God choose how and when
to atone for the blood of His fallen
martyrs. For the living, decency and
integrity remain the primary goals of
social life (*R' Hirsch*).

כַּכָּתוּב בְּתוֹרַת מֹשֶׁה אִישׁ הָאֱלֹהִים — *As it is
written in the Torah of Moses, the man of
God.* Interestingly, this phrase, used here
to introduce a quote from the Torah, is
itself a quote from Scriptures. There the
verse describes how the leaders of Israel
*built the altar of the God of Israel to offer
burnt-offerings upon it, as is written in
the Torah of Moses, man of God* (Ezra 3:2).

Normally, the term תּוֹרַת מֹשֶׁה, *the
Torah of Moses*, denotes both the Written
and the Oral Torah, both of them having
been received by Moses at Sinai. When
Scripture uses the term to refer to the
Pentateuch alone, a limiting phrase is
appended; for example, *the Torah of
Moses, which he wrote* (Joshua 8:32).

The appellation אִישׁ הָאֱלֹהִים, *man of
God*, appears dozens of times in Scriptures.

The *Targumim* invariably render נְבִיָּא דַה׳,
prophet of God.

O — הַרְנִינוּ גוֹיִם עַמּוֹ כִּי דַם עֲבָדָיו יִקּוֹם
*nations, sing the praise of His people for
He will avenge the blood of His servants.*
Clearly, what is promised here is the
future Redemption, which has yet to be
fulfilled. It cannot refer to the return from
the Babylonian exile, because the nations
did not *sing the praise of His people*
during the Second Commonwealth, but
mocked what the 'these feeble Jews do'
[see *Nechemiah* 3:34]. The Jews' leaders
were then still servants in the palace of the
king of Babylonia, and all [the Jews] were
subservient to him. In those days, Hashem
did not 'bring retribution upon His foes'
nor did He 'appease His land and His
people [i.e., forgive their sins]'. . . Rather,
this [verse, and the rest of the] passage
[from which it is taken] stands as an
undeniable assurance of the future Redemption, regardless of what the falsifiers
assert (*Ramban* to *Deuteronomy* 32:40).

וְנִקֵּיתִי דָּמָם לֹא נִקֵּיתִי — *Though I cleanse
[the enemy] — their bloodshed I will not
cleanse.* The prophet Joel describes the
fate that will eventually befall the nations
that have denied God and have oppressed

and their Rock's desire. May our God remember them for good with the other righteous of the world. May He, before our eyes, exact retribution for the spilled blood of His servants, as it is written in the Torah of Moses, the man of God:[1] O nations, sing the praise of His people for He will avenge the blood of His servants and He will bring retribution upon His foes; and He will appease His land and His people.[2] And by Your servants, the prophets, it is written saying: Though I cleanse [the enemy] — their bloodshed I will not cleanse when HASHEM dwells in Zion.[3] And in the Holy Writings it is said: Why should the nations say, 'Where is their God?' Let there be known among the nations, before our eyes, revenge for Your servants' spilled blood.[4] And it says: For the Avenger of blood has remembered them; He has not forgotten the cry of the humble.[5] And it says: He will judge the corpse-filled nations, He will crush the leader of the mighty land. From a river along the way he shall drink — therefore he may proudly lift his head.[6]

(1) *Ezra* 3:2. (2) *Deut.* 32:43. (3) *Joel* 4:21. (4) *Psalms* 79:10. (5) 9:13. (6) 110:6-7.

His people all through the ages. His prophecy ends on this poignant note: Even if God were to cleanse them of their sinfulness in denying His majesty and in constantly looting Israel, He will not cleanse them of the bloodshed they have wreaked, but will exact their blood in return. And when will this take place? *When* HASHEM *dwells in Zion.*

לָמָּה יֹאמְרוּ הַגּוֹיִם אַיֵּה אֱלֹהֵיהֶם — *Why should the nations say, "Where is their God?'* Why do you forsake us in exile so long that the nations become incredulous and ask, what sort of god is this hidden deity of the Jews? If He is truly a god, why does He not champion the cause of His people? (*Metzudas David*).

יִוָּדַע בַּגּוֹיִם לְעֵינֵינוּ נִקְמַת דַּם עֲבָדֶיךָ הַשָּׁפוּךְ — *Let there be known among the nations, before our eyes, revenge for Your servants' spilled blood.* When they see that every drop of Jewish blood is properly avenged, they will recognize that God is

indeed our champion. In addition, let His revenge take place *before our eyes*, so that it will be clear that it is being done for our sake (*R' Avrohom Chaim Feuer*).

כִּי דֹרֵשׁ דָּמִים אוֹתָם זָכָר — *For the Avenger of blood has remembered them.* [The word דֹרֵשׁ, here translated "Avenger," can also mean "investigator."] God investigates and keeps track of every drop of Jewish blood ever shed. Although His vengeance is not swift (for He waits for the proper moment), He remembers every drop, and for each, punishment will be exacted (*Metzudas David*).

עֲנָוִים — *The humble.* According to the Masorah, this word is spelled עֲנִיִּים, *the poor*, but pronounced עֲנָוִים, *the humble*, because the poor are usually humble and meek (*Radak*).

The Midrash (*Shocher Tov* 9) explains that this phrase refers especially to the innocent blood of עֲשָׂרָה הֲרוּגֵי מַלְכוּת, *the ten martyrs murdered by the Roman* government, including Rabbi Akiva, Rabban Shimon ben Gamliel, and other great tzaddikim.[1]

The blood of these, and all others who died עַל קִידוּשׁ הַשֵּׁם, *For sanctification of God's Name*, is especially precious. The Midrash concludes: God will inscribe on His royal mantle the name of every martyr who is slaughtered by the gentiles. In the future, God will demand of the murderers: "Why did you kill so-and-so?" They will deny the accusation. What will the Holy One, Blessed is He, do then? He will take out His royal mantle and show them the names of their innocent victims. This will fulfill the verse: *He has not forgotten the cry of the humble.*

יָדִין בַּגּוֹיִם — *He will judge the ... nations.* God intervenes against the nations who seek to slaughter the Jews. He turns their army into a mass of corpses and crushes their leader. Figuratively, enemy blood flows like a river from which the rescued fugitives can "drink." Spared from danger and shame, Israel "may proudly lift his head."

Alternatively, the nations that Hashem is judging are called *corpse-filled* because their wealth and power were built up through murder and plunder. The arrogant leader of this great and mighty nation did not rise to his prominence by dint of his own abilities. It was Hashem who sent favorable opportunities in his way. All he did was to drink from the *river* of prosperity that *flowed along* his path, yet he *proudly lifts his head* in haughtiness and conceit (*R' Hirsch*).

---

1. The story of the Ten Martyrs is an emotional highlight of the Yom Kippur *Mussaf* service, and of the *Kinnos* (lamentations) of Tishah B'Av. It is the moving and tragic story of ten sages of the Mishnah who were brutally murdered to satisfy the whims of an anti-Semitic Roman ruler.